Dear Brother Ralf,

It has been good to meet you at T.P.S. May the Lord bless your contribution here.

Ron

2-18-03 - accreditation meeting
Tyndale

ISRAEL IN THE DEVELOPMENT OF CHRISTIAN THOUGHT

Ronald Eric Diprose Ph.D.

ISTITUTO BIBLICO EVANGELICO ITALIANO

ISRAEL in the Development of Christian Thought
Author Ronald E. Diprose
Copyright © 2000, Istituto Biblico Evangelico Italiano, Rome, Italy

ISBN 88-85403-07-7

Original title of the Italian version: *Israele e la Chiesa*
Copyright © 1998, Istituto Biblico Evangelico Italiano, Rome, Italy
ISBN 88-85403-06-9

This book is available from:

Istituto Biblico Evangelico Italiano,
Via del Casale Corvio, 50
00132 Rome,
Italy
Fax 0039-06-2070151
E-mail istituto.ibei@flashnet.it

Price 10 Euro

CFI Communications
PO Box 2687
Eastbourne,
E. Sussex BN22 7LZ
England
Fax 0044-1323-410211
E-mail info@cfi.org.uk

This volume contains the first part of a dissertation for which Ronald E. Diprose was awarded the Ph.D. in Theology by the Evangelische Theologische Faculteit, Heverlee (Louvain), Belgium, in September, 1997. The Evangelische Theologische Faculteit has given permission for this material to be published.

TABLE OF CONTENTS

FOREWORD

Everyone knows that modern Israel, especially in its relations with its Arab neighbors, has been continually and conspicuously in the daily news ever since World War II. Less well known, but now amply demonstrated by Dr. Diprose, is the contrasting fact that the concept of "Israel", and the existence and role of the continuing Jewish people, has been hovering in the background while Christians have shaped their doctrinal expressions and the practical consequences resulting from them.

The early church was challenged as to whether Israel's sacred writings were to be considered as Sacred Scripture. The triumphant professing church of the Middle Ages assumed – without bothering to prove it – that it had taken over the promises and blessings (but not the curses) that God had promised Israel. Our own times have seen the culmination of centuries of Christian Anti-Semitism in the Holocaust and the subsequent debate as to whether Jewish people are already saved by virtue of God's covenant with Israel. Dr. Diprose demonstrates that major areas of Christian doctrine have been shaped by the Church's attitudes towards Israel. But tragically for the Jewish people and for the Christian theological tradition, this crucial role of Israel has not been systematically, publicly, and generally reflected upon.

Dr. Diprose is to be commended for undertaking this wide-ranging study in order to demonostrate the need for such reflection to be undertaken. And it is especially fitting that the one who has undertaken this task lives and works in the ancient city of Rome, to whose early Christians the apostle Paul wrote his own sustained reflection on the place of Israel. Sadly, Christians have all too rarely consistently reflected upon the implications of Paul's conclusion: "Just as you... have now received mercy because of their disobedience, so... by the mercy shown to you, they too may now receive mercy" (Ro 11:30,31). In repeated and various ways over the centuries, most Christians, and the Church in its theology, have been anything but merciful to Israel. May this publication of Dr. Diprose's study be one small step toward correcting this ancient and continuing terrible wrong.

Donald Tinder Ph.D.
Professor, Evangelische Theologische Faculteit, Louvain, Belgium
Academic Dean, Tyndale Theological Seminary, Amsterdam, Netherlands

AUTHOR'S PREFACE

I had always been aware that Israel was important for Christian theology. However for a long time it had seemed to me that the question of Israel had become some kind of theological football that two opposing teams of theologians kicked about in accordance with their particular agendas. For dispensationalists it was apparently important that ethnic Israel be given a high profile while for reformed theologians it was apparently important to show that, with the advent of the Church, ethnic Israel's significance had been irrevocably eclipsed. The result: to affirm that there are institutional distinctions between Israel and the Church was another way of declaring oneself to be a dispensationalist while denial of such distinctions was a sign of reformed orthodoxy.

A few years ago I decided that Israel should be considered as a question in its own right and not as an adjunct to a given theological position. Following that decision, I made some interesting discoveries. For example I discovered that two very different views concerning Israel have held sway in Christendom at different times. According to Christian Tradition as it developed during the early centuries, Israel is a renegade nation to be treated with contempt. However, after the *Shoah*[1] and the birth of the modern State of Israel in 1948, a new majority view developed according to which Israel's status as an elect nation exonerates members of this people from the need to exercise faith in Jesus Christ in order to be saved.

The antithetical nature of these two majority views was puzzling and suggested that factors other than the relevant biblical data had determined their development. This was confirmed by reading in the Church Fathers and in the literature pertaining to the current Jewish-Christian dialogue. I also noticed that the neglect of the biblical data concerning Israel had repercussions on Christian theology in general. The effects of the earlier majority view were particularly evident in ecclesiology and eschatology, whereas the new majority view is having serious repercussions in soteriology and missiology, while both views have important implications for hermeneutics.

Many people have helped, directly and indirectly, to make this investigation possible. Conversation with Patrick Sookhdeo, while walking together around a lake in southern Italy, prodded me to think more deeply into some of the relevant issues. Interaction with Professor Donald Tinder was also very fruitful. The footnotes bear witness to my great debt to numerous other scholars. On a practical level special thanks is due to the Board of the Italian Bible Institute for granting me a brief sabbatical in which I was able to begin the project. In particular I wish to thank Bernard Oxenham, who generously shouldered many of my responsibilities, thus allowing me to engage uninterruptedly in research for weeks at a time.

This project would not have been possible without adequate library facilities. In this regard I am grateful to Professor Daniele Garrone for the freedom he gave me to use the excellent Library of the Waldensian Faculty, Rome.

Last, but not least, special thanks is due to my wife Eunice, and to our sons, Andrew and Jonathan, who not only accepted that I be unavailable to them for long hours but who have also offered encouragement and practical assistance during the various phases of the work.

ABBREVIATIONS

1. For the books of the Bible

The same abbreviations are used as are found in the *New International Version* (1985).

2. Ancient works

Augustine
    Civ. — *City of God*
    Barn. — *Barnabas, (pseudonymous) Epistle of*

Clement of Alexandria
    Strom. — *Stromata*

Cyprian
    Testimonies — *Three Books of Testimonies Againt the Jews*
    Unit. eccl. — *On the Unity of the Church*

Cyril of Jerusalem
    Cat. — *Catechetical Lectures*

Eusebius
    Hist. eccl. — *Ecclesiastical History*

Hippolytus
    Antichr. — *On Antichrist*

Irenaeus
    Haer. — *Against Heresies*

Justin Martyr
    Tryph. Jud. — *Dialogue with Trypho*

Origen
    Cant. — *Exposition of the Song of Songs*
    Cels. — *Against Celsus*
    Princ. — *On First Principles*

Tertullian
    Adv. Jud. — *Against the Jews*
    Marc. — *Against Marcion*
    bap. — *On Baptism*

3. Collections, modern pubblication and Journals

ANF — Ante-Nicene Fathers, Alexander Roberts & James Donaldson (eds.); American reprint, A. Cleveland Coxe & Allan Menzies (eds.), 10 vols. Grand Rapids, MI: Eerdmans, 1986.

CH — *Church History*

IBMR — *International Bulletin of Missionary Research*

---

[1] The Hebrew term *Shoah* means "desolation" and refers to the socalled "final solution" worked out by Hitler.

ICC	International Critical Commentaries
JEH	*Journal of Ecclesiastical History*
JES	*Journal of Ecumenical Studies*
NIDCC	*The New International Dictionary of the Christian Church,* J.D. Douglas (ed.), Exeter: The Paternoster Press, 1978.
NIDNTT	*New International Dictionary of New Testament Theology,* translated and revised, with additions, Colin Brown (ed.), 3 vols., Exeter: Paternoster Press,1975-1978.
NPNF fs	Nicene & Post-Nicene Fathers, First Series, 14 vols, Philip Schaff (ed.); Reprint, Grand Rapids, MI: Eerdmans,1979-1987.
NPNF ss	Nicene & Post-Nicene Fathers, Second Series, 14 vols. Philip Schaff & Henry Wace (eds.), Grand Rapids, MI: Eerdmans, 1983.
PG	Patrologia graeca, 162 vols., Paris: J.P. Migne, 1856-1866.
PL	Patrologia latina, 221 vols, Paris: J.P. Migne, 1862-1865; Reprint, Turnbolti, Belgium: Typographi Brepols Editores Pontifichi, n.d.
TCJP	*The Theology of the Churches and the Jewish People: Statements by the World Council of Churches and its member churches,* Comments by Allan Brockway, Paul van Buren, Rolf Rendtorff & Simon Schoon (eds.), Geneva: WWC Publications, 1988.
TDNT	*Theological Dictionary of the New Testament.* Gerhard Kittel and Gerhard Friedrich (eds.); Translated by Geoffrey W. Bromiley, 9 vols., Grand Rapids, MI: Eerdmans, 1964-1972.

4. Other abbreviations

1:459	volume 1, page 459 or volume 1, column 459
Comm.	Commentary
Ep.	Epistle, Epistles
Hom.	Homily, Homilies
sec.	section
Serm.	Sermon, Sermons
WCC	The World Council of Churches

INTRODUCTION

"...we realize that in this question [the relationship of the Church to Israel] the entire self-understanding of the Church is at stake."[1]

Since the tragic events of the *Shoah*[2] and the birth of the modern State of Israel on May 14, 1948,[3] the interest shown in God's ancient people has been widespread and sustained. Awareness of the importance of the minuscule State of Israel for the general well-being of mankind was shown by the presence of seventy prime ministers and heads of state at the funeral of Israeli Prime Minister Yitzhak Rabin, in November, 1995. Furthermore, large sectors of Christendom, such as those represented by the World Council of Churches and the Roman Catholic Church, are now involved in dialogue with the Jewish people. Richard Harries speaks of *the existence of an identical hope of the kingdom, a common mission aimed at sanctifying God's name and... equal dignity in dialogue.*[4]

---

[1] The Commission on Faith and Order, Bristol, 1967, in *The Theology of the Churches and the Jewish People: Statements by the World Councl of Churches and its member churches*, Allan Brockway, Paul van Buren, Rolf Rendtorff & Simon Schoon (eds), Geneva: WWC Publications, 1988 (hereafter *TCJP*), p. 21.

[2] The Hebrew term *Ha Shoah* ("desolation") is used to describe the most notorious of the long series of atrocities perpetrated against the Jewish people. The term identifies the series of events described in German Nazi language as: *die Endlösung der Judenfrage* or "the Final Solution of the question of the Jews" which Nazi Germany planned in order "to ensure that no longer would there be a single Jew upon Planet Earth" (A. Roy Eckardt, "Salient Christian-Jewish Issues of Today: A Christian Exploration," *Jews and Christians*, James H. Charlesworth, Frank X. Blisard & Jeffrey S. Siker (eds), New York: Crossroad, 1990, p. 157). "Holocaust" is a less suitable term to describe these events, as it carries a positive connotation for Jews (see Lev 1:3; 6:1-6).

[3] The birth of the modern State of Israel was described by Teddy Kollek as "perhaps the most significant event of this century" (Norman Solomon, "The Christian Churches on Israel and the Jews," in *Anti-Zionism and Antisemitism in the Contemporary World*, Robert S. Wistrich [ed], London: The Macmillan Press, 1990, p. 144).

[4] Richard Harries, "Dialogo Cristiani-Ebrei", *Dizionario del movimento ecumenico*, a cura di Giovanni Cereti, Alfio Filippi, Luigi Sartori, Bologna: edizioni Dehoniane, 1994, p. 377.

1

Considering the importance of Israel in the Hebrew and Christian Scriptures, Christian theology could be expected to give particular attention to these developments. However, while the *Shoah* and the birth of the modern State of Israel have led some Christian theologians to rethink the question of Israel's relationship to the Church, works of systematic theology continue to be produced which omit Israel altogether or include only marginal mention of her significance for theology.[5] In the words of Gordon Lewis and Bruce A. Demarest, "the notion of institutional Israel is a missing link in much systematic theology".[6]

The absence of Israel in much of Christian theology has a long history. During the formative period of the Christian Tradition[7] this reflected the view that what was promised to Israel finds its ultimate fulfillment in Jesus, the Israelite *par excellence,* or in the Church. It follows that *the Church completely and permanently replaced ethnic Israel in the working out of God's plan and as recipient of Old Testament promises addressed to Israel.* Although this view, variously known as "supersessionism" or "replacement theology",[8]

---

[5] Of sixteen works published between 1980 and 1994, which I have examined, only five make significant mention of Israel, three make marginal reference while eight omit all mention of Israel.

[6] Gordon R. Lewis and Bruce A. Demarest. *Integrative Theology.* 3 vols. Grand Rapids, MI: Zondervan., 1994, 3:336.

[7] Hendrikus Berkhof *(Christian Faith,* Grand Rapids, MI: Eerdmans, 1979, p. 221) writes of the Church: "…she seems to forget Israel almost completely and not need her at all. The latter is especially the case in the creedal statements and systematic theology handbooks."

[8] Gabriel Fackre ("The Place of Israel in Christian Faith," in *Ecumenical Faith in Evangelical Perspective,* by Gabriel Fackre, Grand Rapids, MI: Eerdmans, 1993, pp. 148-153) distinguishes five types of supersessionism: the "Retributive Replacement View," still espoused by the reconstructionist movement which considers Israel to have been repudiated by God on account of her obstinate unbelief; the "Non-retributive Replacement View," probably the most widely held view in historic Christian theology, which sees ethnic Israel as being simply superseded by the person and work of Christ and the community of faith based upon Christ's work; a "Modified Replacement View" which stresses "the role of the Hebrew Scriptures in Christian faith" and "the right of Messianic Jews to incorporate their heritage into their Christian faith"; the "Messianic Replacement View", which sees Christ as the fulfillment of the Jewish hope and seeks to win Jews for Jesus; and lastly Karl Barth's "Christological Election View".

is now widely rejected, both popular opinion and Christian theology remain profoundly influenced by it.

It is conceivable that some avoid theologising about Israel for quite a different reason. They fear that any attempt to take Israel seriously runs the risk of being labelled "dispensationalist". While it is true that Israel occupies an important place in dispensational theology, it is also true that reflection concerning the place of Israel in God's plan predates this school of thought by many centuries. The apostle Paul himself engaged in an in depth study of the relationship of Israel to the rest of the divine programme (Ro 9-11). In the modern era, Puritan theologians such as Henry Finch and Thomas Goodwin attributed great importance to Israel.[9] Moreover the seminal works which, at the beginning of the nineteenth century, led to the reconsideration of the place of Israel in the divine plan, came from very different sectors of Christianity than those generally associated with dispensationalism.[10]

I believe that Christian theology should consider Israel for her own sake and not as an adjunct to some theological system. It is my intention to show that where Christian theology has failed to take into account all of the data concerning Israel contained

---

[9] Henry Finch, *The Worlds Great Restauration, Or The Calling of the Iewes, and (with them) of all the Nations and Kingdomes of the earth, to the faith of Christ,* 1621; Thomas Goodwin (1600-1680), *An Exposition of the First, and part of the Second chapter, of the Epistle to the Ephesians,* Works, 5 vols (1682-1704). In his survey of anti-supersessionist perspectives, Fackre begins with the dispensationalism developed by John Nelson Darby (1800-1882). In reality the historic turning point in attitudes towards Israel, within Protestantism, began with the pre-millennial views of the Reformed German Theologian Johann Heinrich Alsted (1588-1638) and was consolidated by English Puritans (Robert G. Clouse, "The Rebirth of Millenarianism," in Peter Toon [ed], *Puritan Eschatology 1600-1660,* Cambridge: James Clarke, 1970, pp. 42-65); cf. Bryan W. A. Ball, *A Great Expectation: Eschatological thought in English Protestantism to 1660.* Leiden: E. J. Brill, 1975.

[10] Two of the most influential works were: *The Premillennial Advent of Christ demonstrated from the Scripture,* by an Anglican scholar, William Cuninghame, London, 1815, and *Venida del Mesìas en gloria y majestad,* by a Jesuit, Manuel de Lacunza y Diaz and published in 1811. The English translation of the 11th ed. of this work, with Introduction by Edward Irving, was published in 1827 (*The Coming of the Messiah in Glory and Majesty,* 2 vols, London: L.B. Seeley & Sons, 1827).

in the Hebrew Scriptures and the New Testament, much damage has resulted in Christian thought and practice.[11]

After considering the evidence for Israel's uniqueness among the nations, I will address the thorny question of how the radical concept known as *replacement theology* originated. This will be followed by an investigation into the link between *replacement theology* and other aspects of Christian thought, in particular ecclesiology and eschatology.

Ecclesiology and eschatology are not the only areas of Christian theology to have been affected by the Church's views concerning Israel. For example, the basic assumption that the interpretation of the Old Testament was exclusively the prerogative of the Church, linked with the normalisation of the allegorical method, led to the neglect of the Hebrew world view. This resulted in theological thought being set in an essentially Greek philosophical frame of reference.[12] This led, among other things, to the polarisation of the sovereignty of God and the free will of man. Jaroslav Pelikan writes:

---

[11] Jaroslav Pelikan considers the Christian effort to come to terms with the unique and abiding place of the covenant with the people of Israel in the economy of divine revelation "a key to the nature of the Christian message" (Jaroslav Pelikan, *The Christian Tradition*, 5 vols, Chicago: University of Chicago Press, 1971-1989, 5:334); cf. Willem VanGemeren *(The Progress of Redemption,* Grand Rapids, MI: Zondervan, 1988, p. 442), who speaks of the importance of "discussions between church and synagogue that have been suspended since the II century A.D."

[12] This shift in world views and its effect on the whole enterprise of Christian theology is traced by the liberal scholar, Adolf Harnack *Lehrbuch der Dogmengeschichte,* 4th ed, 1909; It. trans., *Manuale di Storia del Dogma,* 7 vols, Mendrisio: Casa Editrice Cultura Moderna, 1912-1914, 1:51-162; 2:175-321; 3:5-144) affirms that everywhere the arsenal of Greek culture passed its weapons and baggage to the Church, so that philosophical theological speculation and the Greek mysteries became the principal factors in the formative process that shaped the Christian church. Harnack adds that significant elements also have their origin in Roman customs, among these the episcopal constitution of the Church. I will argue that this process was also influenced by an indiscriminate takeover of Levitical cultic practice by the Church. Harnack concludes, "Therefore, also in the church perfectly developed in all of its essential structures, we find that the philosophic schools and the Roman empire had chosen to make their home" (1:47). This assessment reflects Harnack's view that metaphysics was an alien intrusion in early Christian thought (Colin Brown, "Harnack", *NIDCC*), however

... the Augustinian tradition has been affected by the loss of contact with Jewish thought, whose refusal to polarize the free sovereignty of God and the free will of man has frequently been labeled Pelagian.[13]

Another serious effect of the loss of constructive contact with the Hebrew world was the position which the Medieval Church assumed in the iconoclastic controversy. A person who favoured the destruction of images was discredited as "one who thought like a Jew".[14] The result was that the Medieval Church supported the use of images in worship despite Scriptural prohibitions to do so.

Following the *Shoah* and the birth of the modern State of Israel a very different view regarding Israel has gained widespread acceptance. Advocates of the new view claim that God's covenant with Israel is sufficient for salvation and discourage sharing the good news of their Messiah with Jewish people. This raises important questions for Christian soteriology and missiology. Underlying the development of both the old and new views there is a common shortcoming: a selective use of Scripture.[15] In the present volume we will focus our attention on the development and effects of the older view.

I have chosen to quote extensively from primary sources so that the reader can see for himself or herself the relationship between the Church's view concerning Israel and the development of Christian thought. Although this approach may prove to be a little tedious at times, it has the considerable advantage of permitting the reader to participate in the evaluation of the data.

it also accurately reflects the phenomenon of Greco-Roman culture replacing the biblical *Hebrew* world view in the development of the Christian tradition; cf. W.H.C. Frend, *The Rise of Christianity,* Philadelphia, PA: Fortress Press, 1984, pp. 367-395.

[13] Pelikan, *Tradition,* 1:22.

[14] According to the church of Rome: "an iconoclast was simply 'one with a Jewish mind ['Ιουδαιοφροῶν]'," (*ibid.,* p. 201).

[15] For a brief presentation of the effects of the new majority view on Christian soteriology and missiology, see my article "The Jewish-Christian Dialogue and Soteriology", *Trinity Journal* 20 NS (1999): 23-37.

Chapter One

A UNIQUE PEOPLE

A. Israel in the Old Testament

1. *The origin of Israel*

The term "Israel" appears over two thousand times in the Old Testament and seventy times in the New Testament. This term refers to a specific ethnic group[1] which believed itself to be united by a covenant with Yahweh, the only true God.[2] The name *Yisra'êl* was conferred on Jacob (Ge 32:28), Abraham's grandson, and means "soldier of God"[3] or "God persists."[4] The significance of Abraham's offspring for general history is explained more fully in the words which God addressed to the patriarch at the moment of his call:

[1] We will not consider here possible exceptions to this rule because the nation of Israel, to which the biblical uses of the name normally refer, still exists and it is the nature of this existence we are considering. See ch. 2 for an examination of the meaning of "Israel" in Romans 9-11.

[2] At the conclusion of a detailed study of the uses of the terms Jews, Hebrews, and Israel in antiquity, Graham Harvey writes concerning the latter:

> Israel is primarily the name of a people. It is linked to an eponymous ancestor, also named "Jacob" whose actions and character (good and bad) are those of the people. Although it is linked with God in the phrase "the God of Israel" (and is distinct from "Jews" in this way also) "Israel" is never a totally pure community: it can be either commended or condemned. "Israel" is an audience for this God and for the authors of the literature discussed (Graham Harvey, *The True Israel*, Leiden: E.J. Brill, 1996, p. 272).

[3] Yisra'êl, "contender," "soldier of God", from saràh "to fight" and 'el "God" (William Gesenius, *Gesenius' Hebrew and Chaldee Lexicon to the Old Testament Scriptures*, trans. S. P. Tregelles, Samuel Bagster & Sons, 1847; Reprint, Grand Rapids, MI: Baker Book House, 1979, p. 370).

[4] Yisra'êl, "Êl persisteth or persevereth" or "Let Êl persist" or "Let Êl contend," *A Hebrew and English Lexicon of the Old Testament*, Francis Brown, S.R. Driver, Charles A. Briggs (eds.), Oxford: Clarendon Press, 1975, p. 975.

> Leave your country, your people and your father's household
> and go to the land I will show you.
> I will make you into a great nation
> and I will bless you;
> I will make your name great,
> and you will be a blessing.
> I will bless those who bless you,
> and whoever curses you I will curse;
> and all peoples on earth
> will be blessed through you (Ge 12:1-3).

The call of Abram and the promises that God made to him at that time were ratified as a solemn covenant described as *everlasting* (Ge 15:1-20; cf. 17:1-10; 22:17-18; 28:13-15). Thus the personal and family history of Abram would always be governed by covenant promise and divine sovereignty. This was immediately evident in the personal history of Abram and his wife Sarai. One year before Isaac – the son of promise – was born, Abram was renamed *Abraham,* meaning: "father of many" (17:1-19). As for Sarai (renamed *Sarah* "princess"), she had been sterile all through the age of childbearing and was very old when Isaac was born (11:30; 18:11; 21:6-7). This circumstance confirmed that Abraham's descendants through her were to be *God's elect people* and not simply a natural offspring. God's special relationship with Israel was recognised by surrounding peoples, despite the human imperfections of Abraham and his descendants (chs 18-20; cf. 26:25-29; 28:15; 31:25-29).

The experiencing of personal blessing under the promises was conditional upon obedience to the God who made the covenant.[5] It should be noted that the blessings contained in the covenant of promise did not include the promise of eternal salvation to all descendants of Abraham by way of Jacob. Rather, according to the terms of the Abrahamic covenant, Israel as a whole was to be the special object of God's love and through them blessing was to flow to the whole earth.

[5] See John Feinberg, "Systems of Discontinuity," in *Continuity and Discontinuity*, John Feinberg (ed.), Westfield, IL: Crossway Books, Good News Publishers, 1988, p. 79.

Because of the promissory,[6] unconditional nature of God's covenant with Abraham, Isaac and Jacob, this covenant was not abrogated when God stipulated a second, conditional, covenant with Israel at the time of Moses (Ex 19:5-8; 24:4-8; cf. Gal 3:15-18). Thus the unconditional covenant blessings promised to Abraham and to his descendants provide a key to understanding the history of this people, who, despite blatant transgression of the Mosaic covenant and the consequent application of its sanctions, continued to be the object of God's love (see Hos chs 1-3).

From being a patriarchal clan which gained the respect of neighbouring peoples (Ge 20,26,31), Jacob's descendants developed into a nation while living in Egypt, where they eventually became slaves of the Egyptian Pharaohs (see Ge 47-50; Ex 1). Following the Exodus,[7] in which God revealed his power and faithfulness to his elect people, the twelve tribes of Israel lived as wandering nomads for forty years. Later, following the partial conquest of the promised land, these tribes remained loosely associated, the tabernacle at Shiloh being the main element of national unity (Jos, Jdg). At the time of Samuel Israel became a powerful monarchy under Saul and David (1-2 Sa). However there was a sharp decline in Israel's fortunes, following the death of Solomon, David's son, characterised by the division of the nation into a northern and southern kingdom, the institutionalisation of idolatry in the northern kingdom, fratricidal wars and two disastrous exiles.

The second exile was followed by the partial restoration of the southern kingdom. This restored kingdom was to enjoy varying degrees of political independence. It was made up of the tribes of Judah and Simeon and those descending from members of the other ten tribes who had either remained in the territory of Judah at the time of the division of the kingdom or

[6] For a discussion concerning the distinctiveness of the promissory covenants, see Thomas Edward McComisky, *The Covenants of Promise: A Theology of the Old Testament Covenants*, Grand Rapids, MI: Baker Book House, 1985, pp. 133-142.

[7] Particular theories concerning Old Testament chronology, such as the date of the Exodus, are not relevant to the purpose of the present work.

had defected to the southern kingdom during the reigns of Rehoboam and Asa (1 Ki 12:16-17; 2 Chr 11:13-17; 15:9). Presumably their choice to identify with the southern kingdom was related to the association of both orthodox religious practice and the Davidic line with Jerusalem.

2. *A nation set apart*

After the name "Israel" was conferred on the patriarch Jacob, the two names were used interchangeably (Ge 46:29-30; Nu 24:17; Ps 146:5; 147:2). Moreover, Jacob's descendants were referred to both as "the house of Jacob" (Isa 2:2-5; Ps 114:1) and "the house of Israel" (Ge 31:33; Isa 5:7) or "Israelites" (Ge 47:27; Ex 14:28). This shows that ethnic identity and divine purpose are closely related in the history of this people group.

It is significant that shortly after Jacob's arrival in Egypt, he blessed the reigning Pharaoh (Ge 47:7). Inasmuch as *the lesser person is blessed by the greater* (Heb 7:7), this act highlights Israel's crucial role in God's plan as an instrument of blessing (Ge 47:7; cf. 12:3). In a prophetic utterance, the aged Jacob went so far as to specify that it would be someone arising from the tribe of Judah that would eventually gain "the obedience of the nations" (49:8-12).

The role God assigned to Israel set the Israelites apart from the other nations. Israel's unique identity was confirmed when God identified her as his "firstborn" at the time of Moses (Ex 4:22-23). It received further, surprising, confirmation when the pagan prophet Balaam was constrained by God to utter blessings upon Israel when hired by Balak, king of Moab, to curse them. In his divinely inspired oracle, Balaam declared:

> From the rocky peaks I see them,
> from the heights I view them.
> I see a people who live apart
> and do not consider themselves one of the nations...
> (Nu 23:9; cf. Dt 23:4-5).

The reason why Israel is not included among the nations is explained by Moses:

The LORD your God... has declared that he will set you in praise, fame and honor high above all the nations he has made and that you will be a people holy to the LORD your God, as he promised (Dt 26:19).

Because God chose to put his name upon Israel, this people had the possibility of being either more blessed or more severely castigated than the nations into whose destinies she could never be fully assimilated. Moreover Moses taught that Israel would never be irreversibly assimilated into other nations (Dt chs 27-28). In fact, because of their particular relationship with God, the Israelites were not allowed to enter into mixed marriages (Dt 25:5-9; Jos 23:12). Furthermore, because of God's close association with Israel, the attitude of other nations towards her would have had a direct bearing upon *their* national fortunes. Thus when Balaam looked out and saw Israel encamped tribe by tribe, the Spirit of God came upon him and he uttered this oracle:

... May those who bless you be blessed
and those who curse you be cursed! (Nu 24:2,9; cf. Isa 54:17).

Awareness of Israel's uniqueness, which depended on her unique relationship with Yahweh, is a recurring theme on the lips of non-Israelites in the course of Old Testament history. For example, Rahab summarised the reaction of the population of Jericho to the mighty acts of God on behalf of Israel, with these words:

When we heard of it, our hearts melted and everyone's courage failed because of you, for the Lord your God is God in heaven above and on the earth below (Jos 2:11).

In the fifth century B.C., Haman the Agagite, a high-ranking official in the reign of Xerxes, the Persian, requested that Israel be annihilated. The terms with which he motivated his request show that the pagan nations of his day perceived Israel's uniqueness. Haman introduced his request to Xerxes with the following statement:

There is a certain people dispersed and scattered among the peoples in all the provinces of your kingdom whose customs are different from those of

11

all other people and who do not obey the king's laws; it is not in the king's best interest to tolerate them (Est 3:8).

Besides affirming Israel's uniqueness, Haman's words imply the impossibility of adopting a neutral attitude towards this people. Either her uniqueness gains her the respect of the nations or she is likely to experience their intolerance. This is futher seen in the sudden turn in fortunes which saw the king honouring Mordecai the Jew for having revealed an assassination plot. At which Haman's advisers and his wife Zeresh made this significant statement:

> Since Mordecai, before whom your downfall has started is of Jewish origin, you cannot stand against him – you will surely come to ruin! (Est 6:13).

3. *The survival of Israel*

It is not part of our purpose to rehearse all the Old Testament prophetic oracles concerning a future messianic age and their implications for Israel. We will limit our attention to the question of whether or not the Hebrew Scriptures envisage a situation in which the special relationship which God had established with Israel could be revoked. We may begin by noting that God's decision to set his affection on Israel was in no way determined by their performance or national greatness but rather by God's free will and his sovereign purposes (Dt 7:7-8; 9:4-5). Similarly the survival of the kingdom of Judah in some shape or form, despite the blatant disobedience of kings such as Jehoram and Ahaziah (2 Ki 8:16-27), depended on the covenant promises which God made to David (2 Sa 7:16; 23:5; Ps 89:3-4; 132:10-18).[8]

The unconditional nature of these earlier statements is paralleled in a surprising statement pronounced by the prophet

---

[8] The Davidic covenant features as the foundation of many prophecies concerning a future Messiah and a messianic age. See: Ps 2; 45:1-7[cf. Heb 1:8-9]; Ps 110 [cf. Heb 1:3; 5:6;]; Ps 118:21-22[cf. Mt 21:42-45]; Mic 5:1-5; Isa 2:1-4; 4:2-6; 9:1-7; 11:1-12; 42:1; 49:5-6; 52:13-53:12; 55:3-5; 59:16-20; 61:1-62:4; Jer 23:5-8; Da 7:13-18 [cf. Mk 14:61-62]; Da 9:26-27; Hos 3:4-5; Am 9:8-15; Zec 2:8-10; 9:9-10; 12:1-13:9. In these passages, the promise theme already present in Genesis (3:15; 12:3; 28:14; 49:9-10) is elaborated, with specific reference to the nature of future fulfillment.

Jeremiah. After insisting on the inevitability of the exile of Judah to Babylon and exhorting those who were already in exile to settle down and serve Nebuchadnezzar, Jeremiah began the constructive phase of his ministry. This began with a prophecy concerning the restoration of Israel and Judah to the land that was peculiarly God's and which he had given as an inheritance to Israel (Jer 30:3; cf. 16:18; 31:10-11, 27-28). There follows what must be rated as one of the most important Old Testament prophecies (31:31-34).[9] It concerns a new covenant which God intends to make at some future time with Israel and Judah, following a period of national repentance (vv. 18-19). The main characteristics of this new covenant are complete forgiveness for sins, the writing of God's law on the hearts of his people and God becoming in a way not yet experienced "*their* God" (vv. 33-34). What interests us at this point is the statement which undergirds this prophecy, making its fulfillment certain:

> This is what the Lord says,
> he who appoints the sun to shine by day,
> who decrees the moon and stars to shine by night,
> who stirs up the sea so that its waves roar –
> the Lord Almighty is his name:
> "Only if these decrees vanish from my sight,"
> declares the Lord,
> "will the descendants of Israel ever cease to be a nation before me."
> This is what the Lord says:
> "Only if the heavens above can be measured
> and the foundations of the earth below be searched out
> will I reject all the descendants of Israel
> because of all they have done," declares the Lord (31:35-37).

Earlier in his prophetic ministry, Jeremiah had insisted that the sin of Judah had made judgment – exile – certain, just as the northern kingdom of Israel had been duly judged. However he now says that Israel's failure to perform according to expectations cannot upset God's plans. Israel's sin can no more thwart God's future purposes *for the nation* than can the heavens be measured

---

[9] This prophecy establishes a basic unity between the Old and New Testaments which allows for both continuity and discontinuity.

and all the secrets of the earth be known. Thus it is clear that God will not reject the descendants of Israel because of the nation's unfaithfulness. But there is more: only in the case of the collapse of God's sovereign control over the physical universe, would Israel cease to exist *as a nation*.

A similar statement is made by God in the prophecy of Malachi, in a context which affirms the immutability of God:

> I the Lord do not change. So you, O descendants of Jacob, are not destroyed (Mal 3: 6).

Thus, though from the time of the patriarchs Israel has continually turned away from God's decrees, yet there is hope for her (v. 7).

It may be argued that, in the Old Testament, expressions suggesting permanence, such as we find here, can refer to a lengthly but limited time.[10] However what cannot be doubted is that the words of Jeremiah mean that Israel will continue to exist *as a nation* until she enters into the new covenant relationship described in the preceding verses. Moreover it is impressive that in Isaiah 66:22 the permanence of Israel, as a distinct nation, is put in relation to the permanence of the predicted new heavens and new earth.

B. The New Testament Witness to Israel's Uniqueness

1. *The problem posed by Israel's unbelief*

The fact that Jesus restricted his own ministry almost exclusively to Israel (Mt 10:5; 15:24) is, in itself, a strong indication of this nation's uniqueness in the counsels of God. It is perhaps not surprising that Jesus' contemporaries were more interested in gaining political advantage from his supernatural powers than they were in taking to heart his insistence on the need for spiritual renewal (Jn 6:14-69). What nation, living

---

[10] An obvious example of this is the covenant that God made with the zealous priest Phinehas (Nu 25:10-13).

under political oppression, would have reacted differently? Despite the failure of the Jewish nation to listen to Jesus, some Jews did become sincere disciples while their number increased significantly after the Pentecost event.

The number of Jews who accepted the message preached by Jesus' apostles, though considerable (Ac 2:41; 4:4; 5:14; 6:1; 21:20), was not noticeably different from that of converts to Israel's Messiah from other nations (Ac 11:19-26; 17:1-4; 1 Th 1:6-9; Ac 18:9-10; 19:8-10). According to the New Testament writers, the unbelief of the majority of the Jews was without excuse, as the ministry of both Jesus and his apostles had been authenticated by the miraculous signs which the Old Testament had taught Israel to expect with the coming of the Messiah (Mt 11:2-6 [Isa 35:4-6; 61:1]; Jn 15:22-24; Ac 2:16-22,32-33; Heb 2:1-4). What is more, unbelieving Jews sought to prevent the Gentiles, who had previously been excluded from the privileges enjoyed by Israel (Eph 2:11-12), from hearing the gospel in order to be saved (Ac 13:44-45; 17:5-9; 1 Th 2:14-16).

Israel's unbelief could lead to two diverse but equally troubling conclusions: that the gospel of God's grace (Ro chs 1-8) was the product of the imagination of the followers of Jesus of Nazareth, or that God had abandoned Israel because of their unbelief. The second of these conclusions is hardly less serious than the first because in Jeremiah's day God had promised that he would not abandon Israel because of her sin (Jer 31:31-37). If it could be shown that he had now done so, not only would that imply the end of Israel's uniqueness, it would also raise questions concerning God's faithfulness. Paul grapples with these problems in Romans chapters 9-11.

2. *The grounds of Israel's uniqueness: election in Romans 9-11*

One of the key concepts in these chapters is the election of Israel. This may be seen in the apostle's paradoxical statement in 11:28. We will begin with a brief consideration of this statement and then seek to clarify the apparent paradox by studying contextually the other uses of the word ἐκλογή ("election") in these chapters.

a. *"Enemies of the gospel" yet "elect" 11:28-29*

> As far as the gospel is concerned, they are enemies on your account (v. 28a).

It is clear from their description as "enemies" that "they" refers to the part of Israel which has been temporarily hardened because of their refusal to believe in Jesus as the Messiah of Israel (see v. 25). Here Paul repeats the concept, already affirmed earlier in v. 13, that unbelieving Israel's opposition to the gospel represents an advantage for the Gentile nations. The apostle then makes a statement which, because it contrasts so strongly with the first half of the verse, must be understood as a basic assumption of Paul's thought:

> but as far as election is concerned, they are loved on account of the patriarchs, for God's gifts and his call are irrevocable (vv. 28b-29).

According to Paul, unbelieving Israel retains her status as an elect people. Does this assertion mean that the majority of ethnic Israelites, although unbelieving, possess salvation? According to the Jewish scholar Raphael Jospe, chosenness and the obtaining of salvation are not identical concepts.[11] Likewise the apostle Paul, following the prophet Isaiah, distinguishes between being members of God's elect people and possessing salvation (Ro 9:27). Yet some Christian scholars treat election and salvation as though they were synonyms.[12] One purpose of our survey of the use of ἐκλογή ("election") in these chapters is to find out whether this is justified.

b. *What Paul teaches in Romans 9 concerning the election of Israel*

The word "election" first occurs in the opening section of this chapter to illustrate the existence of a more authentic Israel

---

[11] Raphael Jospe, "The Concept of the Chosen People: An Interpretation," *Judaism* 43 (1994): 130-135.

[12] For example, Refoulé claims that the reference to the irrevocable call of God in 11:29 is evidence that even in this case salvation is in view; when Paul speaks of election in v. 28b, the apparent paradox being limited to disparity of time. Thus, the elect who are now enemies of the Gospel in the future will respond to God's call,

within historical Israel (v. 6b). Paul then elaborates on God's elective purpose within the context of Abraham's physical descendants (vv. 7-13).[13]

The apostle could have illustrated the concept of an Israel within Israel by appealing to examples taken from the history of his nation, as when some members of the northern kingdom defected to Judah during the times of the reforms promoted by kings Asa and Jehoshaphat (see 2 Ch 15:9, 19:4).[14] However Paul prefers to ground his more nuanced definition of Israel in divine election (ἐκλογὴν, v. 11). He leads up to his statement concerning election by recalling some facts concerning Israel's origin. The expression "children of Abraham" refers to a particular descent that had passed through Isaac rather than through Ishmael. Paul makes the point that not all natural children (τὰ τέκνα τῆς σαρκὸς) are to be considered "children of God," but only the descendants of Isaac, whose existence depends upon divine promise. In other words, a special family relationship exists between God and the children of promise. This relationship held good even when Israel transgressed God's commands. Thus God declared, through his prophet Amos, "You only have I chosen of all the families of the earth; therefore I will punish you for all your sins" (Am 3:2).

God's purpose of election is further seen in the terms of the covenant which He confirmed with Isaac and Jacob (v. 7; cf. Ge 21:12; 26:23-24; 28:13-14). These included the promise of national greatness, a land and the role of bringing blessing to all

showing themselves to be members of true Israel (François Refoulé, "…*Et ainsi tout Israël sera sauvé*", Paris: Les Éditions du Cerf, 1984, pp.191-215). According to the fifth century commentator, Severian of Gabala, Paul's purpose in writing vv. 28-29 was to reprimand the unbelieving Jews, while the phrase "loved on account of the patriarchs" means: "loved because of the fathers, in honor of whom [God] acts benevolently with their descendants and will consider loved those who will believe and will have shown the right of citizenship, whom he will save" (in *Pauluskommentare aus der Griechischen Kirche*, Karl Staab (ed.), 1933; Reprint Münster, Westfalen: Aschendorff, 1984, p. 223).

[13] Robert L. Saucy, "Israel and the Church: A Case for Discontinuity," in *Continuity and Discontinuity*, John S. Feinberg (ed.), Westchester, IL: Crossway Books, Good News Publishers, 1988, p. 245.

[14] This movement of minorities from the northern tribes is reflected in the genealogies of 1 Ch 1-9; 36:22-23.

17

nations (see Ge 12:1-3; 13:14-15). Because God became in a special way "the God of Israel", Isaac and his descendants were put in a position of particular privilege so far as receiving salvation was concerned. However nowhere is it suggested that Israel's advantageous position guaranteed salvation to all members of the nation, neither did it exclude that Ishmael and those who did not descend from Isaac and Jacob, could experience salvation. On the contrary, according to the terms of the covenant, the blessing of salvation was to become available to all families of the earth *through* the elect nation (Ge 12:3; Isa 49:5-6; Gal 3:8-14).

The election of Jacob and his descendants gave expression to God's sovereign will (πρόθεσις, v. 11). The fact that it was already determined "before the twins were born or had done anything good or bad" demonstrates that the election of Jacob rather than of Esau did not depend in any way on the merits or demerits of the persons concerned. The corollary of this truth, often repeated by the Hebrew prophets, is that the full outworking of God's purpose through Israel will not depend upon their faithfulness either (Isa 54:10-17; 65:1-8; Jer 5:10-11,18; 31:35-37; Eze 16:59-63; Hos 1-14; cf. Ro 11:28-29).

Paul brings together two Old Testament passages in order to show that God's way of dealing with Israel is the fruit of sovereign choice:

> "The older will serve the younger" [see Ge 25:22-23]. Just as it is written, "Jacob have I loved but Esau have I hated [see Mal 1:1-3]" (Ro 9:12-13).

When the contexts of these two quotations are kept in mind, it becomes evident that the prediction – "The older will serve the younger" – concerns two nations, Israel and the Edomites, and not the twins as persons. The fact that Esau never served Jacob, in fact it was Jacob who bowed before Esau (Ge 33:1-4), confirms that the *nations* which descended from the two brothers are in view here. Not until the time of David would (descendants of) Esau serve (descendants of) Jacob (2 Sa 8:14).

The subject of the second prophecy, pronounced about 1500 years after the birth of Jacob and Esau, is clearly the nation of Edom and its territory (Mal 1:2-5). During the intervening centuries the descendants of Esau not only had shown hostility towards Israel, they had also tried to prevent the realisation of God's plan through Israel (Nu 20:14-21; cf. Eze 25:12-14). While it is true that God's love for Israel is the result of sovereign choice, Israel has also experienced just judgment and chastisement because of her transgressions. Yet, because God had put his name on Israel and made some solemn covenant promises to Abraham, Isaac and Jacob, he always returned to bless the nation when chastisement induced repentance (Jdg; 2 Ch 7:13-14; Hos 11:7-11; 14:1-9).

We have noted that the last clause of the Abrahamic covenant, "and all peoples on earth will be blessed through you" (Ge 12:3), implied that Israel's election was to be in some way instrumental.[15] However Israel did not always understand her election in these terms.[16] Thus in the continuation of Romans chapter 9 Paul develops the theme of God's mercy, which has in view the blessing of the Gentile nations as well as Israel (9:15-16, 22-24; cf. 11:30-32).

c. *What Paul teaches in Romans 11 concerning the election of Israel*

The chapter opens with a very specific question: "I ask then: Did God reject his people?" The idea that God has rejected Israel is very widespread.[17] Paul's answer is emphatic: "By no means!" (v. 1).[18] Paul confirms this emphatic negation with a biographical

---

[15] Ellison (H.L. Ellison, *The Mystery of Israel*, Exeter: Paternoster, 1966, pp. 41-56) makes a strong case for understanding the election of Israel in this way. He writes, "Here [in Ro 9-11] Paul is concerned with election (national as well as personal, in history rather than in the setting of eternity) as the means whereby He accomplishes His purposes for the world" (*ibid.*, p. 49).

[16] The Book of Jonah was written as an incentive to Israel to fulfil her missionary task.

[17] For example John Calvin (*Romans*, Calvin's Commentaries, John Owen [trans. & ed.], Grand Rapids, MI: Eerdmans, 1947; *Epistles of Paul the Apostle, to the Romans and to the Thessalonians*, Calvin's Commentaries, Reprint, Edinburgh: The Saint Andrew Press, 1961, pp. 190, 238) speaks of the "destruction" and the "rejection" of the Jews.

[18] The particle μὴ in the construction μὴ ἀπώσατο ὁ θεὸς τὸν λαὸν αὐτοῦ; (11:1) has the force of excluding the idea that God has rejected his people.

note: he himself, apostle and servant of Christ Jesus (Ro 1:1), was an Israelite, descendant of Abraham, of the tribe of Benjamin (11:1). He then adds a more general consideration: "God did not reject his people whom he foreknew" (v. 2). In other words, God had put his love on this people, reserving for them a special destiny. Consequently it is unthinkable that he would reject them.[19]

Having excluded categorically that God has repudiated Israel, Paul immediately finds an element of continuity between present events involving the nation and its past history. Elijah the prophet, in a moment of discouragement, thought that he was the only believer left in Israel. In reality there were seven thousand Israelites who had not "bowed the knee to Baal" (1 Ki 19:10-18). Paul then affirms, "So too, at the present time there is a remnant chosen [λεῖμμα κατ᾽ἐκλογὴν] by grace" (v. 5).

According to Refoulé, *the remnant chosen by grace* corresponds to the true Israel of which Paul speaks in 9:6b; moreover the "πᾶς Ἰσραὴλ" of 11:26 corresponds to this elect remnant viewed in its entirety.[20] However Cranfield observes that, if the expression "all Israel will be saved" referred to the sum of the elect chosen by grace during the present time, the statement would repeat something already spelled out in the chapter, which would make vv. 25-27 an anticlimax, whereas in Paul's argument these verses clearly form a climax.[21]

---

[19] According to Kevin Giles (*What on earth is the Church?* Downer's Grove, IL: InterVarsity Press, 1995, p.185), this statement and what follows it, in Ro 11, is not fully representative of Paul's thought, much less of that of other NT writers. Giles writes:

> Right from the beginning he [Paul] designates the Christian community with titles once the sole preserve of Israel, but in the epistle to the Romans he shows himself to be reluctant to concede that God has completely abandoned Israel as his people. He solves his dilemma by predicating a future salvation of 'all Israel'. Later writers were bolder.

Such reasoning neglects both the importance of chs 9-11 in the structure of Romans and the fact that only here in the NT is the question of Israel's present status as an elect people discussed.

[20] Refoulé, *op. cit.*, pp. 142-161.

[21] C.E.B. Cranfield, *The Epistle to the Romans*, 2 vols, ICC, J.A. Emerton (ed.), Edinburgh: T. & T. Clark, 1975-1979, 2:576-577. Cranfield writes:

The attribution of the same value to ἐκλογή ("election") in
11:1-10 as in 9:11 is based on the conviction that these passages
contain parallel treatments of the theme of election.[22] In reality,
in chapter 9 Paul affirms the election of the nation, through Isaac.
The choice of Isaac and, consequently the existence of Israel as
the people of the covenant, depended on the free will of God. In
chapter 11, on the other hand, the term ἐκλογή is qualified by
the words "by grace" (χάριτος, v. 5). This is the first and indeed
only time in Paul's writings that he qualifies "election" in this
way. Moreover it is clear from the context (9:31-11:7a) that
election which is the product of a work of grace is linked with
faith and is *election unto salvation.*[23] That Paul here intends election
unto salvation is confirmed by his emphatic statement in v. 6
which links the present discussion with his teaching in the earlier
part of Romans, that salvation is by grace through faith and not
by works (see especially 3:21-31 and 9:30-10:13). Thus, whereas
in 9:11 "election" refers to God's sovereign choice concerning
the *national* destiny of Israel, in 11:5,7 "election" concerns a
relatively small number of Israelites who have obeyed the Gospel
in the way described in 10:9-13.

There is undoubtedly a tension between the way ἐκλογή is
used in 9:11 and its more restrictive use in 11:5,7. We may ask:
What now of "the others" (v. 7b), are they no longer included in
the special election of Israel? In other words, does Israel's status
as an elect nation now depend on her own faithfulness and no
longer on the sovereign purpose of God? Paul was evidently
aware that his words concerning the election "according to
grace" could be construed as limiting God's interest in Israel to
those Jews who had become members of the Church. Thus,
after distinguishing between "the elect [according to grace]" and

---

The references to πλήρωμα αὐτῶν in v. 12, to ἡ πρόσλημψις in v. 15, and to the
grafting in again of the broken-off branches in vv. 23 and 24, point unmistakably
to something more than what would simply amount to the salvation of the elect
remnants of Israel of all the generations (*ibid.*, p. 577).

[22] Refoulé, "... *Et ainsi*", pp. 163-165.

[23] Cranfield, *Romans*, p. 548; Calvin (*Romans*, p. 414) is also convinced that the
election spoken of here is unto salvation.

"the others" (οἱ δὲ λοιποὶ), he applied himself to defining the present and future status of "the others" – the unbelieving majority of Israel. One of his purposes in pursuing this theme was to prevent his Gentile readers from becoming arrogant (vv. 13,19-21). In the light of the conclusion in v. 28, we can safely say that Paul also is confirming the election of Israel despite the nation's failure to recognise Jesus as their Messiah. Nothing, not even their opposition to the gospel, could cancel the special love of God for this people. It is the election of Israel which makes certain her eschatological salvation affirmed by Paul in vv. 24-27. Likewise her status as an elect people explains why, in the present time, even in her unbelief, Israel contributes to the enrichment and the reconciliation with God of the other nations of the world (vv. 11-15).

C. The Witness of History from A.D. 70 to the Present

The survival of the people of Israel and of its culture over three millennia in almost impossible conditions requires an explanation. In the preceding sections of this chapter we have considered some biblical evidence for Israel's uniqueness. We have seen that Paul reaffirmed this uniqueness, finding its grounds in special election which has not been rescinded despite the refusal of many of his own race to recognise Jesus as their Messiah. In subsequent centuries, however, the uniqueness of this people was contested by some of the most influential members of the Christian Church. Furthermore canon law downgraded the Jews to a status much lower than that of other peoples. Thus it is appropriate to ask whether there continued to be any evidence of Israel's uniqueness during the Christian era.[24]

[24] F. F. Bruce, commenting on those who at the time of the fall of the temple could have thought that the national life of Israel had come to an end, writes, "But the event proved them wrong. The disappearance of the temple order marked the beginning of a new and glorious chapter in Israel's story, which does not come within the scope of this book" (Bruce quotes an historical fragment preserved by Sulpicius Severus, c. A.D. 400, F.F. Bruce, *Romans*, Tyndale New Testament Commentaries, Leicester, England: InterVarsity Press, 2d ed., 1985, pp. 224-225).

Most of the nineteen centuries which have run their course from the destruction of the Jerusalem temple have been marked by intense conflict between rabbinical Judaism and Christendom.[25] Sheer inequality of numerical strength has meant that the Jews have been constrained to play the part of the underdog vis-à-vis a triumphant Church. Too often contempt and abuse meted out on them by representatives of Christendom have fostered uprisings in which instigations, like those of Chrysostom "to hate them and long for their blood",[26] have inspired massacres.

There is a fascinating testimony to the link between religion and persecution of the Jews in the eleventh century in Sir Walter Scott's famous novel Ivanhoe:[27]

> Except perhaps the flying-fish, there was no race existing on the earth, in the air, or the waters, who are the object of such an unintermitting, general, and relentless persecution as the Jews of this period. Upon the slightest and most unreasonable pretences, as well as upon accusations the most absurd and groundless, their persons and property were exposed to every turn of popular fury; for Norman, Saxon, Dane, and Briton, however adverse these races were to each other, contended which should look with greatest detestation upon a people, whom it was accounted a point of religion to hate, to revile, to despise, to plunder, and to persecute....

For their part the Jewish people have maintained their own traditions and "have taken to the whole world the witness, often heroic, of their faithfulness to the one God."[28] Furthermore, in spite of the contempt in which they have been held and repeated waves of aggressive antisemitism,[29] they have found the energy to make significant contributions to human well-being and culture. One example of this was their cultural contribution during

[25] See James Parkes, *The Conflict of the Church and the Synagogue*, New York: Hermon Press, 1934.

[26] Chrysostom, serm. VI, 1 (PG 48:903-905).

[27] Sir Walter Scott, *Ivanhoe*, Nelson Classics, T. Nelson & Sons, 1830, p. 68.

[28] "Sussidi per una corretta presentazione degli ebrei e dell'ebraismo nella catechesi della Chiesa cattolica", *L'osservatore Romano*, June 24-25, 1985, pp. 6-7, quoted by Enzo Bianchi, "Israele e la chiesa", *Storia cristiana* 10 (1989): 95.

[29] The term "antisemitism" does not imply discrimination against people who speak semitic languages (cf. "anti-Semitism"), but rather "hatred and persecution of the Jewish people" (cf. Allan Brockway, *TCJP*, p. 139).

the period known as "the Golden Age of Spain," the eleventh, twelfth and thirteenth centuries. Another was the rapid rise of Jewish scholars to positions of influence in England, after Oliver Cromwell gave tacit permission for Jewish resettlement in 1656. The celebrated career of Isaac Abendana at Oxford university (1663-1699) was but an example of Jewish integration into many different spheres of English life. The first Jewish knighthood was awarded as early as 1700.[30]

But the phenomenon is more general. For example the Jews, often constrained to uproot and resettle, were mediators of different civilizations, philosophic concepts and scientific knowledge. Jews were primarily responsible for the translation of ancient Greek and Roman texts first into Arabic and later into Latin on the eve of the renaissance.[31]

The quality and extent of the cultural contribution of the Jews is reflected, in recent times, in the number of Nobel Prize[32] winners of Jewish origin. A survey of the period 1910-1960 shows that during that half century more than thirty Jews, mostly of German origin, received the Nobel Prize in fields such as Medicine, Physics and Chemistry.[33] In subsequent years further Nobel Prizes in science and literature have been awarded to persons of Jewish origin. Moreover, in 1960 no less than thirty-two Jews were members of the Royal Society, the English Academy of Science.[34] This appears all the more remarkable when it is remembered that most of these Jewish contributions were made in a climate of antisemitism. For example many of the Jewish members of the Royal Society were Jews who had

---

[30] David S. Katz, "The Abendana Brothers and the Christian Hebraists of Seventeenth-Century England," *JEH* 40/1 (1989): 28-52.

[31] Norman Bentwich, *The Jews in our Time*, Penguin Books, 1960, It. trans. by Lia Moggi, *Gli Ebrei nel nostro tempo*, Florence: Sansoni, 1963, pp. 25-26.

[32] Nobel prizes have been awarded yearly since 1901, in accordance with the testament of Alfred Bernhard Nobel (1833-1896), "to those who, during the preceding year, shall have conferred the greatest benefit on mankind" in the fields of physics, chemistry, physiology/medicine, literature and peace (*Enclyclopedia Britannica* [1994], 8:738).

[33] Bentwich, *The Jews*, pp. 141-146.

[34] *Ibid.*, p. 147.

found refuge in England from antisemitic persecution.[35] Even Albert Einstein, who was awarded the Nobel Prize for physics in 1922 and was declared the man of the twentieth century by *Time* magazine[36], drew upon himself a continual stream of verbal abuse and was forced into exile, by reason of his race.[37]

All attempts to exterminate the Jews, whether or not perpetrated in God's name,[38] have met with failure. However there have also been other threats to their survival. These include the physical and cultural constrictions of ghetto existence,[39] the pressure put on them to convert to Christianity *en masse* during the twelth, fourteenth and fifteenth centuries[40], repeated expulsions[41] and attempts to assimilate them into Christian or secular society.

A particularly dangerous development, for the survival of Jewry, was the achievement of the great Jewish scholar Moses Mendelssohn (1729-1786) in the breaking down of the cultural and social barrier between Jew and non-Jew within Germany. Roth summarises his influence as follows:

> In the years following Mendelssohn's death, hundreds of his followers and admirers carried his principles to their logical conclusion by going over to the dominant religion, as he himself had gone over to the dominant culture.[42]

[35] *Ibid.*

[36] "Person of the Century," Elbert Einstein, cover of *Time*, December 31, 1999.

[37] *Ibid.*, p. 31; Cecil Roth, *A Short History of the Jewish People*, London: Horovitz Publishing Co., 5th ed., 1969, p. 425. Norman Bentwich shows that it was common for Jewish scholars and research scientists to encounter antisemitic prejudice (Bentwich, *The Jews*, pp. 142-143).

[38] During the first three Crusades, in 1096, 1147 and c. 1190, Jews as well as Muslims were considered infidels and massacred in great numbers (see Justo L. Gonzàlez, *The Story of Christianity*, 2 vols, San Francisco, CA: Harper, 1984-1985, 1:293-296; James Parkes, *A History of the Jewish People*, Penguin Books, Middlesex: Harmondsworth, 1964, pp. 72-73.

[39] See Roth, *A Short History*, pp. 297-311.

[40] *Encyclopaedia Judaica*, 16 vols, Jerusalem: Encyclopaedia Judaica, (1971), 5:538-539.

[41] Roth, *A Short History*, pp. 221-235.

[42] *Ibid.*, p. 339. Among these were some of his own children. Mendelssohn's grandson, Felix, baptized in infancy, devoted his genius to enriching the music of the Christian church.

Thus in the latter part of the eighteenth century, wholesale assimilation began to be seen in Europe as a viable solution to an age-long problem. This was reflected in the political policies of Joseph II of Austria, Louis XVI of France and the Granduca of Tuscany, Leopoldo I. However assimilation was to prove impossible. While the French revolution held the promise of greater emancipation for the Jews, the *Code Napoléon*, by creating a Jewish Sanhedrin and sundry laws for Jewish citizens, prepared the way for more persecution after the fall of the Napoleonic Empire.[43]

The acme of all attempts to destroy the Jews and, at the same time, the ultimate demonstration that the policy of assimilation had failed, was reached with the policies of the Third Reich (1934-1945). Thus Jewish families who for generations had been assimilated were listed among those to be exterminated. Adolf Hitler was so convinced that he was about to exterminate the Jewish race that he ordered the concentration of objects of Jewish cultural interest in the city of Prague, where he planned to construct a large Jewish museum, in order that Jewish culture would not be totally forgotten by humanity.[44]

While the perpetrators of the pogroms and the Third Reich were bent on destroying the Jewish communities within their reach, a very different movement called Zionism[45] was gaining momentum within Jewry itself. This movement had the ultimate aim of "securing for the Jewish people a home in Palestine guaranteed by public law."[46] This was finally achieved with the birth of the modern State of Israel on May 14, 1948.

---

[43] *Ibid.*, pp. 343-345.

[44] "Sorgente di Vita", RAI Due, 30 Sept., 1995.

[45] The movement was effectively launched by Theodor Herzl (1869-1904) when he wrote and published what was tantamount to the Zionist "manifesto," *Judenstaat*, after witnessing the blatant injustice meted out to Alfred Dreyfus in Paris in 1894. Zionism attracted international attention with the convening of the first Zionist Congress at Basle in 1897. See Howard M. Sachar, *A History of Israel: from the rise of Zionism to our Time*, New York: Alfred A. Knopf, 1993.

[46] The aim of Zionism was thus formulated at the first Zionist Congress, 1897 (Roth, *A Short History*, p. 410). A reflection on the Zionist movement was published by *Judaica*, March-June 1997, for the Centenary of the first Zionist Congress.

The subsequent history of this elect people is common knowledge. Thus it is no longer possible to ignore the surprising survival of this nation.

D. The Place of Israel in God's Plan

At the conclusion of this brief survey of evidence of Israel's uniqueness, it seems appropriate to summarise what the Scriptures teach concerning the purposes which God is working out through this elect people. Israel's special status as an elect nation was never intended to be an end in itself. One of the terms of God's covenant promise to Abraham, Isaac and Jacob was: "all peoples on earth will be blessed through you" (Ge 12:3; 26:4; 28:14). In reiterating this covenant promise to Jacob, God stated explicitly his plan to bless the world "…through you *and your offspring*" (Ge 28:14).

Even in Old Testament times, while the nation of Israel was in the process of learning to know and obey God, God so ordered their existence as to bring blessing to others through them. For example in the book of Genesis there are examples of blessing coming to other peoples through Abraham and his descendants (see chs 14, 26, 29-30, 41 and supremely ch. 47). The subsequent history of Israel contained many more examples of this. To mention just a few: Israel was instrumental in making known the true God to the Egyptians at the time of the Exodus, to the Ninevites at the time of Jonah and to all those living under the dominion of the Babylonian king Nebuchadnezzar, at the time of Daniel (Ex 1-15, Jnh, Da 1-4).

The supreme example of the offspring of Abraham, Isaac and Jacob bringing blessing to the whole of mankind is, of course, the saving work of Jesus the Messiah, "son of David, the son of Abraham", accomplished during his first advent (Mt 1:1, 21; cf. Isa 49:1-7). No blessing can compare with the gift of eternal salvation which is offered to all peoples on the basis of the Jewish Messiah's substitutionary death and resurrection (Ro 3:21-4:25). In this connection it should not be forgotten that it was Jesus himself who insisted that "salvation is from the Jews" (Jn 4:22).

Even the present hardening of unbelieving Israel has, according to Paul, the positive purpose of enriching the Gentile world by favouring its reconcilation to God (Ro 11:15a), much as the Bablyonian captivity brought blessing to pagan kings and their subjects (Da chs 2, 4 & 6). It is no accident that Gentiles who respond in faith to the gospel thereby become "fellow citizens with God's people" (Eph 2:19). In fact by means of their relationship with Israel's Messiah Jews and Gentiles are joined together, sharing the blessing promised to Abraham. The Bible further predicts that the return of unbelieving Israel to the Lord will be a means of exceptional blessing for the rest of the world (Ro 11:12-27).

Finally, if Jeremiah 31:35-37 and Isaiah 66:22 are read in the light of the survival of Israel, it becomes apparent that the history of Israel also constitutes a powerful sign of God's faithfulness.

E. Conclusion

The biblical and historical evidence for Israel's uniqueness fully justifies the following statement which emanated from the inaugural assembly of the World Council of Churches:

> In the design of God, Israel has a unique position. It was Israel with whom God made His covenant by the call of Abraham. It was Israel to whom God revealed His name and gave His law. It was to Israel that He sent His prophets with their message of judgment and of grace. It was Israel to whom He promised the coming of His Messiah. By the history of Israel God prepared the manger in which in the fullness of time He put the Redeemer of all mankind, Jesus Christ...
>
> For many the continued existence of a Jewish people which does not acknowledge Christ is a divine mystery which finds its only sufficient explanation in the purpose of God's unchanging faithfulness and mercy (Rom. 11:25-29).[47]

---

[47] Doc. 1, para. 2, The First Assembly of the World council of Churches, Amsterdam, 22 Aug. - 4 Sept., 1948, *TCJP*, p. 6.

Whatever our conviction concerning the present significance of Israel in the divine plan, we are bound to admit that the nation which God called into being through Abraham, Isaac and Jacob, continues to be a protagonist on the world scene. The best explanation for this is her continuing status as God's *elect* people. It is also because Israel retains her elect status that the Church, in order to not become presumptious, is obliged to take seriously the place of this nation in God's plan.[48]

---

[48] Cf. R. Kendall Soulen, *The God of Israel and Christian Theology*, Minneapolis, MN: Fortress Press, 1996, p. 156: "In the context of God's crowning Sabbath blessing, God's economy is irrevocably embodied in the carnal election of the Jewish people and in the consequent distinction between Jew and Gentile, between Israel and the nations."

Chapter Two

REPLACEMENT THEOLOGY
AND THE NEW TESTAMENT

A. The Present Debate

For over nineteen centuries the Jewish people have been the object of contempt and suspicion. What has come to be called "replacement theology" is widely perceived as being one of the causes of this attitude.[1] According to this concept *Israel has been repudiated by God and has been replaced by the Church in the working out of his plan.*[2] A variation of this idea is that *true* Israel always has been the Church.[3]

It is clear from the New Testament writings that much which was formerly true of Israel is in fact true of the Church. Israel enjoyed a special relationship with God based on election. So does the Church. Just as Israel was called to be a light to the nations, so Christ has entrusted a missionary mandate to the Church. Moreover it would seem clear that Jesus' decision to choose *twelve* disciples had the purpose of convincing Israel that the continuation of salvation history, during the period beginning with the coming of the Holy Spirit at Pentecost, was to be linked primarily with the Church.

Thus no one can deny that the Church stands in continuity with Israel in the working out of God's plan. The question is whether this implies the *cessation* of Israel's special elective status

---

[1] For a helpful survey of the complex phenomenon of antisemitism, see Gavin I. Langmuir, *History, Religion, and Antisemitism,* Los Angeles: Centro di studi medievali e rinascimentali, 1990.

[2] See Hans Ucko, *Common Roots New Horizons,* Geneva: WCC Publications, 1994, pp. 28-29. The term "replacement theology" (cf. "Christian supersessionism") is a relatively new term in Christian theology.

[3] This is summed up in Justin Martyr's description of the Church as "the true Israelitic race" *(Dialogue with Trypho,* cxxxv [PG 6:788]).

and thus the eclipse of her significance in salvation history. It is to this claim that we will be referring when using the expression *replacement theology* in the following pages.

According to some, the roots of *replacement theology* are to be found in the New Testament. According to others its origin is to be sought in post-apostolic times. Which of these two positions is correct? Can it be demonstrated that the New Testament itself teaches the cessation of Israel's special election now that God is calling a people for his name from all nations, or that being part of *true Israel* does not entail physical relationship with Abraham?

If *replacement theology* is taught in the New Testament, we must either accept this concept as an aspect of Christian orthodoxy or adopt a critical attitude towards the New Testament writings themselves. On the other hand, if it turns out that *replacement theology* developed in post-apostolic times, we would expect that its acceptance into the Christian Tradition would modify other aspects of Christian theology as well.

To keep our investigation in focus, it is helpful to remember that *Replacement theology* was an accepted position of a majority within Christendom from postapostolic times until the middle of the nineteenth century. However, just three months after the founding of the modern State of Israel in May, 1948, the First Assembly of the World Council of Churches issued a cautious repudiation of the concept.[4] Subsequent statements emanating from ecumenical circles have included an implicit or overt admission that the Church was partly to blame for the Holocaust, due to the fomentation of anti-Judaic attitudes through its theology of contempt.[5] In 1965, in the context of the Vatican II

---

[4] See *TCJP*, pp. 5-9. Part of this statement is reproduced at the end of ch. 1.

[5] Ecclesiastical groups which have produced such statements include: The Synod of the Evangelical Church in Germany (April 1950), the Netherlands Reformed Church (May 1951), the General Synod of the Netherlands Reformed Church (June 1970), the General Conference of the United Methodist Church in the USA (1972), the General Convention of the American Lutheran Church (October 1974), the Council of the Evangelical Church in Germany (May 1975), the Central Board of the Swiss Protestant Federation (May 1977), the Norwegian Bishops' Conference (November 1977), the Synod of the Evangelical Church of the Rhineland, Germany

Council, the Roman Catholic Church also made a statement[6] judged by Jaroslav Pelikan to be "the most forceful official Christian affirmation of the permanence of the covenant with Israel, at least since the ninth, tenth, and eleventh chapters of the Epistle to the Romans."[7]

Official repudiation of *replacement theology* implied the need to reflect on the origin of the concept. An influential contribution to this discussion was made by the Roman Catholic scholar, Rosemary R. Ruether, wih the publication of her book: *Faith and Fratricide*.[8] According to Ruether, Christology was the key factor in the development of Christian anti-Judaism.[9] The way Ruether builds her case shows the importance of distinguishing between "gospel" and "theological embroidery."[10] In fact the form of Christology criticised by Ruether is coloured by the realised eschatology of later centuries, in particular the claim of the Church to be the normative expression of the Kingdom of God.

A variety of reactions to Ruether's work were published together under the title *AntiSemitism and the Foundations of Christianity*.[11] In his Preface to this book, James Parkes writes,

---

(January 1980), the Texas Conference of Churches (January 1982), the Synod of the Evangelical Church of West Berlin (May 1984) and the General Assembly of the Presbyterian Church in the USA (June 1987). All of these declarations may be found in *TCJP*, 47-120. Moreover a statement of "principles" for the Jewish-Christian dialogue, elaborated by the Main Assembly of the Reformed Alliance in May 1990 was published in *Kirche und Israel* 5 (1990): 88-91, while a Consultation on the Church and the Jewish People of the WCC (4 Nov. 1988) elaborated a statement entitled: "The Churches and the Jewish People: Towards a New Understanding," adopted at Sigtuna, Sweden (*IBMR* 13/4 [1989]: 152-154).

[6] "Nostra Aetate" para. 4, in *Tutti i documenti del Concilio*, Roma: U.C.I.I.M., 1972, pp. 534-537.

[7] Pelikan, *Tradition*, 5:334.

[8] Rosemary R. Ruether, *Faith and Fratricide: The Theological Roots of Anti-Semitism*, New York: Seabury Press, 1974, especially pp. 64-116.

[9] Ruether writes: "In the synoptic tradition, messianic and anti-Judaic midrashim arose as two sides of the same development" (*Fratricide*, p. 64).

[10] Gregory Baum O.S.A., *Is the New Testament Anti-Semitic?* Glen Rock, N.J.: Paulist Press, 1960; Revised ed. 1965, p. 17.

[11] *AntiSemitism and the Foundations of Christianity*, Alan T. Davies (ed.), New York: Paulist Press, 1979, presented to James Parkes, on the occasion of his eightieth birthday.

"the foundations of antisemitism, and the responsibility for the holocaust, lie ultimately in the New Testament".[12] However John Meagher, author of the first essay, does not agree with him. While admitting that there was something very amiss in Christian theology's understanding of the Jews, he believes that its function was "to whitewash and justify an antagonism that sprang mainly from other sources."[13] Monika K. Hellwig[14] also denies that antisemitism is rooted in New Testament Christology. She affirms:

> It is rather a series of unquestioned ethnocentric assumptions arising out of the particular patterns of our history (anachronistically) to read back into the story of Jesus and into the doctrine that he is Christ and Lord [and that this implies] a divinely ordained ending of the covenant of Israel, giving way to the new era of the covenant of Christians.[15]

Debate has continued into the present. In an important contribution, Jeffrey Siker traces the use made of Abraham in New Testament and post-apostolic writings up to the time of Justin Martyr.[16] He concludes that some New Testament writings, in particular the Gospel of John, do anticipate what became the common understanding: that Gentile inclusion in the new covenant implies Jewish exclusion.[17] We will consider the evidence of John's Gospel later in this chapter. At this point I would just mention that, when considering the New Testament evidence, it is important to bear in mind that Jewish particularism and God's universal purpose already coexist in the promise of God to Abraham, as recorded in Genesis 12:1-3.

---

[12] *Ibid.*, "Preface," p. x.

[13] John C. Meagher, "As the Twig was Bent: Antisemitism in Greco-Roman and Earliest Christian Times" (*ibid.*, p. 23). David P. Efraymson, "The Patristic connection," (*ibid.*, pp. 98-117), comes to the opposite conclusion: "The fathers were «carriers» to be sure, and «aggravators» of something that had come into existence earlier."

[14] Monika K. Hellwig, "From the Jesus of Story to the Christ of Dogma" (*ibid.*, pp. 118-136).

[15] *Ibid.*, p. 132.

[16] Jeffrey S. Siker, *Disinheriting the Jews; Abraham in Early Christian Controversy*, Louisville, KY: Westminster/John Knox Press, 1991.

[17] *Ibid.*, pp. 185-198.

It follows that an emphasis on either Jewish particularism or God's universal purpose for mankind elsewhere in Scripture does not in itself imply the exclusion of the other aspect.

In another important contribution published about the same time as Siker's book, James Dunn argues that most if not all of the conflict between the Church and the Synagogue, witnessed to in the New Testament, was in reality an in-house debate comparable to other such debates within Second Temple Judaism.[18] However reputable evangelical theologians continue to consider some form of *replacement theology* axiomatic to a correct interpretation of Scripture.[19] For this reason and considering the role of this concept in the general development of Christian thought,[20] it is appropriate to re-examine the evidence for its origin in apostolic or post-apostolic times. In the present chapter we will consider some New Testament passages thought to contain evidence for *replacement theology*. In the next chapter we consider the tensions which developed between the Church and non-Christian Jews in the years following the fateful Jewish war of A.D. 66-70, before consulting the post-canonical writings, beginning with pseudo *Barnabas* and terminating with the writings of Origen.[21]

[18] James D.G. Dunn, *The Partings of the Ways,* London: SCM, 1991.

[19] For example Edmund Clowney writes: "In the history of revelation, the Old Testament people of God become the Church of the Messiah" (Edmund P. Clowney, *The Church,* Contours of Christian Theology, Gerald Bray [ed.], Downers Grove, IL: InterVarsity Press, 1995), p. 29. Thus the Church, which is said not to have begun but rather to have been renewed at Pentecost (*ibid.,* p. 53), is "the new and true Israel in Christ" (*ibid.,* p. 163). Similarly Colin Chapman writes: "The one and only fulfilment of all the promises and prophecies was already there before [the eyes of the New Testament writers] in the person of Jesus" (Colin Chapman, *Whose Promised Land?* Berkhamsted, Herts: Lion Publishing, 1983, p. 153). Wayne Grudem, in a brief section on the Church and Israel, makes the following statement: "the church has now become the true Israel of God and will receive all the blessings promised to Israel in the Old Testament" (Wayne Grudem, *Systematic Theology: An Introduction to Biblical Doctrine,* Leicester: InterVarsity Press, 1994, pp. 859-862).

[20] See chs. 4 and 5.

[21] Lee Martin McDonald surveys the phenomenon of anti-Judaism in the patristics in "Anti-Judaism in the Early Church Fathers", in *Anti-Semitism and Early Christianity,* Craig A. Evans and Donald A. Hagner (eds.), Minneapolis, MN: Fortress Press, 1993, pp. 215-252.

B. The New Testament and the Present Status of the Jewish People

1. New Testament passages thought to support replacement theology

John 8:30-59

Jeffrey Siker believes that "the contrast between σπέρμα Ἀβραάμ ('descendants of Abraham'] and τέκνα Ἀβραάμ ('children of Abraham') points to the heart of the dispute in John 8:31-47."[22] The Jews describe themselves as σπέρμα Ἀβραάμ in 8:33 and Jesus concedes this (v. 37). But, in Siker's opinion, by describing his Jewish opponents as *"descendants* of Abraham" while excluding that they are *"children* of Abraham" (v. 39), Jesus denies that Abraham is their father "in any meaningful way" (cf. v. 15). Siker then proceeds to link 8:39 with 1:12 and suggests that in the fourth Gospel τέκνον Ἀβραάμ and τέκνον θεοῦ ("child of Abraham" and "child of God") are equivalent terms. Thus anyone who meets the conditions of 1:12, whether a physical descendant of Abraham or not, becomes both a child of God and a child of Abraham. Unbelieving Jews, on the other hand, are "children of the Devil" (v. 44).[23] Siker concludes that, according to the fourth Gospel, Jewish opponents of the Johannine community "have no legitimate claim to being *children of Abraham*".[24]

Some comment is called for. The Greek text of John 8:44, which links Jesus' Jewish opponents with the Devil, does not contain the word τέκνα ("children"), as Siker avers.[25] The text reads: ὑμεῖς ἐκ τοῦ πατρὸς τοῦ διαβόλου ἐστέ (lit. "out of your father the devil you are"). Thirdly it is an exaggeration to say that Jesus denies that Abraham is the father of these Jews "in any

[22] Jeffrey Siker, *Disinheriting the Jews,* p. 136; cf. D.A. Carson: "In short, Jesus resorts to a moral and ethical notion of descent as being of far more importance than merely physical descent, and as being already supported by Scripture" (*The Gospel According to John,* Grand Rapids, MI: Eerdmans, 1991, p. 351).

[23] Siker, *Disinheriting the Jews,* pp. 136-191.

[24] *Ibid.,* pp. 142-143.

[25] *Ibid.,* p. 139.

meaningful way" considering that Jesus addresses them with the words Ἀβραάμ ὁ πατὴρ ὑμῶν ("Abraham your father") in v. 56. While the Jews who opposed Jesus were not, according to John, "children of God" (1:12) and could not be described as spiritual "children of Abraham",[26] there still was a real sense in which they could legitimately call Abraham their father (8:56).

When evaluating what some contemporary writers consider anti-Judaic attitudes in the fourth Gospel, it should be remembered that it was no novelty to deny the status of "children of God" to disobedient Jews. In Deuteronomy 14:1-29 Moses makes it clear that being "children of God" implies obedience to the covenant. Moreover the "Song of Moses" contains the following statement: "They have acted corruptly toward him; to their shame they are no longer his children, but a warped and crooked generation" (Dt 32:5). So the issue turns not on language but rather on whether Jesus is really the Christ, as the writer of the fourth Gospel has set out to demonstrate (Jn 20:30-31). If he is, those who fail to recognise this fact are disobedient and thus cannot be considered children of God according to Deuteronomy 32:5. Moreover if the words: "you belong to your father, the devil" (Jn 8:44)[27] are understood in the light of the Jewish way of speaking in Jesus' time, they no longer appear to be anti-Judaic nor a sign that unbelieving Israel has been repudiated by God. In fact, a little later in the same conversation Jesus' Jewish opponents express the conviction that *he* has a demon (v. 52). A wider study of Johannine terminology concerning unbelievers further confirms that the words attributed to Jesus in John 8:44 are not anti-Judaic. In 1 John 3:10 *all* of humanity, not just the Jewish people, are divided into τέκνα θεοῦ ("children of God") and τέκνα τοῦ διαβόλου ("children of the devil"), to indicate those who are born of God and those who are not (v. 9). Further on in the same Letter, John affirms, "We know

---

[26] The same distinction between σπέρμα Ἀβραάμ and τέκνα Ἀβραάμ found in John 8:37-39 is made by Paul in Rom 9:7.

[27] Cf. Siker's discussion (*Disinheriting the Jews*, pp. 136-143). Rosemary Ruether also uses John 8:43-47 (*Fratricide*, pp. 113-114) to argue that the NT teaches the rejection of the Jews.

that we are children of God, and that the whole world is under the control of the evil one" (5:19). Thus it is faulty exegesis to take the phrase "you belong to your father, the devil", used by Christ in the fourth Gospel, in isolation and read anti-Judaic attitudes into it, while failing to consider the parallel expressions used elsewhere in John's writings.[28] It is certain that the words "children of the devil" used in 1 John 3:10 do not have anti-Judaic connotations. Neither is John the only one to report Jesus' use of strong language. In Matthew (16:23) we read of Jesus using the word "Satan" to describe, not opponents, but no less a follower than Peter.

Perhaps the most significant of all references to "the Jews" in John's Gospel are those found in chapter four. Here Jesus himself features as a Jew (v. 9) while his answer to the Samaritan woman's question concerning the right place to worship includes this statement: "we [Jews] worship what we do know, for salvation is from the Jews" (v. 22). According to Jesus, the Jews have a unique knowledge of God; furthermore *only as a Jew* could Jesus contribute to God's saving work (cf. v. 42). Thus the fourth Gospel, which contains the clearest statements concerning the incarnation (1:14; 16:28), also contains the clearest statement concerning the whole world's indebtedness to the Jewish nation.

---

[28] In the longer version of Ignatius' *Epistle to the Philadelphians* there is the following allusion to John 8:44: "If anyone preaches the one God of the law and the prophets, but denies Christ to be the Son of God, he is a liar, even as also is his father the devil, and is a Jew falsely so called, being possessed of mere carnal circumcision (ANF, 1:82). Cyprian understands this verse to teach that the Jews "cannot now call God their Father," *On the Lord's Prayer,* 10 (5:450). The verse is used in support of anti-Judaic sentiment in the *Constitutions of the Holy Apostles* I, 21 (7:405) where Jews, as a class, are linked with the heathen and atheistic heretics and described as "not men, but wild beasts in the shape of men… destroying wolves". In general John 8:44 is used with reference to the Jewish people. This is always the case in the writings of Augustine except when he identifies in those who took Jesus to be the subject of Ps 17:11 (NPNF fs 8:50) and where he identifies the subject of the phrase "You are of your father the devil" and the "strange children" of Ps 18:46 with those who reject the NT, choosing rather to follow their own traditions (NPNF fs 8:54).

Matthew 21:42-44

Jesus addressed the Jewish leaders who rejected him, with these words: *Therefore I tell you that the kingdom of God will be taken away from you and given to a people who will produce its fruit.* According to Chrysostom, the whole parable of the tenants and in particular this conclusion, teaches the repudiation of the Jews.[29] In reality the subject of the sentence is not the Jews themselves but rather the kingdom with which they had enjoyed a special relationship.

According to Scot McKnight, this announcement reflects the thrust of Matthew's Gospel: "the message of the kingdom is for all, and one of the major foundations for this offer is the suspension of national privilege".[30] On the other hand, David Hill agrees with Chrysostom when he writes, "the Jewish nation, as a corporate entity, had now forfeited its elect status."[31] Hill reaches this conclusion in spite of having previously observed that "Matthew intentionally differentiates between the eschatological Kingdom (which the Jews never possessed, in any case) and the 'sovereignty of God' over Israel, expressed in terms of the special covenantal relationship".[32] The denial that Israel possesses the eschatological Kingdom does not imply that her special covenantal relationship with God has terminated.

D.A. Carson understands the announcement to refer to Israel's role as agent in the administration of the kingdom:

> Strictly speaking, then, v. 43 does not speak of transferring the locus of the people of God from Jews to Gentiles, though it may hint at this insofar as that locus now extends far beyond the authority of the Jewish rulers (cf. Acts 13:46; 18:5-6; 1 Peter 2:9); instead, it speaks of the ending of the role the Jewish religious leaders played in mediating God's authority.[33]

[29] Chrysostom, *Homilies on the Gospel of Matthew*, 68 (PG 58:631-634).

[30] Scot McKnight, "A Loyal Critic", in *Anti-Semitism and Early Christianity*, p. 77. McKnight observes: "It is a fact that the traditions of Israel consistently explain destructions of cities in Israel and deportations as God's judgment" (p. 75). He concludes, "Matthew... is no more anti-Semitic than Amos or Jeremiah" (p. 77).

[31] David Hill, *The Gospel of Matthew*, The New Century Bible commentary, Matthew Black (ed.), Grand Rapids, MI: Eerdmans, 1972, p. 301.

[32] *Ibid.*

[33] D.A. Carson, *Matthew*, The Expositor's Bible Commentary, Frank E. Gaebelein (ed.), 12 vols, Grand Rapids, MI: Zondervan, 1984, 8·454.

The post-resurrection mandate which Jesus entrusted to his followers spelt out the exact nature of the authority conferred upon them and their mediatorial role in the administration of God's rule (Mt 28:18-20). Although the Jewish people, as such, do not feature in this mandate, the overwhelming majority of the first generation of Christ's witnesses were Israelites. Moreover we are reminded in various parts of Acts that the Church's role in the present administration of the kingdom must not be confused with the eschatological kingdom (Ac 1:6-8; 3:19-31; 14:21-23).

Acts 15:1-18

The question addressed at the Jerusalem Conference was whether Gentile converts were required to accept circumcision and embrace the Mosaic law, in order to be saved (Ac 15:1-5). Peter's negative answer (vv. 7-11) was based on the way he had seen God work in the house of Cornelius, where he had witnessed the purification of the hearts of Gentiles who had believed the Gospel, through a direct work of the Holy Spirit. It is significant that Peter does not mention water baptism as essential to salvation, in the place of Jewish circumcision, although he had in fact baptised the converts at Caesarea (10:47-48).

The distinctiveness of James' contribution to the discussion (vv. 14-18) lies in his use of the term λαός ("people") and in the fact that he puts the Gentile mission into eschatological perspective. According to Kevin Giles, the fact that James "can transfer the title [λαός] to Christians, irrespective of their nationality, shows that a theological transition in his thinking on the status of Christians is well under way".[34] According to Giles, the understanding of the New Testament writers concerning the status of Christians was paralleled by the corresponding demise of ethnic Israel's status as the people of God.[35]

---

[34] Kevin Giles, *What on earth is the Church?* Downers Grove: InterVarsity Press, 1992, p. 88.

[35] Thus the choice of twelve apostles shows that "Jesus had come to reconstitute Israel" (Giles, *Church*, p. 32); the Church, as "restored Israel" is understood to be "the heart of *Luke's unique ecclesiology*" (p. 51; following J. Jervell, *Luke and the People of God* [Minneapolis, MN: Augsbury, 1972], p. 95), and "the Christian

There is no doubt that James' description of those called from the Gentile nations as a people (λαόν) for his name "was for Jewish ears an astounding and even a revolutionary saying."[36] This is due to the unprecedented juxtaposition of ἐθνῶν and λαόν, which in Jewish thinking had been mutually exclusive terms (Ex 19:5; 23:22; Dt 14:2; 28:9-10; Am 3:1; Isa 43:1). However this need not imply that the Church supplants Israel. According to Strathmann:

> The circle of the word λαός is given a new centre. Only faith in the Gospel decides. The title is not herewith taken from Israel. But another λαός now takes its place along with Israel on a new basis.[37]

Strathmann's observation that the use of λαόν to describe Gentile believers does not imply disinheriting Israel of the title, finds support in the fact that the definite article is not used with λαόν in Acts 15:14 whereas the definite article is still used to describe Israel in Acts 28:17,26-27. Furthermore we know from other passages in Acts and the New Testament Epistles that the new people that God is calling to himself is composed of Jewish *as well as* Gentile converts.[38]

James' statement in v. 15, "the words of the prophets are in agreement with this", is clearly a generalisation. The fact that God is calling from the Gentiles a people for his name, should not come as a surprise to readers of the Old Testament. After all, the Abrahamic covenant and the Hebrew prophets had envisaged Israel being a means of blessing to all peoples. As an example of the agreement between "the words of the prophets" and God's work of "taking from the Gentiles a people for himself", James quotes part of a prophecy relating to the re-establishment of the Davidic

community, the church, in Colossians is the eschatological people of God, the new Israel" (p. 132). "The quoting of Leviticus 19:2 [in 1 Pe 1:16]... illustrates how completely the church has supplanted historic Israel" (p. 167), while the negative references in Revelation to Jews (2:9; 3:9) and Jerusalem (11:8), are understood to prove that "the church completely supplants the old entity" (p. 175).

[36] Strathmann, *TDNT,* 4:54.
[37] *Ibid.*
[38] Cf. my discussion on Eph 2:11-3:6 (below).

dynasty (vv. 16-18, [Am 9:11-12]). The modification of the Amos prophecy from: "so that they may possess the remnant of Edom" to: "that the remnant of men may seek the Lord" (v. 17a), tends to confirm that Israel's involvement in history, whatever form it may take, is in view of the furthering of God's salvation purpose (cf. Ge 12:3 [Gal 3:8]; Isa 49:5-6).[39] The identification of Jesus as "the son of David" and Israel's promised messianic king, in Matthew 1:1-2:6; 21:9; 27:37, fully justifies James' conviction that "David's tent" was being rebuilt by the victorious conclusion of Messiah's first advent. The continuation of the prophecy in the book of Amos (9:13-15) and such New Testament passages as Matthew 23:39 and Acts 1:6-7; 3:19-21, suggest that the rebuilding of David's tent will also have positive signficance for Israel as a nation, at the time of Messiah's second advent.

James' concluding words: "For Moses has been preached in every city from the earliest times and is read in the synagogues on every Sabbath" (v. 21), suggest that the attention he gives to God's wider purpose does not imply unawareness of the particular role of his own race in God's programme. It must be remembered that James' primary concern was to give his opinion concerning "the Gentiles who are turning to God": whether or not they should be asked to accept circumcision and to observe the law of Moses (vv. 5,19). According to James, such a request ignores an important part of the purpose which God was working out through the Davidic line: in the benevolent plan of God there is room for the Gentile nations *as well as* for the people of Israel.

---

[39] J.A. de Waard has shown that while the rendering of Amos 9:11-12 in Acts 15:16-17 differs somewhat from the MT in meaning and from the LXX in form, it agrees, both in meaning and form, with the Hebrew of the Qumran scroll, 4QFlor 1:12 (J.A. de Waard, *Comparative Study of the Old Testament Text in the Dead Sea Scrolls and the New Testament,* Leiden: E.J. Brill, 1965, pp. 24-26,47,78-79). Moreover the pesher type exegesis seen here is paralleled in 4QFlor, where parts of the same text from Amos are applied to the situation of the Qumran community (I. Howard Marshall, *The Acts of the Apostles,* Tyndale N. T. Commentaries, R.V.G. Tasker [ed.], Grand Rapids, MI: Eerdmans, 1980, pp. 252-253). However the basis of James' use of Amos is his conviction that *God has already acted* (not that he was *about* to act) in a way that is eschatologically significant.

Galatians 3:26-29; 6:16

Galatians is a particularly polemical letter. In fact the reason why Paul wrote it was to refute the error of Jewish Christians who attributed a similar importance to "the works of the law" for salvation as the apostle attributed to justification "by grace through faith in Christ". Paul met this challenge first by an appeal to his personal history and the experience of the Galatians themselves (1:11-3:5) and secondly by considering some key elements of salvation history (3:6-18). The passage which interests us concludes with these important statements:

> There is neither Jew nor Greek, slave nor free, male nor female, for you are all one in Christ Jesus. If you belong to Christ, then you are Abraham's seed, and heirs according to the promise (3:28-29).

According to H.D. Betz, the thrust of Paul's argument is that non-Christian Jews are excluded from the Abrahamic promises. In other words, the Church has taken the place of Israel.[40] Is this so? A straightforward reading of Galatians does not require this conclusion. The question being discussed is not the status of Israel, as such, but whether justification can be attained by "the works of the law" as Paul's opponents believed. Siker, who examines Paul's polemic in Galatians as possible evidence of the disinheriting of the Jews, writes:

> Paul's fight in Galatians is not with non-Christian Jews but with a rival group of Christians whom he views as opponents because of their understanding of the law's centrality to the gospel. Indeed, Paul's dispute with the Teachers appears to have been primarily over the necessity of law observance for Gentile Christians.[41]

The idea that, when Paul insists that "God's grace" (χάριν τοῦ θεοῦ) manifested in the death of Christ and "righteousness of the law" (νόμου δικαιοσύνη) are mutually exclusive, he is also proclaiming the demise of Israel as an elect people, is based on too narrow an understanding of first century Judaism. Dieter

---

[40] H.D. Betz, *Galatians*, Philadelphia, PA: Fortress Press, 1979, pp. 116, 142, 146, 250-251.

[41] Siker, *Disinheriting the Jews*, p. 48.

Georgi has discovered parallels, within first-century Judaism, to Paul's teaching on grace in Galatians[42] and to his polemic with Torah centred Judaism.[43] Dunn concurs that Paul's argument and appeal in Galatians "reflect the concerns and language of intra-Jewish polemic."[44]

In order to understand Paul's argument in 3:26-29, it is necessary to consider his statement in v. 16, concerning Abraham's seed (σπέρματι). F.F. Bruce writes:

> There is no need to make heavy weather of Paul's insistence that the biblical text has σπέρματι (singular) and not σπέρμασιν (plural). The essence of his argument can be expressed quite acceptably if it is pointed out that the biblical text uses a collective singular ("offspring") which could refer either to a single descendant or to many descendants.[45]

That "seed" can have a plural connotation, as well as referring to a single individual, is evident from the following passages in Genesis: 12:7; 13:15; 17:7; 24:7 and from Isaiah chapters 42-53. Thus the word "seed" in Galatians 3:16 can be understood as referring to a single descendant, Christ, without excluding reference to the people to which he belonged (cf. 4:4 and Jn 4:22). Through Jesus the Jew the promised blessing comes to all the Gentile nations (Gal 3:8). The second use of the term (v. 29) refers to all who receive this blessing, that is, to all who belong to Christ and are thereby included in Abraham's spiritual offspring. Thus Paul can write, "You are all sons of God through faith in Christ Jesus, for all of you who were baptized into Christ have

---

[42] Dieter Georgi, "The Early Church: Internal Jewish Migration or New Religion?" *Harvard Theological Review* 88/1 (1995): 35-68.

[43] An analogous polemic is witnessed to in IV Ezra, an apocalyptic work. The writer of this work contests the restoration programme of the Pharisaic rabbis following the A.D. 66-70 Jewish war.

[44] Dunn, "Echoes of Intra-Jewish Polemic in Paul's Letter to the Galatians", *Journal of Biblical Literature* 112/3 (1993): 459-477. Dunn concludes:

> Our findings above do indicate a movement still in process of coming to terms with itself regarding its identity as heirs of the promises to Abraham, where the differences between Christian Jews were of a piece with the extension of polemical disputes elsewhere among the factions of Second Temple Judaism (*ibid.*, p. 477).

[45] F.F. Bruce, *Commentary on Galatians*. New International Greek Testament Commentary, I. Howard Marshall & W. Ward Gasque (eds.), Grand Rapids, MI: Eerdmans, 1982, p. 172.

clothed yourselves with Christ" (vv. 26-27). Being "clothed with Christ" is the secret of Gentiles becoming heirs of the promise made to Abraham.

It is at this point that Paul writes, "There is neither Jew nor Greek, slave nor free, male nor female, for you are all one in Christ Jesus" (v. 28). *In Christ* believers feature neither as Jews (people whose standing depends on privileges, such as those mentioned in Romans 9:1-5), nor as Greeks (people without any standing before God according to Ephesians 2:11-12), but rather as Abraham's seed and, as such, heirs of the promise. Thus the attempt of Paul's opponents to put the Gentile converts of Galatia under law was ill-conceived.

It is instructive to consider the other distinctions – slave/free and male/female – which are eclipsed by the relationship of believers in Christ (v. 28). The interesting thing is that both of these distinctions still subsisted, even though the social distinctions thus indicated did not carry over into the relationship of these various categories of people *in Christ*. It follows from a comparison of these three pairs: Jew/Greek, slave/free, male/female, that Paul is not insinuating the demise of Israel, as a nation. What is new is that the distinction between Jews and Gentiles does not carry over to the standing in grace of believers in Christ.

We conclude that this passage does not allude to the Church substituting Israel. Rather Paul's purpose here, as elsewhere in Galatians, is to demonstrate to his Jewish-Christian opponents, as well as to those Galatians who had been influenced by their teaching, that Gentiles, *as well as* Jews, become "heirs according to the promise" by placing their faith in Jesus the Messiah (cf. Ac 15:10-11).

We must now consider one of the concluding statements of Paul's letter to the Galatians. The expression καὶ ἐπὶ τὸν Ἰσραὴλ τοῦ θεοῦ, which appears only in Galatians 6:16, is variously interpreted *"and* upon the Israel of God" (King James Version), *"even* to the Israel of God" (New International Version) and "They are the new people of God" (New Living Translation). E. D. Burton understands the Greek text to mean that Paul invokes peace on those who walk according to the rule summarised in Galatians 6:14-15 and mercy upon the Israel of God, understood as "those within Israel who even though as yet unenlightened are the true Israel of God."[46] Bruce compares Paul's desire that Israel experience "peace and mercy" (Gal 6:16) both with his teaching concerning the hope of Israel in Romans 11:26 and with the closing words "Peace be upon Israel" of Psalm 125:5, the eighteenth ascription of the Eighteen Benedictions, used as a prayer in Jewish synagogues.[47] According to Bruce the phrase is to be understood as having an eschatological connotation. He writes: "For all his demoting of the law and the customs, Paul held good hope of the ultimate blessing of Israel".[48] On the other hand J.B. Lightfoot understands the statement καὶ ἐπὶ τὸν Ἰσραὴλ τοῦ θεοῦ to contrast with the expression *Israel after the flesh* found in 1 Corinthians 10:18, giving the following sense: "spiritual Israel generally, the whole body of believers whether Jews or Gentiles".[49]

Several recent writers insist that we read the words καὶ ἐπὶ τὸν Ἰσραὴλ τοῦ θεοῦ in the light of Paul's polemic with the Judaisers. Harvey Graham writes of the phrase:

> Since "Israel" has always been associated with "the people of God" it will now, in this polemic, serve to demonstrate that when all the barriers are down God has one people regardless of their origin. Outside of this polemic "Israel" is not used of the new group. In as much as this polemic interacts with other uses of "Israel" the name cannot be said to have been usurped by the Christian group at this date.[50]

James D. G. Dunn's position is similar:

> It will have been no accident, then, that Paul concludes this, his most polemical letter, with a blessing on "the Israel of God" (6:16), itself a

---

[46] E. D. Burton, *The Epistle to the Galatians,* I C C, S.R. Driver, A. Plummer, C.A. Briggs (eds.), Edinburgh: T. & T. Clark, 1921; Reprint, 1957, pp. 357-358.

[47] Bruce, *Galatians,* pp. 273-275.

[48] *Ibid.,* p. 275.

[49] J.B. Lightfoot, *The Epistle of St. Paul to the Galatians,* 1865; 20th reprint, Grand Rapids, MI: Zondervan, 1982, p. 225.

[50] Harvey Graham, *The True Israel,* Leiden: E.J. Brill, 1996, p. 236.

final polemical shot summing up the claim (chaps. 3-4) that the Israel of covenant promise is the Israel defined by that promise as including Gentles as well as Jews.[51]

Gutrod concludes that "the expression is in a sense to be put in quotation marks".[52] On the other hand, Kevin Giles maintains that the Church can properly be called "the Israel of God" and that Paul is stating as much here, polemics apart.[53]

We may sum up the evidence as follows: the expression καὶ ἐπὶ τὸν Ἰσραὴλ τοῦ θεοῦ appears only once in the New Testament writings, the letter in which it appears is admittedly polemical, moreover the translation *"even* upon the Israel of God"*, although possible, is not the most straightforward rendering of καὶ, otherwise translated "and" or "also". Thus we conclude that Galatians 6:16 is insufficient grounds on which to base an innovative theological concept such as understanding the Church to be the *new* and/or *true* Israel.

Ephesians 2:11-22

This section of Ephesians treats the change in status of Gentiles who have become part of the Church. Our question is: Does this mean any significant change in status for the Jewish nation? Commenting on the term τῶν ἁγίων "of the saints" in v. 19 a century ago, T.K. Abbott wrote:

> The clear reference to the πολιτεία of Israel shows decisively that the ἅγιοι are those who constitute the people of God. Such formerly had been the Jews, but now are all Christians. These are now the Israel of God...
> The ἅγιοι, then, are not the Jews, nor specially the patriarchs or Old Testament saints...[54]

---

[51] James D.G. Dunn, "Echoes of Intra-Jewish Polemic in Paul's Letter to the Galatians," *Journal of Biblical Literature* 112/3 (1993): 477.

[52] Gutrod, *TDNT,* 3:387-388.

[53] Giles, *Church,* p. 109.

[54] T.K. Abbott, *The Epistles to the Ephesians and to the Colossians,* ICC, S.R. Driver, A. Plummer, C.A. Briggs (eds.), Edinburgh: T. & T. Clark, 1897; 5th reprint, 1956, p. 69.

Markus Barth, commenting on the same passage three quarters of a century later, had a different perspective on the matter. He writes:

> First the Gentiles are reminded that they are received into the house of God, the community of Israel.[55]

Abbott's comment reflects the majority view of the Church before the Shoah and the birth of the modern State of Israel: that the Church has entirely replaced Israel. Barth's comment, on the other hand, reflects the renewed attention given to "the place of Israel and the Jew in God's purpose for the salvation of the world, and... the relationship of Israel to the Christian Church" which followed these events.[56] But is this all there is to it? Which of the two comments reflects more closely the meaning and flow of the Greek text?

Abbott's statement only apparently follows the text. The word πολιτεία does not occur in v.19, where the new status of Gentile Christians is defined, but rather in v.12, where it is affirmed that, in former times, the Gentiles "were... excluded from citizenship [πολιτεία] in Israel and strangers to the covenants of promise". The word in v.19 is συμπολῖται, meaning "fellow-citizens". The whole phrase, συμπολῖται τῶν ἁγίων means: "fellow-citizens of the saints". In other words, Gentile Christians were accepted in the community of saints which was already in existence. In this way they also become "members of God's household", which is "the household of faith" (Gal 6:10).

In v. 17 Israel is characterised as being "near" (ἐγγύς) while the pagan nations are characterised as being "far away" (μακρὰν). But being near did not mean that all Israelites were "saints". Both before and after the advent of Christ and the subsequent birth of the spiritual temple, the Church (Jn 4:21-24; Mt 16:18b),

---

[55] Markus Barth, *Ephesians 1-3,* The Anchor Bible, New York: Doubleday & Co, 1974, p. 314.

[56] Howard Taylor, "The Continuity of the People of God in Old and New Testaments", *The Scottish Bulletin of Evangelical Theology* 3/2 (1985): 13.

only believing, obedient Israelites are counted among the saints (Eph 2:18; cf. Heb 3:7-19; 11:1-38; Mal 3:16). What is new is the realisation of God's eternal purpose of uniting Jews and Gentiles in the Church (Eph 3:1-12). This "mystery" had only been partially revealed in former times, for example in the last clause of the Abrahamic covenant (Ge 12:3; cf. Isa 49:5-6). Now it is fully revealed. In Christ, believing Gentiles share in the honour of being God's household, while all in this household have greater privileges than in former times, having become the temple of the Holy Spirit (vv. 21-22; cf. Heb 11:39-40). Dunn's comment on vv. 17-19 sums it up:

> The point is that Israel has not been cast off; its blessings have not been taken away from them and given to others (contrast even Mark 12:9 pars.). Rather the Gentiles have been brought in to share the blessings previously confined to Israel.[57]

There is further confirmation of this in v. 20. The foundation of the new temple, besides being Christ himself, consists of twelve Jewish apostles, together with prophets. So it is incorrect to speak of a Gentile church. Rather God, through the preaching of the gospel, calls people *from* the Gentiles (Ac 15:14), as well as from among the Jews, to salvation and sanctification. So far as those *not* belonging to the Church are concerned, Paul does not suggest that Israel has lost her privileged status among the nations.

Hebrews 8:1-13

If the traditional opinion concerning the addressees of Hebrews is assumed,[58] this book appears irrelevant to the question of the

---

[57] James D. G. Dunn, "Anti-Semitism in the Deutero-Pauline Literature", in *Anti-Semitism,* Evans/Hagner, p. 158.

[58] While the opinion that Hebrews was addressed to Jews continues to enjoy widespread support, it is not universal. James Moffatt, *Epistle to the Hebrews,* ICC (1924; 3d reprint 1957) xv-xvii, believes that the first readers were mainly Gentile Christians. More common is the view espoused by F. F. Bruce that the first readers were Hellenistic Jews, F.F. Bruce, *The Epistle to the Hebrews,* The New International commentary on the New Testament, F.F. Bruce (ed.), Grand Rapids, MI: Eerdmans, 1964; Reprint, 1981, pp. xxiii-xxx.

origin of *replacement theology.* Siker notes that this letter does not contain either "any direct critique of non-Christian Judaism" or "any explicit appeal to Abraham to argue for Gentile inclusion".[59] That is not to say that there is no room for Gentile inclusion in the Church, the question is simply not raised. Robert W. Wall and William L. Lane write:

> The pastoral strategies adopted in Hebrews were all designed to stir the members of a Jewish-Christian assembly to recognize that they could not turn back the hands of the clock and deny their Christian understanding and experience ... this is not anti-Judaism; it is the reflection of a distinctive reading of Scripture in the light of the writer's convictions about Jesus.[60]

However not everyone agrees with Wall and Lane. Clark M. Williamson writes:

> Whatever its purpose, Hebrews put forth a supersessionist argument against Judaism, claiming that the covenant between God and the Israel of God had been abolished.[61]

This statement is not fair to the writer to the Hebrews for right at the centre of his homily he makes it clear that he is describing the *fulfillment* of Old Testament prophecy (Heb 8:8-12; cf. Jer 31:31-34). Readers who were acquainted with the book of Jeremiah knew that, in a moment of extreme weakness in the life of Judah, God had announced that he would, in the future, make a *new* covenant with the whole house of Israel. In the same context God spoke of the unconditional nature of promised blessing on the nation (Jer 31:35-37). This prophecy is quoted at length in Hebrews 8:8-12 and again at the conclusion of the writer's discussion on the new covenant (10:15-17). Wall and Lane observe that "the argument developed in Hebrews on the basis of Jeremiah 31:31-34 exhibits the writer's ability to

---

[59] Siker, *Disinheriting the Jews,* p. 97.

[60] Robert W. Wall and William L. Lane, "Polemic in Hebrews and the Catholic Epistles", in *Anti-Semitism,* Evans/Hagner, pp. 184-185.

[61] Clark M. Williamson, *A Guest in the House of Israel,* Louisville, KY: Westminster/John Knox Press, 1993, pp. 109-110.

recognize a significant hint in Scripture that was overlooked by contemporary writers".[62]

The concern of the writer to the Hebrews is that his readers grasp the nature of this new, better, covenant of which Christ is the great high priest (8:1-2). While he shows great respect for all that has preceded the new covenant, he insists that the new is better, as indeed does Jeremiah. The chief purpose of his "hortatory discourse" (τοῦ λόγου τῆς παρακλήσεως, 13:22) was to warn his own generation against making the same mistake as the generation of Israelites which Moses led out of Egypt, by failing to believe God (see 2:1-4; 3:7-19; 6:4-6; 10:26-29).

It is true that much of the book is devoted to showing that the new covenant, and what pertains to it, are better than the old Levitical covenant. However it is crucial to realise that this difference depends upon a solid fact of salvation history: the new covenant is based on the better, final sacrifice of Jesus the Messiah. Williamson takes particular issue with the biblical author's conviction that the old covenant has been abolished, a position which he describes as "supersessionist".[63] But, as Bruce observes:

> The very words "a new covenant" antiquate the previous one. In saying this our author does not go beyond Jeremiah, who explicitly contrasts the new covenant of the future with the covenant made at the time of Exodus, and implies that when it comes, the new covenant will supersede that earlier one.[64]

What needs to be stressed is that this is not a case of the Church pretending to supersede the Israel of God, but rather of one (presumably Jewish) Christian seeking to convince his fellow Jews that the new covenant has been established through Jesus and that there is no turning back. His readers are encouraged to join those of their own nation who have already entered the new covenant through faith. It is not part of his purpose to consider

---

[62] Wall and Lane, "Polemic", in *Anti-Semitism*, Evans/Hagner, p. 181.

[63] Willliamson, *Guest*, p. 108.

[64] F.F. Bruce, *Hebrews*, p. 177.

the status of non-Jews who are admitted into the new covenant by virtue of their relationship with Israel's Messiah.

While claiming that "we are receiving a kingdom that cannot be shaken" (12:28), this writer is aware that not all kingdom promises have yet been fulfilled (10:12-13). Thus he envisages Christ appearing "a second time to bring [complete] salvation to those who are waiting for him" (9:28).

1 Peter 2:4-10

This passage has in common with James' speech in Acts 15:14-18 that it attributes the dignity of "people of God" (λαός) upon converts to the Christian faith. Because of the deliberate way in which this is done (v. 10), it has been taken as evidence for *replacement theology.* For example, in view of all that God is said to have bestowed on the followers of Christ in vv. 4-10, Wayne Grudem concludes his comment with this rhetorical question:

> What more could be needed in order to say with assurance that the church has now become the true Israel of God?[65]

Peter H. Davids agrees with Grudem, but goes further by suggesting that the apostle's interest in these verses is exclusively in the experience of the Gentile component of the churches to which he writes:

> Unlike Israel these Christians never experienced themselves as unfaithful to a covenant, but they did realize that they were once outside God's favor, that is, rejected... But now these Christians know they are elect – not just a people of God, but *the* people of God.[66]

Certainly the transposition of titles of honour in vv. 9-10 is impressive:

---

[65] Wayne Grudem, *1 Peter,* Tyndale New Testament Commentaries, Downers Grove, MI: InterVarsity Press, 1988; Reprint, 1992, p. 113.
[66] Peter H. Davids, *The First Epistle of Peter,* The New International Commentary on the New Testament F.F. Bruce (ed.), Grand Rapids, MI: Eerdmans, 1990, p. 93.

But you are a chosen people, a royal priesthood, a holy nation, a people belonging to God, that you may declare the praises of him who called you out of darkness into his wonderful light.
Once you were not a people, but now you are a people of God;
once you had not received mercy, but now you have received mercy.[67]

In considering the apostle's transposition to the Church of titles of honour used by the prophet Hosea (Hos 2:23; cf. 1:6,9-10), it must be remembered that Christian Jews were among the addressees to whom the letter was written (1 Pe 1:1-2; cf. Gal 2:8-9).[68] For these Jewish Christians, the words of Hosea would have had much the same meaning as they had for the Israelites of Hosea's own time. The name *Lo-Ammi* (Hos 1:9), meaning "not my people", stood for a severing of the covenant relationship between God and Israel through Israel's acting like an unfaithful wife. However God's faithfulness toward unfaithful Israel meant that there was a future for the nation. Thus Hosea prophesied:

Yet the Israelites will be like the sand of the seashore, which cannot be measured or counted. In the place where it was said to them, "you are not my people," they will be called "sons of the living God" (Hos 1:10).

To understand how Peter could legitimately apply this prophecy to Jews who had come to faith in Christ, it is helpful to bear in mind the theme of repentance and forgiveness in Hosea (14:1-4) and the following parts of Jeremiah's prophecy concerning the new covenant:

I will be their God,
and they will be my people...
For I will forgive their wickedness
and will remember their sins no more (Jer 31:33-34)

John the Baptist, the forerunner of Jesus, addressed the nation of Israel, calling them to repentance, in the spirit of Hosea 14:1-4. Many of his countrymen not only flocked to hear him preach

---

[67] Translation mine.
[68] Grudem agrees that the first readers included Christian Jews, Grudem, *1 Peter*, pp. 37-38.

but also showed their repentance by submitting to baptism (Lk 3:1-18). Andrew, brother of Simon Peter, was among the disciples of John who left him in order to follow Jesus (Jn 1:35-41).

While the first part of Jesus' earthly ministry was similar to that of his predecessor (Jn 3:22-30; Mk 1:14-15), it concluded with the stipulation of the new covenant prophesied by Jeremiah, by means of the shedding of his own blood (Lk 22:14-20; cf. Mk 10:45; 1 Pe 3:18a). After his resurrection, Jesus entrusted the Good News to his apostles and Joel's prophecy began to be fulfilled at Pentecost (Ac 2:1-21). To those Jews who believed the gospel, God became their God in a new, more intimate way and they became his people in a new way, just as Hosea and Jeremiah had prophesied (Ac 2:38-47; 3:19-26; 4:23-31). These Jews, born again of the Spirit, now had a new standing with God based on the finished work of Christ (Jn 1:12-13; 3:3-8; Ro 8:1-16; cf. Eze 36:26). Georgi writes:

> The Jesus believers identified themselves as the beginning and center of the eschatological people of God; Israelites and Jews knew this idea from the prophetic predictions of the end times when a renewed covenantal community would grow out of the people of Israel.[69]

We may presume that there were also Gentile Christians among the first readers of Peter's letter. Both Grudem and Davids feel that the application of the Hosea prophecy to these non-Jews is proof that the Church has, to all intents and purposes, replaced Israel as the people of God. But this is not a necessary conclusion. Peter knew that Gentile Christians had been admitted into the new covenant. We are informed concerning the occasion in which "the apostle to the Jews" was constrained by God to recognise Gentiles who believe in Christ as having the same status as their Jewish brothers (Ac 10:1-11:18; 15:7-11). By applying the Hosea prophecy to the whole Church, Peter gave further demonstration of having accepted this fact.

It is not part of Peter's purpose to force a decision that either the Church or Israel is to be understood as *the* people of God.

[69] Georgi, "Early Church", p. 41.

While Davids is emphatic that the Church is "*the* people of God", Peter himself carefully avoids using the definite article in vv. 9-10.[70] It would seem then that Peter uses Old Testament titles of honour analogically, without attributing exclusiveness to them. If we bear in mind what Peter himself said elsewhere about the future fulfillment of God's promises to Israel (Ac 3:19-21), his avoidance of the definite article when describing the nature of the Church as a people of God appears to be deliberate.

Finally, nowhere does Peter make a statement like: "The Church is *the* new/true Israel". Such statements have to be added by commentators. In my opinion Peter himself would not have made such a statement, despite his recognition that the Church, as God's people, had much in common with Israel.

Philippians 3:4-9 and 1 Thessalonians 2:15-16

It has been suggested that these two Pauline passages are radically anti-Judaic.[71] However that assumes that Paul should have always used the kind of diplomatic language which is more in vogue in our pluralistic society than it was in the first century. In reality the radical nature of Paul's language is paralleled in Romans 11:28, where he describes the unbelieving majority of Israel as *enemies of the gospel* (11:28a). In the same letter he writes, "Pray that I may be rescued from the unbelievers in Judea..." (15:31). The strong language used in Paul's letter to the Thessalonians was well known to readers of the Hebrew prophets. Such invective was actually a confirmation of the special love of God for unfaithful Israel (Am 3:1-2).[72]

According to Williamson, Paul's negative evaluation of his former life in Philippians 3:4-9 is directed against pious Jews.[73]

---

[70] His readers were: γένος ἐκλεκτόν, βασίλειον ἱεράτευμα, ἔθνος ἅγιον, λαὸς εἰς περιποίησιν ... λαὸς θεοῦ. (1 Pe 2:9-10).

[71] See Ernst Käsemann, "Paul and Israel", in Ernst Käsemann, *New Testament Questions of Today*, Philadelphia, PA: Fortress Press, 1969, pp. 183-187.

[72] Giancarlo Rinaldi, "Osservazioni sull'epistola ai Romani", *EmmanuEL*, 3 (1997):10; cf. the love of Paul for his own people (Ro 9:1-5; 10:1).

[73] Williamson, *Guest*, p. 79.

This reading of the passage neglects the fact that Paul continued to consider himself a devout Jew even after his conversion to Jesus on the Damascus road (Ac 21:20-26; 24:10-18). Paul's polemic is rather with those who sought to construct a personal righteousness derived from the law *rather than* "the righteousness that comes from God and is by faith" (Php 3:9). Thus the real question, as in the case of Jesus' polemic in John chapter 8, becomes whether or not Jesus is to be considered the promised Messiah. According to Ruether, the root cause of *replacement theology* is the conviction that Jesus of Nazareth is the Messiah and the consequent obligation that Israel accept him as such.[74] In reality the fact that the head of the Church is Israel's Messiah constitutes a strong element of continuity between Judaism and Christianity and a strong affirmation of the uniqueness of the Jewish people.

2. Passages which seem to exclude replacement theology

a. Romans 9-11

In this section of Romans Paul conducts a thorough examination of Israel's place in the outworking of the divine plan. It follows that no serious examination into the legitimacy of *replacement theology* can ignore these chapters.[75] This is not the place to attempt a full-scale exegesis of these chapters, rather we will consider one of its leading features, the repeated use of the term "Israel". In fact while the term "Israel" is used eleven times in Romans 9-11, it does not appear at all elsewhere in

---

[74] See Ruether, *Fratricide*, pp. 246-251. The centrality of the historical figure of Jesus in the Jesus movement was not a unique phenomenon in first century Judaism: "The Qumran sect also put a historical figure – the Teacher of Righteousness – into a comparable central hermeneutical position" (Georgi, "Early Church", p. 43).

[75] This section of Romans is invoked repeatedly in support of the *new* majority view. For example, Romans 11:25-29 is cited in the statement made by the First Assembly of the WCC (August 1948) in support of the assertion that "For many the continued existence of a Jewish people which does not acknowledge Christ is a divine mystery which finds its only sufficient explanation in the purpose of God's unchanging faithfulness and mercy" *(TCJP*, p. 6). These chapters are also alluded to five times in paragraph 4 of "Nostra Aetate" promulgated by the Vatican II Council on 28 October 1963.

Romans and is used only six times in the rest of Paul's writings. The main question we will seek to answer is: Did Paul use the term *Israel* deliberately in these chapters in order to maintain the sense of Israel's uniqueness or was it his purpose to enlarge its field of reference to include the Church and thus Gentile Christians?

There is no doubt that in Paul's opening statement (9:1-5) the term *Israel* refers to the ethnic people with whom the plan of God is closely associated in the Hebrew Scriptures.[76] The passionate nature of this statement finds correspondence in Paul's prayer "for the Israelites… that they may be saved" (10:1). After listing the privileges enjoyed by Israel, Paul denies that the Word of God has failed. In order to prove this he makes the following statement: "For not all who are descended from Israel are *Israel*" (9:6). According to Ulrich Luz the second use of the term indicates here the extension of Israel's privileges to the Christian community, however without implying that the Church takes Israel's place in the divine plan.[77] Arethas, in his comment on the Greek text, expresses substantially the same conviction. He interprets the words "not all who descended from Israel are Israel" in the light of the preceding statement: "It is not as though God's Word had failed" (v. 6a). He adds this exhortation, "Let no-one, observing the entrance of the Gentiles, suppose that God's Word has fallen to the ground".[78] Thus, for Arethas, it is the entrance of the Gentiles which ensures that the Word of God does not fail. However, in

---

[76] In Romans 9:4 "the people of *Israel*" are those to whom belong the adoption (cf. Hos 11:1; Am 3:1-2), to whom God has made known his glory (cf. Ex 16:15-18; 38:34-38), with whom he has stipulated the biblical covenants (Ge 12:1-3; 15:7-18; 35:10-11; Ex 24:1-8; 2 Sa 7:12-16; 23:5; Jer 31:31-34), to whom God has given a legislation (Ex 34:28, Dt), a ritual which allowed them to have access to His presence (Ex chs 19-40; Lev chs 1-16) and the promises regarding messianic times (Isa 11:1-12:6; 49:5-23; 52:13-55:5; Jer 31:31-37; 32:37-44; Eze 36:24-28 etc.). In all this *Israel* is distinguished from other peoples (cf. Eph 2:11-12).

[77] Ulrich Luz, *Das Geschichtsverständnis des Paulus*, Beiträge zur evangelischen Theologie, Theologisch Abhandlungen, Herausgegeben von E. Wolf, vol. 49, München: Chr. Kaiser Verlag, 1968, pp. 269-274.

[78] μηδεὶς ὁρῶν τὴν τῶν ἐθνῶν εἰσαγωγὴν οἰέσθω τὸν τοῦ θεοῦ λόγον διαπεσεῖν… Arethas of Caesarea, in Staab, *Pauluskommentare*, p. 657.

order to demonstrate that *Israel* in v. 6b denotes the entrance of the Gentiles, Arethas finds it necessary to add the word μòνοι, modifying the phrase as follows, "In fact not all descendants of Israel are, *only they,* Israel".

Arethas's addition of μονοί to the text throws some doubt on the claim that Gentile Christians, understood as the *true* Israel, are alluded to in v. 6b. There is in fact no concrete evidence in the immediate context corroborating the interpretation according to which *Israel* includes those converted from paganism. Gutbrod is of the opinion that "the distinction at Romans 9:6 does not go beyond what is presupposed at John 1:47 ['Here is a true Israelite in whom there is nothing false']".[79] According to François Refoulé, Paul's more restrictive use of *Israel* in 9:6b corresponds to elect Israel which is to be found within physical Israel.[80]

R. Mayer approaches this more restrictive use of the term Israel by comparing it with a wider phenomenon within first century Judaism. Different groups made the claim to be the *true* Israel, while at the same time refraining from identifying themselves with eschatogical *total-Israel.*[81] He writes:

> Each individual group relied on the fact that it was the separated remnant of Israel which would lead to the eschatological community of the saved...[82]

Mayer understands Paul's treatment of Israel in Romans 9-11 to reflect that of contemporary Jewish sects. In this case the more restrictive use of the term *Israel* in 9:6b does not exclude that the same term can be used to describe a wider category corresponding to the eschatological *total-Israel.*[83] C.E.B. Cranfield finds the key to the meaning of the phrase, *For not all*

---

[79] Gutbrod, *TDNT* 3:387.

[80] Refoulé, "...*Et ainsi*", p. 181.

[81] *NIDNTT* 2:304-316. Mayer mentions the Sadducees, the baptisers, the apocalyptic movement, the Pharisees, the Zealots and quotes from the literature of Qumran.

[82] *Ibid.*, p. 312.

[83] Contra Refoulé ("...*Et ainsi*", pp. 142-161) according to whom "πᾶς Ἰσραὴλ" in 11:26 corresponds to the whole of the "elect remnant".

who descended from Israel are Israel (9:6b), in the statements contained in vv. 7-8. In these verses "Abraham's children," "God's children" and "Abraham's offspring" are distinguished from the more general categories described as "Abraham's descendants" and "natural children."[84] In other words, the more nuanced use of *Israel* in 9:6b refers to ethnic Israelites who were both natural and spiritual children of Abraham.[85]

The restriction of a title *Israel* to those Israelites who are spiritually attuned to God's purpose has precedents in the teaching of both Moses and Jesus, who respectively narrow the meaning of *"children* of God" and *"children* of Abraham" to those who lived as such (Dt 32:5; Jn 8:39-44). Moreover Paul himself had already narrowed the meaning of "Jew" and of circumcision in Romans 2:28-29, in a similar way (cf. Lev 26:41).

Israel is used three other times in Romans 9, always with reference to the descendants of Jacob. The first two uses (v. 27) are linked with the quotation of Isaiah 10:22-23 which refers to the salvation of only a remnant of the nation. Paul identifies this limited return to God with the limited response of his own generation to the preaching of the gospel. In v. 31 *Israel* is used as a collective noun with reference to the error committed by the majority of his contemporaries who sought righteousness on the basis of works, rather than by faith.

The first use of *Israel* in Romans 10 is in the rhetorical question: "Did Israel not understand?" (v. 19), with a view to demonstrating that the nation is inexcusable. Israel's guilt derived from the fact that she had not obeyed the proclamation of the gospel even though the prophecy of Deuteronomy 32:21 had been fulfilled. The name *Israel* is used again in v. 21 to distinguish between this people and the other nations. In all of these cases the term *Israel* is used to identify the descendants of Jacob.

---

[84] Cranfield, *Romans*, p. 305.

[85] According to Bruce W. Longenecker, it is the "faithful remnant" of the nation that is indicated, "Different Answers to Different Issues: Israel, the Gentiles and Salvation History in Romans 9-11", *Journal for the Study of the New Testament* 36 (1989): 96.

In chapter 11, the terms "Israelite" and "Israel" are used in two distinct ways. In vv. 1-6 "Israelite" is used with reference to "a remnant chosen by grace" while in vv. 7-29 "Israel" is used with reference to the unbelieving majority of the nation. The chapter opens with a rhetorical question requiring a negative answer: "I ask then, Did God reject his people? By no means!" (11:1). Paul proceeds to identify himself as an Israelite and to use the seven thousand faithful Israelites of Elijah's time as an analogy. This is followed by the assertion that "in the present time there is a remnant [of Israel] chosen by grace" (v. 5), that is those who have recognised in the saving work of Jesus the only grounds of their justification (v. 6; cf. 3:21-4:25).

Paul then addresses the problem posed by the unbelieving majority (οἱ δὲ λοιποὶ..., v. 7b), by speaking of a hardening which will continue "until the full number of the Gentiles has come in" (v. 25). Much of Paul's argument in this section turns on the distinction between Israel and the Gentiles while a recurring theme is the inappropriateness of the Gentiles boasting because their place in "the olive tree" is based entirely on faith and does not depend on natural rights (vv.13-14, 20-24).[86]

In his presentation of the place of Israel in God's plan, Paul uses an *a fortiori* argument (vv. 12,15) in order to show the effects on the rest the world of both Israel's present unbelief and her future return to the Lord. Regarding their present unbelief (v. 12), Israel's "transgression" or "loss" (ἥττημα) is producing riches for the "world"/"the [other] nations". Regarding Israel's future return to the Lord, described here as her "fullness" (πλήρωμα, cf. v. 26), it is expected that it will produce even "greater riches".[87] In this whole section Paul is concerned to demostrate

---

[86] Refoulé finds Paul's description of the salvation of the Gentiles and the salvation of "all Israel" parallel but distinct ("...*Et ainsi*", pp. 142-143).

[87] The concept suggested by the terms "fullness" and "whole bunch" (vv. 12,16) finds an echo both in the final part of the parable of the olive tree: πόσῳ μᾶλλον οὗτοι οἱ κατὰ φύσιν ἐγκεντρισθήσονται τῇ ἰδίᾳ ἐλαίᾳ (v. 24) and in the words πᾶς Ἰσραὴλ in v. 25.

that the function of Israel, as a chosen instrument, is constant in history and is not eclipsed by the entrance of the Gentile nations (cf. vv. 24-27).

The same kind of reasoning is repeated in v. 15, where he asks: If the exclusion (ἀποβωλὴ) of Israel from its position of privilege means the reconciliation of the world, what can be the expected effect of her re-admission (πρόσλημψις[88]) if not *life from the dead*? The eschatological nature of this statement becomes evident when the concept of rejection with which Paul characterises the present experience of Israel is compared with his statement in v. 25 where the partial hardening of Israel is said to continue "until the full number of the Gentiles has come in". Mention of "the world" in the first part of verses 12 and 15 suggests that the expression "life from the dead", which describes the effect of Israel's future re-admission (v. 15), also has to do with world history.

Not all interpreters agree that Paul's discussion in Romans 11 concerns two distinct periods. For example, in his treatment of vv. 25-27, Luz appeals to the fact that the conversion of Israel is more important than the order of events, reaching the conclusion that it is not necessary to consider the parousia a distinct moment in salvation history. According to Luz a careful study of the prophecies cited in vv. 26-27 shows that Paul is thinking mainly in terms of the first advent of Christ and has in mind the work of Christ viewed in its entirety.[89] This interpretation neglects the fact that the temporal references in vv. 25-27 are a basic element in the "mystery" revealed in these verses, suggesting that at v. 26 the apostle introduces a new stage in the history of salvation. That Paul has in mind two different stages in salvation history is also suggested by his distinction between present and future in v. 15 and by his statement in v. 24 that, in the future, the natural branches "will... be grafted into their own olive tree!"

---

[88] πρόσλημψις is a NT hapaxlegomena and thus, to determine its meaning, particular attention must be given to the immediate context.

[89] Luz, *Paulus*, pp. 288-295.

Whereas Luz considers the mystery passage (vv. 25-27) an integral part of vv. 11-32, Christoph Plag considers it an extraneous element which may have been extrapolated from another of Paul's writings. Plag reaches this conclusion on the basis of his conviction that Romans 11 presents two different ways in which Israel reaches salvation. The first of these ways envisages Israel returning to God by conversion (vv. 11-24, 28-32).[90] The second way, which Plag considers incompatible with the first, is prophesied in vv. 25-27. This second way is thought to depend entirely upon God both in the choice of the moment and in its realisation.[91]

Plag is right when he asserts that vv. 25-27 have a unique quality. In fact in introducing them Paul speaks of a "mystery". However there are numerous elements in common between these verses and the rest of the chapter which suggest that throughout the passage Paul has in mind two distinct moments in Israel's return to God. For example in v. 11 Paul affirms that the part of Israel which has stumbled has not fallen *beyond recovery* while, at v. 24, he affirms that this part *will* be grafted in again. Besides, nothing in vv. 25-27 leads the reader to doubt that some Israelites will be saved during the present time in which God is bringing in "the full number of the Gentiles". The expression *"all* Israel" not only emphasises the exceptional nature of the event described in vv. 26-27, it also presupposes the conversion of *some* Israelites in the present.

The term *Israel* appears twice in vv. 25-27. The fact that the content of these verses is described as a μυστήριον ("mystery") makes the reader aware that Paul is about to present something which could not be imagined without the help of special revelation. For the ancient Greeks the word μυστήριον indicated *that which must not or cannot be said*.[92] In the New Testament the emphasis shifts to what cannot be known without divine revelation.[93]

---

[90] Christoph Plag, *Israels Wege zum Heil*, Eine Untersuchung zu Römer 9 bis 11, Stuttgart: Calwer Verlag,1969, pp. 49-54,61.

[91] *Ibid.*, pp. 56-61.

[92] Colin Brown, "Secret", *NIDNTT,* 3:501.

Grasping the meaning of the term *Israel* in these verses is particularly important because of the future reference of the passage. If the object of this special work of God is ethnic Israel, it follows that this nation still figures as the object of God's special love, despite the existence of the new people of God made up of both Jews and Gentiles.

The first part of the "mystery" clarifies the relationship between the partial hardening of Israel in the present time and world evangelism: "Israel has experienced a hardening in part *until* the full number of the Gentiles has come in" (v. 25b). This brings us to the central statement of the revelation: καὶ οὕτως πᾶς Ἰσραὴλ σωθήσεται ("And so all Israel will be saved", NIV). This phrase, and the passage of which it is the centre piece, have provoked much thought. Refoulé lists seven ways, besides his own, in which it has been understood.[94] The first three of these have in common that they seek to define the *content* of the "mystery". This has been variously understood to concern: the *fact* that "all [historical] Israel" will be saved,[95] the *time sequence* by which "all Israel" will be saved[96] and the *manner* in which the salvation of Israel will be achieved.[97] According to the fourth view, the "mystery" teaches the mutual dependence of the salvation of pagans and Jews.[98] According to exponents of the fifth view, for example Oscar Cullmann,[99] the passage teaches how the pagan nations, by

[93] *Ibid.*, 3:504. This is particularly evident in the following passages: Mk 4:11; 1 Co 15:51 and Eph 3:4-6. In all μυστήριον is used 28 times in the NT.

[94] Refoulé, "...*Et ainsi*", pp. 25-30, 179-182.

[95] This is the most common view and was already held by Gennadius of Constantinople in the fifth century (Staab, *Pauluskommentare*, p. 401).

[96] Thus Douglas J. Moo, *The Epistle to the ROMANS*, The New International Commentary on the New Testament, Gordon Fee (ed.), Grand Rapids, MI: Eerdmans, 1996, p. 716.

[97] So Luz (*Paulus*, p. 295), according to whom Israel will be saved suddenly by divine grace after the period of her hardening whose aim was to favour the salvation of the pagan nations.

[98] This is taught by B. Mayer, *UnterGottes Heilsratschluss, Prädestinationsaussagen bei Paulus*, (Würsbourg, 1874); quoted by Refoulé ("...*Et ainsi*", p. 29).

[99] Oscar Cullmann, *Le Salut dans l'Histoire*, Neuchâtel, 1966, p. 162; quoted by Refoulé (*ibid*).

becoming part of "all Israel", enter salvation history and thereby give meaning to history in general. According to the sixth view, held by Karl Barth, the passage has to do with the constitution of "the Israel of God".[100] As in the case of Cullmann's view, "all Israel" is understood to be made up of both pagan converts and Jews.[101] According to the seventh view, the object of the "mystery" is to announce the different way Israel will be saved, not through faith in Christ but rather through a special intervention of God.[102] Refoulé's own view[103] is that πᾶς Ἰσραὴλ is elect Israel, which he understands to be the sum total of the remnant of Israel of each succeeding generation. In his opinion, elect Israel includes the part of Israel which has been temporarily hardened. The latter is not to be confused with historical Israel, which Refoulé believes to be under the judgment of God (1 Th 2:15-16).[104]

I have three difficulties with Refoulé's view. In the first place the language of 1 Thessalonians 2:14-16 is no more severe than that used in Ephesians 2:3 – "objects of wrath" – to describe God's former attitude toward people destined to become his "workmanship, created in Christ Jesus…" (v. 10). That there was still hope for disobedient Israelites is clear from Peter's appeal on the day of Pentecost and from the immediate inclusion in the

[100] Karl Barth, *Der Römerbrief,* Zürich: Evangelischer Verlag Zollikon, 1954; It. trans. *L'epistola ai Romani,* Giovanni Miegge (ed.), Milano: Feltrinelli, 1962, pp. 397-399.

[101] This was the conviction of Theodor of Mopsuestia (Staab, *Pauluskommentare,* p. 159) who speaks of Israel consisting of "not only those who are naturally related to Israel… but also those who by means of this faith have shown themselves to be worthy of the title… whose provenience is from the Gentiles".

[102] So Plag (see above) and W.D. Davies, "Paul and the People of Israel," *New Testament Studies* 24 (1977-1978): 4-39.

[103] Refoulé, "…*Et ainsi*", pp. 79-82.

[104] *Ibid.,* pp. 26-27. Refoulé writes:: "*C'est le Reste qui sera sauvé* et *tout Israël sera sauvé* n'est donc nullement contradictoire: c'est bien seulement le Reste qui sera sauvé, mais *tout le Reste,* celui qui est déjà dans l'Eglise, et celui encore présentement endurci. Tel est le mystère annoncé par Paul" (*ibid.,* p. 181). Appollinaris of Laodicea held a similar view, as may be seen in his comment on Ro 11:25: "Up until the exodus of all the peoples that have been foreknown, an insensitivity hinders Israel, but after this, the remnant of the nation, which follows that which is called Israel, will be saved" (Staab, *Pauluskommentare,* p. 75).

Church of some Jews who shared responsibility for the death of Jesus, following their repentance (Ac 2:36-42). Romans 11:26-27 envisages a similar transformation of unbelieving Israel at the parousia. My second objection has to do with the identification of "the others" (Ro 11:7b). Refoulé limits this group, and similarly the Israelites for whom Paul prays (10:1) to *the remnant of each generation of Israelites who will eventually come to faith in Christ.* This appears arbitrary, because it presupposes that of every generation of Israelites, including the generation which will be alive at the time of the parousia, God will harden only those who will later come to faith. If the others are not hardened, it is not clear why they do not come to faith in Christ, particularly those living at the moment of Christ's return in glory. My third objection has to do with Refoulé's understanding of election. His exegesis presupposes that "election" is virtually a synonym of "salvation". But God's sovereign purpose in the election of Israel (Ro 9:7-13) has more in view than the salvation of individual Israelites.[105] In any case in vv. 7b-27 Paul writes concerning the majority of Israel, who were *not* part of the "remnant according to the election of grace" (11:5). Following the logic that a revelation normally concerns something previously unknown, I find the second of the above views most satisfactory: that the "mystery" concerns the sequence by which "all Israel" will be saved.

Paul introduces the phrase "all Israel will be saved" with the conjunction καί, followed by the adverb οὕτως. In the past this adverb was widely understood to have temporal significance, giving to καὶ...οὕτως the sense: "and then", but the presence of the temporal proposition "until the full number of the Gentiles has come in", at the end of the previous sentence (v. 25b), makes such a meaning superfluous.[106] According to Gie Vleugels, the sense of the adverb is concessive, with reference to the immediate context: "notwithstanding Israel has experienced a hardening..."[107]

---

[105] Cf. Isa 44:28-45:3.

[106] Henry George Liddell & Robert Scott, *A Greek-English Lexicon*, 1897; 8th revised ed.., Oxford: Clarendon Press, 1901, p. 1098.

[107] Gie Vleugels, "Οὕτως", unpublished notes, Evangelische Theologische Faculteit, Heverlee (Louvain), Belgium, n.d., p. 2.

Bruce understands the sense to be modal, implying "that 'in this way' – by the operation of the divine purpose that the gospel should be received by the Gentile first, and then also by the Jew – the salvation of 'all Israel' will come about".[108] Douglas Moo concurs, understanding the reference to be to the process outlined in vv. 11-24 and summarised in v. 25b. Moo further observes that οὕτως, "while not having a temporal *meaning,* has a temporal *reference:* for the manner in which all Israel is saved involves a process that unfolds in definite stages".[109] Bauer, who also takes οὕτως to be an adverb of manner, understands it to be used correlatively with καθὼς,[110] with reference to what follows: the occasion and manner of the eschatological salvation of "all Israel" (vv. 26b-27). The Old Testament prophecies quoted in these verses certainly contribute to our understanding of the manner and the occasion of the salvation of "all Israel".[111] Understanding οὕτως to be an adverb of manner fits best with the flow of Paul's thought, whether it is understood to refer to what precedes or to what follows the words "all Israel will be saved". In both cases the description of manner involves a time reference.

So far as the meaning of *Israel* in v. 26 is concerned, the interpreter is obliged to attribute to it the same meaning it bears in v. 25. As there is no doubt that the reference in v. 25 is to ethnic Israel, we may conclude that Paul is speaking about the salvation of ethnic Israel in v. 26.[112] The use of the proper name

---

[108] Bruce, *Romans,* p. 209.

[109] Moo, *Romans,* p. 720.

[110] *A Greek-English Lexicon of the New Testament and Other Early Christian Literature,* W. Baur, W.F. Arndt & F.W. Gingrich (eds.); Revised ed.; F.W. Gingrich & F.W. Danker (eds.), Chicago: The University of Chicago Press, 1979, s.v. "Οὕτως", 2., p. 602.

[111] The same correlative of manner, οὕτως... καθὼς, appears in Php 3:17.

[112] John Murray, *The Epistle to the Romans,* The International Commentary on the New Testament, 2 vols., F.F. Bruce (ed.), Grand Rapids, MI: Eerdmans, 1959, 2:96, writes: "It is exegetically impossible to give to "Israel" in... verse [26] any other denotation than that which belongs to the term throughout this chapter. It is of ethnic Israel Paul is speaking and Israel could not possibly include Gentiles." Bruce *(Galatians,* p. 209) agrees: "It is impossible to entertain an exegesis which understands 'Israel' here in a different sense from 'Israel' in verse 25 ('a hardening has come upon part of Israel')"; so Cranfield *(Romans,* p. 576) and Hodge *(Romans,* p. 372).

Jacob in one of the passages quoted by Paul (v. 26), provides further confirmation of this.

Understanding *Israel* in v. 26 to refer to *ethnic* Israel raises the question as to whether "all Israel" is to be understood in an absolute sense. Zerwick and Grosvenor render πᾶς Ἰσραὴλ "all (=the whole of) Israel".[113] But does this mean that *every* Israelite, without exception, alive at the time of the parousia, will be saved and will enter into a new covenant relationship with God? In this regard it is helpful to note that, although the term *Israel* refers to historical Israel as a whole in v. 7, exception is made for Israelite believers. Similarly we may presume that, in the case of the re-admission of the nation into the olive tree (vv. 12,15,24,26-27), the nation *as a whole* is in view even though there may be exceptions in this case as well. Murray sums up the evidence:

> ... the salvation of Israel must be conceived of on a scale that is commensurate with their trespass, their loss, their casting away, their breaking off, and their hardening.[114]

On the basis of this survey of Paul's use of *Israel* in Romans 9-11, we concur with Siker when he writes concerning these chapters:

> [Paul] denies that Jewish rejection of Christ implies God's rejection of the Jews (Ro 11:1,11). Although their rejection of Christ shows their

---

[113] Max Zerwick and Mary Grosvenor, *An Analysis of the Greek New Testament*, Rome: Biblical Institute Press, 1981, p. 485.

[114] John Murray, *Romans*, p. 98; cf. Moo (*Romans*, p. 723): "Paul is probably using the phrase *all Israel* to denote the corporate entity of the nation of Israel as it exists at a particular point in time". Bruce (*Galatians*, p. 209), writes: "*All Israel* is a recurring expression in Jewish literature, where it need not mean *every Jew without a single exception*, but *Israel as a whole*. Thus *all Israel has a portion in the age to come*, says the Mishnah tractate *Sanhedrin* (10.1), and proceeds immediately to name certain Israelites who have no portion therein." According to William L. Osborne, "all Israel" must be understood as a technical term, indicating a group representative of the whole, "The Old Testament Background of Paul's *all Israel* in Romans 11:26a," *Asia Journal of Theology* 2 (1988/2): 282-293. Hodge (*Romans*, p. 374) writes, "Πᾶς Ἰσραὴλ should not be understood here to mean all the true people of God, as Augustine, Calvin and many others explain; nor as all the elect Jews but rather as the entire nation, as a nation."

current disobedience, the Jews remain included within God's promises because God is faithful (Ro 11:28-31).[115]

b. Other New Testament evidence

Romans 9-11 contains the only extended discussion of the problem posed by unbelieving Israel and the implications of such unbelief for the continuance of Israel as God's elect people. However there are other elements in the New Testament which appear to imply the permanence of Israel as God's special covenant people. Paul's own apostolic ministry reflected his conviction that Israel continued to be unique among the nations. Despite the obstinate unbelief of many of his own nation, the apostle to the Gentiles continued to go to the Jew *first* (Ac 13:14,46; 17:1-2; 18:4, 19-20; 28:16-17). That this custom was not only dictated by good missionary strategy is clear from the following passages of Romans: 1:16; 2:9-10; 3:1-4; 15:25-32. Paul would have even been ready to make the supreme sacrifice in order to facilitate the conversion of his own race (Ro 9:1-5; 10:1). Furthermore he described the Gentile Mission as an "offering" which he hoped would provoke to envy his own people in order to save some of them (Ro 15:16; cf. 11:13-14).

There are also other New Testament passages which seem to envisage a distinctive future for physical Israel, thus excluding the logic of *replacement theology.* Two affirmations made by Jesus containing the adverb "until" appear to be particularly significant. The first of these concerns the relationship of the Jews and the city of Jerusalem to what Jesus calls "the times of the Gentiles":

> They will fall by the sword and will be taken as prisoners to all the nations. Jerusalem will be trampled on by the Gentiles until the times of the Gentiles are fulfilled (Lk 21:24).

The use of the adverb "until" (ἄχρι) does not, in itself, prove that there will be a period of historical time following "the times of the Gentiles." However, it is clear that the idea of fixed periods of time is present. I. Howard Marshall suggests that the reference

---

[115] Siker, *Disinheriting the Jews,* p. 187.

is to one of the "allotted times" of prophetic scripture[116] and he links the theme with early church teaching reflected in Romans 11:25-27.[117]

In the second passage Jesus makes the following affirmation concerning unbelieving Israel:

> Look, your house is left to you desolate. For I tell you, you will not see me again *until* you say, "Blessed is he who comes in the name of the Lord" (Mt 23:38-39).

This statement presupposes that the people of Israel will see Jesus again and will pronounce this benediction upon him. Furthermore it implies that this occasion will coincide with the end of the prophesied state of desolation of the house of Israel.

Such statements as these may have helped to convince Jesus' disciples that the period of world mission, into which they were introduced by the coming of the Holy Spirit at Pentecost (Ac 1:5-8; 2:1-36; cf. Mt 28:18-20; Mk 16:15-16; Lk 24:44-47; Jn 20:21) was to be followed by the realisation of another dimension of kingdom promises. The following statement made by Peter denotes such a prospect: "[Jesus] must remain in heaven until the time comes for God to restore everything, *as he promised long ago through his holy prophets*" (Ac 3:21).

C. Assessment

According to some scholars, a number of the New Testament passages which we have examined require us to accept the logic of *replacement theology*. This seems to be reading too much into the text. Although several of these passages, taken on their own, especially Galatians 6:16 and 1 Peter 2:4-10, may be said to be

---

[116] See the juxtapposition of ἄχρι χρόνων... in Ac 3:21 where a distinction between present and future time is clearly intended.

[117] I. Howard Marshall, *The Gospel of Luke*, The New International Greek Testament Commentary, I. Howard Marshall & W. Ward Gasque (eds.), Exeter: The Paternoster Press, 1978, pp. 773-774; cf. Hodge (*Romans*, pp. 372-373) who compares the use of ἄχρις οὗ in Ro 11:25 with its use in Rev 15: 8 and 17:17.

compatible with *replacement theology,* they do not require it. Moreover, in order for *replacement theology* to qualify as a biblical option, passages which *allow* such an interpretation are not enough. There need to be, positively, passages which clearly teach it and, negatively, no passages which actually exclude it. I believe that the teaching of Romans 9-11 and the other New Testament affirmations which we have just considered do in fact exclude *replacement theology.*

Someone might object that even if the New Testament cannot be said to teach *replacement theology,* as such, it does display anti-Judaic attitudes, which after all have been one of the driving forces behind antisemitism. But here the issue really concerns the general presupposition of the New Testament writers, that Jesus of Nazareth is the Messiah whose coming was predicted by the Hebrew prophets. To those who do not accept this, much in the New Testament will appear anti-Judaic. Furthermore passages in which Jews and Gentiles alike are said to share in something more glorious than what had been formerly entrusted to Israel (Eph 2:11-21; Heb 11:39-40), or that describe the Church as *a chosen people* and *a royal priesthood* (1 Pe 2:9), will seem to be both illegitimate and arrogant. Similarly, statements according to which Gentiles are admitted into the sphere of God's blessing on grounds other than *personal* faithfulness to the Torah (Ac 15:7-11; Ro 3:21-31) will almost certainly be perceived as a seed of *replacement theology.*

On the other hand, a Jewish reader who shares the conviction that Jesus is the Messiah would be surprised if he found no evidence in the New Testament writings of the gospel being taken to the Gentiles (see Ge 12:3; Isa 49:5-6; cf. Ac 13:46-47; Gal 3:8). Similarly, talk of a *new* covenant and of the purifying work of the Holy Spirit, will not have the appearance of innovations to those acquainted with the prophecies of Jeremiah, Isaiah, Ezekiel and Joel, *once it is accepted that Jesus is the Messiah.* Moreover, when confronted with unfulfilled elements of Old Testament promise, perplexed readers will find reassurance when they read of a *second* coming of Christ (Ac 3:20-21; cf. Mt 13:36-43; 23:23; Lk 19:11-27; Jn 14:1-3).

What we find in the New Testament is a climate of debate within Judaism and a critical attitude towards those Jews who did not accept Jesus as the promised Messiah. On the other hand even in a context of heated debate, such as that described in John 8:31-58, Israel is not repudiated as a nation. Joel Marcus writes, "the very same New Testament polemics against Jews could be construed as either anti-Semitic or not, depending on the ethnic identity and sociological setting of the narrator and his audience".[118] According to Marcus, the polemic against Jews in the New Testament "is mostly... a criticism formulated by Jews against other Jews, and the audience for whose benefit the criticism is enunciated also includes a sizeable number of Jews [Jewish Christians]".[119] Moreover the fact that Paul attributes the status of elect nation to Israelites who are "enemies of the Gospel" (Ro 11:28) shows that the continuing elect status of Israel does not depend on her faithfulness, any more than it did in the times of the Hebrew prophets (see Jer 31:35-37).

If our findings are valid, it follows that the origin of *replacement theology* must be sought in the post-apostolic period.

---

[118] Joel Marcus, "Epilogue", in *Anti-Semitism,* Evans/Hagner, p. 292.
[119] *Ibid.*

Chapter Three

THE DEVELOPMENT OF REPLACEMENT
THEOLOGY IN POSTAPOSTOLIC TIMES

A. The Pattern of History

While it is dangerous to generalise concerning the movement
of history, few would dispute that the disastrous Jewish war of
A.D. 66-70, which witnessed the destruction of Jerusalem and
the Second Temple, began a process which changed the face
of Judaism and Jewish-Christian relations.[1] Although Jewish
apocalypticism continued to be an influential rival to Pharisaic
Judaism during the following decades, the failure of the Jewish
revolt led by Bar-Kochba in A.D.132-135 strengthened the
position of Rabbinical Judaism as the only enduring form of the
Jews' historical faith. Other earlier rivals, such as the parties of
the Zealots, the Essenes and the Sadducees, had been either
crushed or rendered obsolete by the earlier Roman victory.[2] At
the same time the importance of *Jewish* Christianity was greatly
reduced by the forced exile of the Jerusalem Christians to
Transjordan in A.D. 66 and the loss of prestige which Jewish
Christianity suffered due to the destruction of Jerusalem.[3]

During this period both Christianity and Judaism experienced
hostility because both were monotheistic and opposed to the use
of images. The consequent struggle for survival produced a spirit
of rivalry between these communities of faith. Georgi sees a link

---

[1] Dunn (*Partings*, pp. 230-259) shows that, in the complex pattern of relationships
following the events of A.D. 66-70, Jewish Christianity was more of a force than has
generally been thought.

[2] See F.F. Bruce, *The Spreading Flame*, The Paternoster Church History, vol. 1,
Exeter: The Paternoster Press, 1958, pp. 261-267.

[3] Inasmuch as the Romans forbade Jewish Christians to live in Jerusalem after
A.D. 135, the church there was purely Gentile in nature (Bruce, *ihid*, p. 272).

between this spirit of rivalry and the growing exclusivism of both monotheistic communities. He writes:

> Toward the end of the first century CE, Jews and Christians began to develop their own identities; not only against each other but also against the huge range of other options available to them both. These options were suddenly considered deviant.[4]

So far as Christianity was concerned, Jaroslav Pelikan observes that:

> the appropriation of the Jewish Scriptures and of the heritage of Israel helped Christianity to survive the destruction of Jerusalem and to argue that with the coming of Christ Jerusalem has served its purpose in the divine plan and could be forgotten. It also enabled Christianity to claim an affinity with the non-Jewish tradition as well as with the Jewish...[5]

The vastly decreased dependence of Christianity on its Jewish roots and the freedom with which it absorbed elements from the Greco-Roman cultural tradition is reflected in the fact that, while

> only one of the writers of the New Testament, Luke, was not a Jew, as far as we know, none of the church fathers was a Jew, although both Hermas and Hegesippus, for example, may have been.[6]

With Judaism engaged in a struggle for survival, and Christianity moving more and more into the milieu of Greco-Roman culture, it is hardly surprising that these two faiths increasingly saw themselves as rivals.[7] Thus at Jamnia, where Yohanan ben Zakkai had received permission from Rome to set up a school for rabbinical study, the rabbis developed puns to distort the meaning of the word εὐαγγέλιον ("gospel").[8] Moreover

---

[4] Dieter Georgi, "Early Church", p. 65.

[5] Pelikan, *Tradition*, 1:26.

[6] *Ibid.*, 1:12; cf. Gillian R. Evans, "The Beginning of Christian Philosophy," in *The Science of Theology*, Gillian R. Evans, Alister E. McGrath, Allan D. Galloway, vol. 1 of *The History of Christian Theology*, Paul Avis (ed.), Basingstoke: Marshall Pickering, 1986, pp. 26-40.

[7] Thus Frend, *Rise of Christianity*, pp. 135-136.

[8] George F. Moore, *Judaism in the First Three Centuries of the Christian Era. The Age of the Tannaim*, 2 vols, 1927; 3d ed., New York: Schocken Books, 1971, 1:244.

the *Birkath ha-Minim,* a pronouncement against heretics which is part of the twelfth "benediction" in the Jewish liturgical prayer, *Eighteen Benedictions,* is thought to be directed against Christians.[9] There is evidence of this in Justin Martyr's *Dialogue with Trypho,* written about A.D. 150. At a certain point Justin accuses the Jews of "cursing in your synagogues those that believe on Christ".[10] Such attitudes were not unilateral. Ignatius of Antioch, writing around A.D. 115, instigated his readers to oppose all things Jewish. He claimed that the Hebrew prophets had lived according to Jesus Christ and *not* according to the Jewish law.[11]

Lee Martin McDonald suggests that another factor contributing to "the Christians' strong negative stance against Jews and Judaism... around the turn of the first century... may have been the vast difference in the size of their religious bodies". He estimates that Christians may have numbered fewer than 100,000 while Jews numbered somewhere between six and seven million.[12] The negative stance of Christians against Jews and Judaism consolidated into an *Adversus Judaeos* tradition[13] which permeated much of the writings of the Church Fathers, favouring *replacement theology.*

---

[9] Bruce, *Spreading Flame,* p. 267; Lee Martin McDonald, "Anti-Judaism in the early Church Fathers", in *Anti-Semitism,* Evans/Hagner, p. 246.

[10] καταρώμενοι ἐν ταῖς συναγωγαῖς ὑμῶν τοὺς πιστεύοντας ἐπὶ τὸν Χριστόν, *Tryph. Jud.*. 16,4; PG 6:512.

[11] *To the Magnesians,* VIII, 10.

[12] McDonald, "Anti-Judaism", in *Anti-Semitism,* Evans/Hagner, p. 242.

[13] The *Adversus Judaeos* writings include Dialogues, Books of Testimonies and Homilies. Ferdinandus Cavallera (PG 162:128-129) lists 22 such works written in Greek, beginning with the II century work, *Epistle of Barnabas,* and ending with a XIII century work by Euthymius Zigabemus, *Panoply of Dogmatics,* ch. 8 (PG 162:128-129). Moreover 11 of the "Scripta Polemica" in Latin (PL 218:1059-1064) belong to this tradition and bear such titles as *An Answer to the Jews,* Tertullian's seminal work dating from c. 200 (PL 2:595-642) and *A Tract against the Jews,* an anonymous work written in the XII century (PL 213:747-808).

The following are some of the more important contributions to the *Adversus Judaeos* tradition, listed in chronological order: Justin Martyr, *Dialogue with Trypho* (PG 6:471-799); Tertullian, *An Answer to the Jews* (PL 2:595-642); Hippolytus, *Expository Treatise Against the Jews* (PG 10:787-794), Novatian, *"On Jewish Meats"*

A particular area of rivalry between Christianity and Judaism concerned the Old Testament Scriptures. For their part, the Rabbis rejected the Christian interpretation of the Hebrew Scriptures when these were used to demonstrate that Jesus was the Messiah of Israel.[14] On the other hand Christians freely appropriated to themselves much in the Hebrew Scriptures that was originally addressed to Israel.[15] This was facilitated by the practice of allegorical interpretation.[16]

B. Replacement Theology in Early Christian Writings

1. The *Epistle of Barnabas: The disinheriting of Israel*

One of the main purposes of this pseudonymous second century writing was to show that the Jews, by interpreting the Old Testament ceremonial law literally, lost sight of its true import.[17] To gain a perspective on this unknown writer's opinion concerning ethnic Israel, we may begin by observing his reasoning

(ANF 5:645-650); Cyprian, *Three Books of Testimonies Against the Jews* (PL 4:703-810); Ephraem of Syria, *Rhythm Against the Jews* (Library of the Fathers, J.B. Morris (ed.), Oxford, 1847, pp. 61-83); Aphrahat of Persia, *Demonstrations Against the Jews*, (see J. Neusner, Aphrahat and Judaism, Leiden: Brill, 1971); John Chrysostom, *Demonstrations to the Jews and Gentiles that Christ is God* (PG 48:811-838) and *Eight Orations Against the Jews* (*ibid.*, cols 839-942); Augustine, *Tract Against the Jews* (PL 42:51-64); Maximus the Confessor, *Treatise Against the Jews* (Edited text by C.H. Turner, *Journal of Theological Studies* 20 [1919]: 289-310); Isidore of Seville, *Against the Jews* (PL 83:449-538); John Damascene, *On the Orthodox Faith*, 4:23 "On the Sabbath, Against the Jews," (PG 94:1201-1206); Martin Luther, *The Jews and their Lies* (1543).

Around the eighth century many pseudo *Dialogues* were composed, following the general pattern of Justin Martyr's *Dialogue with Trypho,* in which the Jewish interlocutors were figments of the imagination of the Christian writer. Despite the unilateral nature of these Dialogues, they not only represented but also influenced medieval Christian thought concerning the Jews.

[14] Bruce, *Spreading Flame,* pp. 263-267.

[15] Pelikan, *Tradition,* 1:14-27.

[16] See also the section "The Christian Synagogue," in Frend, *Rise of Christianity,* pp. 120-160.

[17] Bruce, *Spreading Flame,* p. 236. According to Bruce, *The Epistle of Barnabas* was written between 70 and 135.

in chapter XIV, 3-4. Commenting on the historical data concerning the golden calf and the fact that Moses broke the original tables of stone when he became aware of the nation's transgression, the writer concludes that the Lord never did give the promised testament to unworthy Israel; rather it has been given to the Church which, through Christ, has received the promised inheritance.

> He was manifested, in order that they [the Israelites] might be perfected in their iniquities, and that we, being constituted heirs through Him, might receive the testament of the Lord Jesus (XIV, 5).[18]

This disinheriting of Israel is evident throughout *Barnabas*. For example, alluding to Exodus 33:1-3, the author treats God's promise to Abraham, Isaac and Jacob of a land, as a parable of the Christians' inheritance through Christ and regeneraton by the Spirit *(Bar.* VI, 6-17). In IX, 3-4 he claims that the practice of physical circumcision was in reality a transgression which an evil angel misled them to do, whereas God's command concerned only *spiritual* circumcision. Levitical food laws are similarly discredited in chapter X.

Of particular significance for our study is the use *Barnabas* makes of Genesis 25:21-23. Chapter XIII begins:

> But let us see if this people is the heir, or the former, and if the covenant belongs to us or to them (XIII,1).

The chief point in discussion is the phrase "the older will serve the younger" quoted by Paul in Romans 9:12. In Genesis the *older* is clearly Esau (and his descendants) while the *younger* is Jacob (and his descendants). Paul quotes this prophecy in Romans to show that Israel's position as the elect nation depends upon God's purpose and not upon human works. The author of *Barnabas* completely ignores the way the phrase is used both in Genesis and Romans and links it with Genesis

[18] The Latin text reads, "Apparuit vero, ut tum illi [Judaei] in peccatis consumarentur, tum nos per ipsum haeredes facti Domini Jesu testamentum acciperemus, qui destinatus erat, ut per adventum suum praecordia nostra, iam a morte assumpta et tradita erroris iniquitati, redimens e tenebris verbo [suo] disponat in nobis testamentum" (PG 1:1221),

48:17-19, contending that in both cases the younger child refers to the Church, the true heir to the covenant.

Barnabas shows little respect for Old Testament institutions. For example in chapter XVI, 7 a temple made with hands is likened to a habitation of demons, full of idolatry. The writing, as a whole, manifests the latent presupposition that *the Church, the true heir of the promises, occupies the place that Israel had always been unworthy of occupying.*

2. The *Letter to Diognetus: Is the Old Testament canonical?*

This anonymous writing[19] is an apology for the Christian way of worshipping God. It dates from around the middle of the second century when the Christians began to feel the need to defend and explain the faith in a way that was comprehensible to pagan neighbours and philosophers. In this writing Levitical offerings are compared with idolatry (III, 5) while food laws, Sabbath keeping, circumcision and fasting are called "superstition" and "utterly ridiculous and unworthy of notice" (IV, 1). Thus depreciation of the Jews is extended to depreciation of the Torah. Circumcision, which was particularly offensive to Greco-Roman culture,[20] is singled out for particular comment:

> ...to glory in the circumcision of the flesh as a proof of election, and as if, on account of it, they were specially beloved by God, how is it not a subject of ridicule? (IV, 4).[21]

---

[19] ANF 1:25-30/PG 2:1167-1186.

[20] Bruce *(Spreading Flame,* pp. 14, 270) informs us that circumcision hindered many men from becoming Jewish proselytes and featured among the bodily mutilations that were prohibited by law under emperor Hadrian. Josephus, himself from the ranks of the Pharisees, recounts how he withstood his fellow Jews when they tried to force two men from the region of Trachonitis to be circumcised (*The Life of Flavius Josephus,* in Works of Josephus, 4 vols, trans. William Whiston, Grand Rapids, MI: Baker Book House, 1974, vol. II, sec. 23). Martin Hengel (*Judentum und Hellenismus,* Tübingen: J.C.B. Mohr [Paul Siebeck], 1973; Eng. ed.. *Judaism and Hellenism,* trans. John Bowden, 2 vols, London: SCM Press, 1974, 1:74, 278, 289; 2:96) draws attention to the attempts of Jewish ephebes to remove the signs of their circumcision in the period preceding the Maccabean revolt (1 Macc. 1:15).

[21] The Greek text reads, τὸ δὲ καὶ μείωσιν τῆς σαρκὸς μαρτύριον ἐκλογῆς ἀλαζονεύεσθαι, ὡς διὰ τοῦτο ἐξαιρέτως ἠγαπημένους ὑπὸ Θεοῦ, πῶς οὐ κλεύης ἄξιον; (PG 2:1172-1173).

By lumping together "the superstition of the Jews" with pagan idolatry (I,1) and treating as superstition what is prescribed by the Mosaic law (chapters III-IV), the author, besides showing contempt for the Jews, is ignoring the canonical status of the foundational part of the Old Testament.

3. The writings of Justin Martyr: *The Church is the "true Israelitic race"*

Although our interest will focus mainly on the *Dialogue of Justin with Trypho, a Jew,* Justin's presentation of the concept of "logos" in his *First Apology* is also relevant to our purpose. His theory of the eternity of the logos is invoked to answer objections regarding the relatively recent appearance of Christ on the scene of history.[22] He writes:

> We have declared above that…[Christ] is the Word of whom every race of men were partakers; and those who lived reasonably are Christians, even though they have been thought atheists; as, among the Greeks, Socrates and Heraclitus, and men like them; and among the barbarians, Abraham, and Ananias, and Azarias and Misael, and Elias, and many others whose actions and names we now decline to recount, because we know it would be tedious.[23]

It is noteworthy that Justin adopts a typically Greek attitude towards Abraham, Elijah and Daniel's three friends, calling them "barbarians". It is important to follow Justin's reasoning here. By understanding Christianity to be a product of the logos, "the most ancient philosophy and father of all rational thought", he finds no reason for attaching particular importance to physical Israel.

Justin's *Dialogue with Trypho*[24] is more of a monologue than a dialogue. In fact while Justin freely presents his point of view, Trypho is allowed little room for voicing his. This imbalance

---

[22] According to Arthur J. Droge, the logos theory is introduced by Justin "primarily to refute the charge of novelty and at the same time to appropriate the Jewish scriptures as a Christian book" (Arthur J. Droge, "Justin Martyr and the Restoration of Philosophy," *CH* 56 [1987]: 315).

[23] Justin Martyr, *First Apololgy* , 46:3, ANF 1:178 (PG 6:334) cf. 63:10,16 (PG 6:378-379).

[24] ANF 1·194-270/PG 6:471-799.

reflects the fact that, by the time Justin was active as a Christian apologist (c. 150), the Jews were at a distinct disadvantage when debating with Christians. This is seen in the exchange between Justin and Trypho concerning the words "from the wood," which introduce into Psalm 96:10 the idea that Jesus reigns, as God and Lord, from the cross. Justin assures the Jew that the words, now thought to be a gloss,[25] were part of the original text of Psalm 96:10 and had been deleted by Jews who did not believe in Jesus. Trypho's comment is:

> Whether [or not] the rulers of the people have erased any portion of the Scriptures, as you affirm, God knows; but it seems incredible (LXXIII).

The tendency to christianise the Old Testament can be seen throughout the *Dialogue*. Another characteristic of the writing is the definition of Christians as "the *true* Israelitic race". For example, in commenting on Isaiah 42:1-4, Justin writes:

> Christ is the Israel and the Jacob, even so we, who have been quarried out from the bowels of Christ, are the true Israelitic race (CXXXV).[26]

The people of Israel are correspondingly held in contempt, as may be seen in the following statement:

> God has from of old dispersed all men according to their kindreds and tongues; and out of all kindreds has taken to Himself your kindred, a useless, disobedient, and faithless generation; and has shown that those who were selected out of every nation have obeyed His will through Christ, whom He calls also Jacob, and names Israel (CXXXV, 3-4).

---

[25] The Hebrew text of Ps 96:10 reads:

אָמְרוּ בַגּוֹיִם ׀ יְהוָה מָלָךְ אַף־תִּכּוֹן תֵּבֵל בַּל־תִּמּוֹט יָדִין עַמִּים בְּמֵישָׁרִים

imᵉru baggôyim YHWH malak, 'ap-tikkôn tebel bal-timmot yadîn 'ammîm bᵉmêsharîm ("Say among the nations: Yahweh reigns. Certainly the world will be established firmly, it will not be moved; He will judge the people righteously"); neither does the LXX contain anything which corresponds to the words "from the wood": εἴπατε ἐν τοῖς ἔθνεσιν Ὁ κύριος ἐβασίλευσεν καὶ γὰρ κατώρθωσεν τὴν οἰκουμένην, ἥτις σὺ σαλευθήσεται, κρινεῖ λαοὺς ἐν εὐθύτητι (Ps 95:10).

[26] The Greek reads, Ὡς οὖν Ἰσραὴλ τὸν Χριστὸν καὶ Ἰακώβ οὕτως λέγει, καὶ ἡμεις ἐν τῆς κοιλίας τοῦ Χριστοῦ λατομηθέντες, Ἰσραηλιτικῶν τὸ ἀληθινόν ἐσμεν γένος (PG 6:788). Graham Harvey comments as follows on the first surviving occurrence of the association of "Israel" with "true" here and in ch. CXXIV of Justin's work: "This clearly exemplifies Christianity's separation of itself from

Throughout the *Dialogue* Abraham is presented as an exemplary Christian believer of whom Justin idealises the state of uncircumcision (XI, 3-4; XXIII, 3-4). So far as the sign of circumcision is concerned, Justin states its purpose as follows:

> For the circumcision according to the flesh, which is from Abraham, was given for a sign; that you may be separated from the other nations, and from us; and that you alone may suffer that which you now justly suffer... (XVI, 2).[27]

This negative connotation which Justin attributes to circumcision, accompanied by contempt for the circumcised people, is further accentuated in these words which he addressed to his Jewish interlocutor:

> Noah was the beginning of our race; yet, uncircumcised, along with his children he went into the ark. Melchizedek, the priest of the Most High, was uncircumcised; to whom also Abraham, the first who received circumcision after the flesh, gave tithes, and he blessed him: after whose order God declared, by the mouth of David, that He would establish the everlasting priest. Therefore to you alone this circumcision was necessary, in order that the people may be no people, and the nation no nation; as also Hosea, one of the twelve prophets, declares (XIX).[28]

We have seen that Justin uses Scriptural terms very loosely, as when he identifies Christians as "the true Israelitic race" and regards circumcision as a sign of inferiority instead of the positive covenant sign that it was (Ge 17:12-14). Furthermore he argues from silence when he asserts that Melchizedek was not circumcised, as the practice of circumcision was not unknown in the ancient world outside of Israel. Thus it would seem that the basis of his evaluation of the Jews was not so much the

---

Judaism whilst claiming the entire inheritance of the earlier Israelite tradition" (Harvey, *True Israel*, p. 1). Harvey makes this further insightful statement: "The fact that at this stage they begin to use the phrase *true Israel* of themselves strongly suggests that [Christians] suspect that God remains interested in some sort of dialogue with a Jewish (non-Christian) *Israel*" (pp. 272-273).

[27] Ἡ γάρ ἀπὸ Ἀβραὰμ κατὰ σάρκα περιτομὴ εἰ σημεῖον ἐδόθη ἵνα ἦτε ἀπὸ τῶν ἄλλων ἐθνῶν καὶ ἡμῶν ἀφωρισμένοι· καὶ ἵνα μόνοι πάθητε ἃ νῦν ἐν δίκῃ πάσχετε... (PG 6:509, cf. p. 516).

[28] ANF 1:204/PG 6:516-517.

Scriptures of the Old and New Testaments as the opinions concerning the Jews which he gleaned from such sources as the *Epistle of Barnabas* and the *Letter to Diognetus* or from sources common to all three writings. Justin read and interpreted Scripture in the light of these opinions. Thus *replacement theology,* as taught by Justin, may be seen to arise from what Gregory Baum has termed "theological embroidery."[29] We may presume that this development represents a response to the challenge posed by Judaism which, although it did not recognise Jesus as the promised Messiah, showed no sign of disappearing from the scene.

4. Irenaeus' *Against Heresies:*[30] *God's promises to Israel are for the Church*

Irenaeus, bishop of Lyons from c.178 until his death in c.195, was an important figure in second century Christianity who, while still a young man, had heard Polycarp speak about his conversations with the apostle John. He is probably best known for his strong defence of the orthodox faith against Gnosticism.[31] In order to defend orthodoxy, Irenaeus distinguished between the canonical writings of the New Testament, particularly the four Gospels,[32] and extra-canonical writings, so making an important contribution to the definition of the New Testament canon.

In book 5 of his famous work, *Against Heresies,* Irenaeus applies four Old Testament prophecies to the gathering into the Church of "those that shall be saved from all the nations".[33] The first of these is Isaiah 26:19, where the prophet predicts the resurrection of the dead. Some commentators have seen in this verse a veiled reference to the restoration of Israel from captivity.[34] In the second passage quoted (Eze 37:12-14) God foretells that he will

[29] Gregory Baum, O.S.A., *Is the New Testament Anti-Semitic?* Glen Rock, NJ: Paulist Press, 1960, p. 17.

[30] PG 7:433-1224.

[31] *Against Heresies,* bks I-II (PG 7:433-842).

[32] *Ibid.,* bk III (PG 7:843-972).

[33] *Ibid.,* bk V, 34 (PG 7:1221-1224).

[34] Franz Delitzsch, *Isaiah,* in the series *Commentary on the Old Testament,* C. F. Keil & F. Delitzsch, 10 vols; Reprint, Grand Rapids, MI: Eerdmans, 1980, 8:452.

miraculously resurrect the whole house of Israel, by means of his Spirit, and will resettle her in her own land. The third quotation draw from several passages in Ezekiel, including 36:24-25, in which the regathering and resettling of Israel in her own land is said to be followed by purification. The last of the series is an abbreviated quotation of Jeremiah 23:6-7 where the future salvation of Judah is predicted and, consequently, "people will no longer say, 'As surely as the Lord lives, who brought the Israelites up out of Egypt,' but they will say, 'As surely as the Lord lives, who brought the descendants of Israel up out of the land of the north and out of all the countries where he had banished them'."

Irenaeus finds the fulfilment of all these passages in the salvation of people from the Gentile nations. By so doing he disinherits Israel of promises which are clearly addressed to her and at the same time manifestly makes the Church the new or true Israel. In other words he bases his exegesis on the assumption that the Old Testament should be read in the light of what we have called *replacement theology* which he apparently considered to be a part of orthodox Christian thought.

5. Tertullian's *Answer to the Jews*:[35] *Israel must serve the Church*

Tertullian's contribution to Christian theology was unique in a number of ways. Living in the period c. 160 - 225, he was the first theologian to write extensively in Latin. Furthermore he coined numerous theological terms which proved useful in the formulation of classical trinitarian and Christological statements. He was also the only orthodox theologian of the early centuries to leave the official church. In his opinion the official church had come to lack moral vigour and its episcopal structure had become overbearing, to the detriment of its essential, pneumatic nature.[36]

Considering Tertullian's capacity for original, rigorous thinking, it is reasonable to expect from him an original contribution to the Church's understanding of its relation to the Old Testament people of God. To some extent his contribution

[35] PL 2:595-640.
[36] *NIDCC*, s.v. "Tertullian."

was original. In fact in his *An Answer to the Jews* he appears more concerned to defend the Christian faith than to list the errors of the Jews. Moreover, as the "clue to the error of the Jews," he correctly presents the doctrine of the two advents of Christ – one characterised by humility and suffering and the other by honour and glory (chapter XIV).

Yet some of the themes which we have found in previous writings recur in Tertullian's *Answer,* in particular the tendency to minimise the importance of the Mosaic law and to consider physical circumcision a sign given to mark Israel out as a "contumacious people" (chapters II-III).

What is most significant for our study is Tertullian's use of Genesis 25:21-23 in the opening paragraphs of his *Answer,* where he follows the kind of allegorical exegesis which we have already met with in the *Epistle of Barnabas.* Here is his comment on the phrase, "the older will serve the younger":

> Accordingly, since the *people* or *nation* of the Jews is anterior in time, and "greater" through the grace of primary favor in the Law, whereas ours is understood to be "less" in the age of times, as having in the last era of the world attained the knowledge of divine mercy: beyond doubt, through the edict of divine utterance, the *prior* and "greater" people – that is, the Jewish – must necessarily serve the "less"; and the "less" people – that is, the Christian – overcome the "greater".[37]

So, if Israel has any continuing role, it is as servant of the Church (cf. Ro 11:11-15). Tertullian proceeds to adduce reasons for this inversion of roles, finding the main cause in Israel's idolatrous practices. He concludes:

> For thus has the "less" – that is the posterior – *people* overcome the "greater people", while it attains the grace of divine favor from which Israel has been divorced.[38]

Tertullian wrote in Latin. It is instructive that commentators of the Greek text of Romans did not follow *Barnabas* and Tertullian

---

[37] Tertullian, ANF 3:151/PL 2:598.
[38] *Ibid.*, p. 152/*ibid.*

in identifying the "older" people with the Jews and the "lesser" people, that is the posterior, with the Christians. In fact the comments on Romans 9:12-13 dating from the fourth to the ninth centuries, of commentators whose works are in Greek, do not contain any mention of Χριστιανοί, ἡ ἐκκλησία or ἔθνη ("Christians", "the Church" or "Gentile nations").[39] These commentators link the Genesis quotation strictly with Paul's reasoning concerning God's elective purpose.[40]

Although, as we have seen, Tertullian held to the main tenets of *replacement theology*, he also wrote positively concerning the place of Israel in God's plan. For example, in his treatise *Against Marcion,* he used Romans 10:2-4 and 11:33 to demonstrate that the God who had been known imperfectly during Old Testament times was the same God who had now revealed Himself more fully in Christ.[41] In this context Tertullian makes reference to Paul's recognition of Israel's zeal for God. Furthermore in one of his later writings, entitled *On Modesty,*[42] he greatly modified what had become the standard interpretation of the parable of the prodigal son, according to which the younger *prodigal but repentant* son represents the Church while the older unrepentant son represents Israel. According to Tertullian the older son represents the Church just as much as Israel and, following Israel's loss of the land, the younger son represents Israel as much, if not more, than the Church. He concludes as follows:

[39] Akazius of Caesarea (d. 366), on Ro 9:11-14, in Staab, *Pauluskommentare,* p. 54; Theodor of Mopsuestia (350-428), on Ro 9:9-13, *ibid.,* pp. 143-144; Gennadius of Constantinople (d. ca. 471), on Ro 9:10-13, *ibid.,* pp. 389-390; Photius of Constantinople (c. 820-891), on Ro 9:10-13, *ibid.,* pp. 516-517.

[40] Akazius held the view that the divine choice was related to foreknowledge of the good and bad works which Jacob and Esau would have performed: διὰ τὸ προγινώσκειν ἀμφοτέρων τὰ ἔργα, ὥσπερ αὐτὸς ὁ Παῦλός φησιν ἀνωτέρω ὅτι οὓς προέγνω, καὶ προώρισεν καὶ τὰ ἑζῆς (Akazius, in Staab, *Pauluskommentare,* p.54). For the other three commentators, the election of Jacob and his descendants was to be understood in terms of divine purpose.

[41] PL 2:503-508.

[42] PL 2:979-1030.

...it will be fitting for the Christian to rejoice, and not to grieve, at the restoration of Israel, if it is true, (as it is), that the whole of our hope is intimately united with the remaining expectation of Israel (VIII).[43]

It is possible that Tertullian's disenchantment with the Catholic Church, which occurred before he wrote his tract *On Modesty*, is linked with this change of attitude. All we can say for sure is that, in his interpretation of the parable of the prodigal son, Tertullian's criticism of the official church is paralleled by a return to a more Pauline view of the future of Israel.

6. The contribution of Origen: *corporeal and spiritual Israel*

The work of Origen (c.185 - c.254),[44] Clement's successor as head of the catechetical School of Alexandria, strengthened the theoretical basis of *replacement theology* by grounding it in biblical exegesis.[45] However his exegetical methodology was profoundly influenced by the intellectual climate in which he grew up. The Greeks had used allegorism to make the mythical content of ancient works, such as those written by Homer and Hesiod, acceptable to readers with a more philosophical turn of mind. Origen was also influenced by the example of Philo, a first century Alexandrian Jew who had interpreted the Old Testament Scriptures allegorically in order to make them harmonise with Platonism.[46] Allegorism played an important part in Origen's theory of interpretation and, as he was the first biblical scholar

[43] ANF, 4:82/PL 2:996 "Christianum enim de restitutione Iudaei gaudere, et non dolere conveniet; sequidem tota spes nostra cum religua Israelis exspectatione coniuneta est (Rom.xi)." A. Cleveland Coxe assumes that Tertullian alludes here to the teaching of Romans 11:11-36 (ANF, 4:82, n. 9).

[44] For a good introduction to the nature of Origen's scholarship and a critical appraisal of his allegorism, see R.P.C. Hanson, *Allegory and Event, A study of the sources and significance of Origen's Interpretation of Scripture,* Richmond, VA: John Knox Press, 1959.

[45] *Ibid.*, pp. 160-161. As an exegete, Origen owed much to the Gnostic, Heracleon.

[46] Daniel P. Fuller, "Interpretation, History of," in *The International Standard Bible Encyclopedia,* fully rev., Geoffrey W. Bromiley (gen. ed.) 4 vols, (1982), 2:865; cf. Hanson, *Allegory and Event,* pp. 217-218.

to work out "a complete hermeneutical theory",[47] his work was destined to exert great influence on the Christian approach to the Hebrew Scriptures, for centuries to come. It appears ironical that, in applying the allegorical method to the biblical text, Origen was inspired in part by the example of a Jewish scholar. Allegorism allowed Origen to freely apply to the Church Old Testament passages where ethnic Israel is clearly intended while denigrating the Jewish people themselves.

Origen is remembered for his philosophical speculation and as the allegorist *par excellence* among Biblical interpreters. However, to be fair, it must be said that allegorical interpretation was widely practised by Christian writers before Origen's time. Moreover part of Origen's purpose was to refute the heretical teachings of Marcion. The latter, while insisting on a *literal* interpretation of the Old Testament, had taught that the "god" who speaks in these Scriptures is not the God and Father of our Lord Jesus Christ.[48]

Origen offered his own rationale of allegorism in book IV,1 of his work *On First Principles*.[49] According to this Alexandrian Father, Proverbs 22:20 authorises interpreters to seek a three-fold meaning in each passage of Scripture: fleshly, psychic and spiritual.[50] In practice, Origen insisted mainly on distinguishing between the literal and spiritual meaning of the Biblical text. According to Origen the spiritual meaning belongs to a higher order of ideas than the literal. He motivated this view by appealing to the principle of divine inspiration and by affirming that often statements made by the biblical writers are not literally true and that many events, presented as historical, are inherently

---

[47] Fuller, "Interpretation", 2:864. The allusion is to bk IV of Origen's work *On First Principles*. It is significant that Fuller begins his survey of the history of biblical interpretation with Origen (*ibid.*, 2:864-874).

[48] See Hanson, *Allegory and Event*, pp. 133-142.

[49] For a critical text of this work, see *Die griechischen Christlichen Schriftsteller der ersten drei Jahrhunderte,* Berlin, 1927-, vol. 22.

[50] *On First Principles,* bk IV, ch. I, sec. 2, (ANF 4:359-360); cf. Hanson, *Allegory and Event*, pp. 235-258.

impossible.[51] Thus only simple believers will limit themselves to the literal meaning of the text.[52]

Of course Origen recognises that some of the events mentioned in Scripture must be considered historically true, if the reader is to make any sense at all out of the text.[53] Thus it is the task of the interpreter to decide which events are to be taken literally and which are not. He writes:

> the exact reader must, in obedience to the Saviour's injunction to "search the Scriptures", carefully ascertain in how far the literal meaning is true, and in how far impossible; and so far as he can, trace out, by means of similar statements, the meaning everywhere scattered through Scripture of that which cannot be understood in a literal signification.[54]

The words, "in how far the literal meaning is true, and *in how far impossible,*" reveal an inherent weakness in Origen's hermeneutical theory because it leaves the door open for cultural prejudice and the limited experience of the reader to determine what God can and cannot do and whether events described, or biblical prophecies, are to be taken literally or not. A good example of what cultural prejudice can do to interpretation is Origen's view that thinking of "God as he deserves to be thought" means interpreting all Scriptural passages which speak of his wrath in the light of his presumed impassibility.[55] From this example it is clear that, once the centre of the hermeneutical process shifts from the Scriptures themselves to the cultural milieu in which the interpreter operates, philosophy can influence a reader's decision regarding "that which cannot be understood in a literal signification."

Origen exemplifies his hermeneutical theory by discussing the difference between a "bodily" race of Jews and those who are "Jews inwardly." With reference to *bodily* Israel and Judah, he writes:

---

[51] Origen, *Princ.,* bk IV, I, 1-9,15-21 (ANF 4:349-358,364-369). An example of when Origen discounts the literal nature of an event is the story of Adam, as reported in the book of Genesis (*ibid.,* sec. 16 [ANF 4:365]).

[52] *Ibid.,* sec. 12 (ANF 4:360).

[53] *Ibid.,* sec. 20 (ANF 4:369).

[54] *Ibid.,* sec. 19 (ANF 4:369).

[55] *Ibid.,* II, IV, 4 (ANF 4:277-280).

And do not such promises as are written concerning them, in respect of their being mean in expression, and manifesting no elevation (of thought), nor anything worthy of the promise of God, need a mystical interpretation? And if the "spiritual" promises are announced by visible signs, then they to whom the promises are made are not "corporeal".

...are not the "spiritual" Israelites, of whom the "corporeal" Israelites were the type, sprung from the families, and the families from the tribes, and the tribes from some one individual whose descent is not of a "corporeal" but of a better kind, – he, too, being born of Isaac, and he of Abraham, – all going back to Adam, whom the apostle declares to be Christ?[56]

An attitude of contempt towards Israel had become the rule by Origen's time. The new element in his own view of Israel is his perception of them as "manifesting no elevation [of thought]". It follows that the interpreter must always posit a deeper or higher meaning for prophecies relating to Judea, Jerusalem, Israel, Judah and Jacob which, he affirms, are "not being understood by us in a 'carnal' sense."[57]

In Origen's understanding, the only positive function of *physical* Israel was that of being a type of *spiritual* Israel. The promises were not made to *physical* Israel because she was unworthy of them and incapable of understanding them.[58] Thus Origen effectively disinherits physical Israel. In the continuation of the section of *On First Principles* in which Origen distinguishes between *physical* and *spiritual,* he presents a platonic concept of the Church. According to this view, every family which is related to God took its commencement from Christ. Moreover Adam and Eve are considered to be "types of the Church, inasmuch as in a pre-eminent sense they are ... descended from the Church."[59] The Church itself is conceived of in non-temporal, heavenly terms. This platonic understanding of the Church implies the secondary nature of historical realities, including Israel. Thus the Church's appropriation of the Old Testament appears to be legitimate, while the importance that Scripture itself attributes to history is ignored.

[56] *Ibid.* sec. 22 (ANF 4:370).
[57] *Ibid.*
[58] *Ibid.*, but see Ro 9:3-4; Eph 2:12.
[59] Origen, *ibid.*, sec. 21 (ANF 4:370-371).

Applications of Origen's hermeneutical principles to *physical* and *spiritual* Israel may be found both in his Commentary on Matthew and in his Old Testament *Homilies.* For example, commenting on Matthew 19:6-8, Origen likens Israel to a divorced wife in whom an unseemly thing had been found.[60] He writes:

> And a sign that she has received the bill of divorce is this, that Jerusalem was destroyed along with what they called the sanctuary.[61]

The "unseemly thing" of which Origen speaks was the request that Jesus be crucified and Barabbas be released.[62] Origen pushes the analogy of divorce still further by suggesting that Israel has joined herself to another husband, "Barabbas the robber who is figuratively the devil, or some evil power," while Christ has joined himself to a new wife, the Church.[63] Furthermore Origen takes Christ's words, "the lost sheep of Israel" (Mt 15:24), in the narrative concerning the faith of the Canaanite woman, as referring to intelligent Gentiles who respond to the gospel, while "the wise of this world" and "the things that are" (1 Co 1:27-28) are taken to refer to unbelieving Israel.[64]

The concept that the promises were not addressed to physical Israelites but rather to *spiritual* Israelites (the Church), is repeated in Origen's Old Testament *Homilies.* For example, in his *Homilies on Genesis,* he distinguishes sharply between Jacob and Israel.[65] In his comment on Leviticus 24:10-14 he states that he who is a Catholic Christian and also accepts the spiritual meaning of the Scriptures is an Israelite "by both mother and father."[66] It

---

[60] Origen, *Commentary on Matthew,* ANF 9, Allan Menzies (ed.), pp. 507-508 (PG 13:830-1600 contains bks 10-17 and fragments of bks 1,2 & 7).

[61] ANF 9:507-508.

[62] *Ibid.*

[63] *Ibid.*, p. 508. Origen's analogy presupposes the normativity of remarriage, following divorce, an aspect of the question not addressed by Christ in Mt 19:1-12.

[64] *Ibid.*, pp. 445-447.

[65] For example, commenting on Ge 50:3, the act of burying "Israel" is taken to symbolise the detestation of all good and of all heavenly intelligence (PG 12:242-244).

follows that all that Israel *according to the flesh* prefigured, is fulfilled in the true and heavenly Israelites.[67] Thus all who see God – angels and members of the church of the firstborn (Heb 12:18-20) – are "children of Israel."[68]

Origen warns the Church, which he considers to be the *true* Israel,[69] to not take from the events the meaning that they have for Jews and heretics.[70] Jews, as a race, are viewed as obtuse and inferior to members of the Catholic church who are able to interpret the Old Testament allegorically. *True* Israel is the heir of all that was promised and given to physical Israel.[71]

In the light of the above, it is unclear what Origen means when he writes that, after the fullness of the Gentiles comes in, "the whole of Israel, whom Celsus does not know, may be saved"[72]. In this writing he certainly depicts the Jews as more honourable than other ancient races, inasmuch as the whole of their history and polity were administered by God. Moreover, by their fall salvation has come to the Gentiles (Ro 9:11-12).[73] Thus when he speaks of "the whole of Israel" attaining to salvation, either Origen intends the reader to understand a change of subject when he switches from the name "Jews" to "Israel," the latter indicating *spiritual* Israelites, or we must conclude that he did hold out the possibility of physical Israel still receiving divine blessing. The latter is possible because, in his comment on the "mystery" passage in Romans 11,[74] he takes the indications of vv. 26-27 quite literally and expresses the belief that a certain "Israel" will be saved after what he calls the period of "blindness" (cf. v. 25). However he

---

[66] PG 12:553-554.

[67] *Hom. on Numbers* XI,4 (PG 12:647-648; cf. Hom. XV,3 (PG 686-688) e XVI,3 (PG 12:695). In Hom. XVIII (PG 12:718), "Israel" becomes a synonym of "soul".

[68] *Hom. on Joshua* IX,4 (PG 12:874).

[69] *Hom. on Ezekiel* II,2 ...*vero Israel, id est Ecclesia...* (PG 13:682).

[70] *Ibid.*, Hom. XV,1 (PG 12:897).

[71] *Ibid.*, Hom. XXVI, 3 (PG 12:948).

[72] In *Cels.* VI, 80 (PG 11:1120).

[73] *Ibid.*

[74] Origen, *Commento alla Lettera ai Romani*, Introduction, trans. and notes by Francesca Cocchini, 2 vols, Genoa: Marietti, 1986, 2:79-84. Some fragments of this commentary are preserved in PG 14:1195-1202.

remains unsure whether the reference is to those who have been blinded – natural Israelites – or to people from the nations not calculated in the *fullness* mentioned in v. 25.[75]

Even if Origen did envisage a future conversion of the Jewish people, this would not substantially modify his portrayal of ethnic Israel as an unworthy subject of Christian theology.

C. Major Shapers of Christian Thought and Practice

1. *Ambrose and Augustine*

Origen's contribution to *replacement theology* was particularly incisive because of his exegetical prowess and because he was the first Christian writer to attempt making a complete statement of the Christian faith.[76] Even though a number of Origen's speculations, such as the pre-existence of souls and the doctrine of universal salvation, were later anathematised,[77] this did not significantly lessen his influence. Thus, for churchmen who read his commentaries and Homilies during subsequent centuries, the idea that *true* Israel had always been the Church, appeared to be something taught by the Bible itself.[78]

Origen's view, that physical Israel is not a subject of theological reflection, found authorative confirmation in the teaching of Augustine, whose influence on the development of Christian theology is without parallel. Pelikan writes:

---

[75] *Ibid.*, pp. 82-83/PG 14:1195-1198.

[76] The best expression of this attempt is Origen's seminal work *On First Principles* (ANF 4:239-384).

[77] An edict, issued by the Synod at Constantinople (543), put into effect the anathemas pronounced against Origen in a letter written by emperor Justinian to Mennas of Constantinople, moreover the V general council at Contantinople (553) listed Origen among ancient heretics *(NIDCC* s.v. "Origenism").

[78] Cf. Soulen (*The God of Israel and Christian Theology*, pp. x, 1-5,12-13,16-19,29,31-34,48-50,54-58,77-79,82-84) who makes the point that *replacement theology* became the unexamined presupposition of much of Christian theology. According to Soulen, the standard model provides a narrative construal of the Christian Bible that gives powerful expression to the church's central confession "in a manner that is profoundly supersessionist in both doctrinal and structural ways" (p. 109).

In Augustine of Hippo Western Christianity found its most influential spokesman…
The role of Augustine in the evolution of Christian thought and teaching affected the history of every doctrine…"[79]

So far as his understanding of Israel is concerned, we may presume that Augustine was influenced by the ideas of his spiritual mentor, Ambrose of Milan, so it is with the latter that we must begin.

Soon after Augustine's arrival at Milan towards the end of A.D. 384, he began listening to the preaching of Ambrose, who had been catapulted into the role of bishop ten years earlier. About the same time as Augustine was baptised by Ambrose, around the time of Easter 387,[80] Ambrose delivered his "Exameron"[81] in a series of nine orations. In the ninth discourse, delivered on the sixth day, the bishop applied Jeremiah's rhetorical question, "Can the Ethiopian change his skin or the leopard its spots?" (Jer 13:23), to the soul of the Jewish people, considered irrevocably perverse and incapable of any good thought.[82] Another feature of this and other writings of Ambrose is his use of "Jews" as a type of the infidel.[83]

That the antisemitism of Ambrose was entrenched in his thinking is evident from the famous letter he wrote to Theodosius I (c. 346-395, Roman emperor from 379) in December 388.[84] The local bishop of Callinicum, in Syria, had apparently ordered the burning of the local synagogue and the Emperor had ordered him to have it rebuilt at his own expense. Ambrose ordered the emperor to change his mind on the grounds that burning a Jewish synagogue was not a crime. It is reported that on the following Sunday Ambrose not only pitted the Church against the

[79] Pelikan, *Tradition,* 1:292-293.
[80] D.F. Wright, *NIDCC,* s.v. "Augustine of Hippo."
[81] Giovanni Coppa calculates it being during the same holy week (*Opere di Sant'Ambrogio,* Giovanni Coppa (ed.), Classici delle religioni, Turin: U.T.E.T., 1969; Reprint 1979, p. 49. The term "Exameron" refers to the "six days" of creation.
[82] *Six Days of Work,* Serm. IX, 15 (PL 14:247).
[83] *Ibid.,* bk II,3,11; 3;16 (PL 14:149,153) *et passim.*
[84] Ep. XL (PL 16:1102 1113).

Synagogue in a sermon but also publicly enjoined the Emperor to annul the sentence previously issued against the bishop of Callinicum. Ambrose refused to continue the order of service until Theodosius had given him his word![85]

There is no record of Augustine using his office to sanction anti-Jewish activity, as Ambrose had done. Nevertheless in his major apologetical work, *The City of God*, there is evidence that he shared the view of Origen and Ambrose concerning physical Israel. At the first mention of the "kingdom of the Jews" in book IV, he attributes their downfall to their "impious curiosity, which... drew them to strange gods and idols, and at last led them to kill Christ."[86]

Augustine's *Tract Against the Jews* was one of the most influential anti-Judaic writings emanating from the centuries following Origen.[87] Because of the almost canonical status enjoyed by Augustine's writings during medieval Church history, the dominant form of the anti-Jewish polemic during this period is commonly called "Augustinian". In this tradition, *replacement theology* and the consequent normativity of Jewish subservience to Christians, were understood to be certain. This did not exclude the toleration of Jews, because they preserved the original form of the Old Testament and because their eschatological conversion was envisaged.[88]

2. *John Chrysostom* (347-407)

This popular church father is important for our study because as a preacher he influenced public opinion both at Antioch and later at Constantinople, where he was patriarch from 398. His fame as a preacher later merited him the name Chrysostomos,

[85] Parkes, *Conflict*, pp. 166-167.

[86] Augustine, *Civ.* bk IV, xxxiv (NPNF, f.s., 2:83/PL 41:140). In *The City of God*, Augustine's greatest work, he reviews world history from a theological, and thus eschatological, stand-point.

[87] PL 42:51-64.

[88] D.E. Timmer, "Biblical Exegesis and the Jewish-Christian Controversy in the Early Twelfth Century." *CH* 58 (1989): 310-311.

"golden mouthed." Among the hundreds of his sermons that survive, eight are directed against the Jews. [89]

Chrysostom's anti-Jewish sermons were delivered at Syrian Antioch, in the year 387. Despite their virulent nature, they contain little indication of the circumstances that gave rise to them. But even allowing that there could have been some circumstantial justification for them, Chrysostom's vehemence is surprising. He accuses the Jews of murdering their offspring,[90] and of worshipping devils and not God.[91] Furthermore he insists that Jews are hated by God and, since they have murdered Jesus, they are no longer given the opportunity to repent.[92] God's purpose in concentrating all their worship in Jerusalem was to facilitate its destruction,[93] moreover the suffering inflicted upon them was an expression of the wrath of God, and his absolute rejection of the Jewish people.[94] Finally, since God hates them, Christians are also duty bound to hate them.[95]

It is remarkable that neither Chrysostom nor those who before and after him accused the Jews of deicide, balanced this accusation with a recognition of the necessity of Christ's death.[96] This omission implies that the Church would have been better

---

[89] PG 48:843-942.

[90] Serm. 1, 6 (PG 48:852).

[91] Serm. I, 3 (PG 48:847).

[92] Serm. VI, 1 (PG 48:903-905): Such reasoning ignores Peter's appeals to Jews in Ac 2:36-38 and 3:17-19. Paul's strongest statement concerning Jewish guilt is found in 1 Th 2:14-16, which includes the words "...the Jews, who also killed the Lord, even Jesus, and the prophets...". H.L. Ellison *(The Mystery of Israel,* Exeter: The Paternoster Press, 1966, p. 18) notes, "Paul is affirming that the actions of the Jewish leaders were merely the continuation of those of their ancestors... Paul is not accusing them of killing Jesus in particular."

[93] Serm. IV, 6 (PG 48:879-881).

[94] Serm. VI, 3 (PG 48:907-908).

[95] Serm. VI, 1 (PG 48:904-905).

[96] This omission was corrected by the Vatican II Council in the document "Nostra Aetate" which received formal approval on October 28, 1965. After deploring all kinds of persecution and manifestations of antisemitism directed against the Hebrews in all epochs and whatever their origin, the document draws attention to the fact that Christ submitted himself voluntarily to suffering and death in view of making salvation possible for sinful mankind *(Tutti i documenti del Concilio,* Roma: U.C.I.I.M.; 5th ed., 1972, p. 536).

off had the Christ of God never taken the sinner's place on the cross. There was also a general failure to recognise that believing *Jews* had taken the Christian gospel to the rest of the world.[97]

The anti-Jewish attitudes evident in the preaching of Chrysostom were part of a general trend that can be traced through the *Adversus Judaeos* literature.[98] Many of these writings were motivated by the desire to prove that the Jesus of the Gospels was the Christ prophesied in the Old Testament and that the Jews were culpable in not recognising his Messiahship. However most of these writings also manifest a general antagonism towards all things Jewish and very often a theology of contempt.

The fact that Chrysostom's study of Romans 9-11[99] did not induce him to take a stand against this trend is surprising when it is remembered that he stood in the Antiochene tradition which favoured the literal interpretation of Scripture.[100] Moreover, at Constantinople, he evidenced a readiness to suffer for the sake of what he considered needful reforms.

3. *Cyril of Alexandria* (c. 370 - 444)

Cyril is remembered as a major forerunner of the Council of Chalcedon but also as a bellicose ecclesiastic greedy for power.[101] His position as Patriarch of Alexandria from 412 till his death in 444 meant that he could wield considerable influence. For our

---

[97] The statement which perhaps comes closest to an exception to this rule is found in Augustine's *On Christian Doctrine,* III, 6 (NPNF, fs, 2:559):

But those [Jews] who did believe, from among whom the first church at Jerusalem was formed... because they were very near spiritual things... were filled with such a measure of the Holy Spirit that they sold all their goods, and laid their price at the apostles' feet to be distributed among the needy, and consecrated themselves wholly to God as a new temple...

Now it is not recorded that any of the Gentile churches did this, because men who had for their gods idols made with hands had not been so near to spiritual things.

[98] See note n. 13.

[99] See his *Hom. on Romans* (PG 60:547-596).

[100] *NIDCC* s.v. "Chrysostom, John."

[101] *NIDCC* s.v. "Cyril."

purposes it is significant that this important figure in the development of Christian orthodoxy was also anti-Jewish. For example, on one occasion he led Christians in pillaging the city's Jewish quarter. This resulted in many Jews being killed while the remainder were expelled from the city.[102]

Cyril's opposition to Jews had a theoretical basis. This may be seen from the way he begins his commentary on Romans chapter 9:

> In the beginning, God made Israel a chosen one and therefore he called him «first born» [Ex 4:22]. But they have become arrogant and reckless and even worse: murderers of the Lord. Therefore they have perished, for they have become exiles and outcasts, and because they have lost their close relationship to God altogether, they have been placed behind the nations and have been alienated from the hope of the fathers.[103]

This was not only the opinion of Cyril; by his time it had become the official position of the Church, as we shall see when we consider the development of anti-Jewish legislation.

4. *Pope Gregory I* (540-604)

Gregory I is known to history as Gregory *the Great* because his careful administration and astute diplomacy[104] enabled him to consolidate the Roman papacy during the years 590-604. Furthermore he reformed the Roman liturgy and, as a doctor of the Roman Catholic Church, popularised the teaching of Augustine,[105] developing what has been called "Augustinian traditionalism."[106]

---

[102] James Parkes, *Conflict*, pp. 234-235.

[103] Cyril of Alexandria, PG 74:820.

[104] 708 of Gregory the Great's letters are listed in "Epistolarum ordo antea vulgatus ad novum reductus" (PL 77:1379-1390) and published elsewhere in the same volume (cols 431-1352).

[105] Robert G. Clouse, *NIDCC*, s.v. "Gregory The Great".

[106] Pelikan, *Tradition*, 1:350-351. This is particularly true of Gregory's *Four Books of Dialogues on the Life and Miracles of the Italian fathers and on the Immortality of Souls* (593-594), which contain a simplification of many themes found in Augustine's *The City of God*.

Along with occasional condemnatory allusions to the Jews based on allegorical interpretation, in the writings of Gregory,[107] some of his Epistles deal with matters affecting Jews. These letters throw light on the way that exclusion of ethnic Israel from Christian theology affected the attitudes of the clergy. In fact Pope Gregory found it necessary to admonish the bishops of Terracina, Palermo, Cagliari and Naples for having made threats to the Jews and for having confiscated synagogues and other goods from them. He insisted that they be granted the rights that the Theodosian Code reserved for them.[108] Gregory was in favour of the Jews converting to Christianity but insisted that sincere conversions can be effected only by preaching, not by force.[109] At the same time, he was against granting the Jews more privileges than those envisaged in the Theodosian Code.

This reference to the Theodosian Code reminds us that the Church's theological understanding of the Jews found expression both in Canon laws and State legislation. Such official rules, regulating the relations of Christians with Jews, gave legal warrant to a growing feeling of mistrust towards the Jewish minority. This in turn facilitated the development of lists of accusations and a general attitude of contempt on the part of followers of the dominant religion. In the following survey we consider only Canon laws because of their more direct link with Christian thought.

5. *Emperor Constantine and canon law*

In A.D. 325 Constantine wrote a letter to those bishops who had not been present at the Council of Nicea concerning the

---

[107] Such allegorical interpretation is particularly evident throughout his Homilies on Ezekiel where everywhere Jerusalem is assumed to be heavenly and God's people the Church (PL 76:785-1072). For condemnatory statements and the concept that the Church has replaced physical Israel in the divine plan, see in particular: bk I, Hom. 12,18 (PL 76:926-927); bk II, Hom. 5,2 (PL 76:985-986); Hom 6,23 (PL 76:1011); Hom. 8,13 (PL 76:1035-1036).

[108] Ep. VII, bk XIII (PL 77:1262-1265).

[109] Ep. XII, bk. XIII (PL 77:1267-1268).

date of Easter.[110] The following consideration contained in this letter, "We ought not, therefore, to have anything in common with the Jews," sums up one of the key ideas behind much subsequent legislation against the Jews: *All things Jewish were understood to be totally incompatible with Christianity.* This concept is reflected in the confessions which, in later centuries, Jewish converts to Christianity would be required to make at the moment of their baptism.[111]

The theory of the total incompatibility of Christian faith and Judaism contrasts sharply with the testimony of the New Testament, according to which the apostle Paul could declare, at an advanced stage of his ministry, "I am a Pharisee" (Ac 23:6) and clearly considered the practice of Jewish customs compatible with Christian faith (1 Co 9:20; Ro 14:1-8; cf. Ac 18:18; 21:20-26). The theory of the total incompatibility of Christian faith and Judaism also ignores the fact that the God of Israel is the God worshipped by Christians while the Jewish Scriptures make up three quarters of the biblical canon accepted by the Church. The following samples of canon law show that the Church was not prepared to recognise the fact that Judaism and Christianity have much in common:

According to Canon I of the Synod of Antioch (341), whoever observes Easter at the same time as the Jews, makes himself "an alien from the Church, as one who not only heaps sins upon himself, but who is also the cause of destruction and subversion of many."[112]

The Synod of Laodicea, which met sometime between 343 and the Council of Constantinople (381), decreed:

> It is not lawful to receive portions sent from the feasts of Jews or heretics, nor to feast together with them.[113]
> It is not lawful to receive unleavened bread from Jews, nor to be partakers of their impiety.[114]

---

[110] PG 20:1074-1080.
[111] Parkes (*Conflict*, pp. 394-400) gives a sampling of such confessions.
[112] The Seven Ecumenical Councils, in NPNF, ss, 4:108.
[113] Canon XXXVII, *ibid.*, p. 151.
[114] Canon XXXVIII, *ibid.*

The legal rights of Jews were greatly restricted by "The Code of Canons of the African Church," issued by two hundred and seventeen "fathers" assembled at Carthage, in A.D. 419. In Canon CXXIX Jews, along with all those who have the stain of infamy, heretics and heathen, are forbidden the right to bring legal accusations (apart from in their own suits).[115]

The Council of Chalcedon also gave attention to relations with Jews. A new restriction was the stipulation that no Christian parent was to give his child in marriage to a Jew.[116]

More complete ostracism of the Jews was decreed by the Council which met at Trullo in 692:

> Let no-one in the priestly order nor any layman eat the unleavened bread of the Jews, nor have any familiar intercourse with them, nor summon them in illness, nor receive medicine from them, nor bathe with them but if anyone shall take in hand to do so, if he is a cleric, let him be deposed, but if a layman, let him be cut off.[117]

Moreover, one of the so-called "Apostolic" canons, approved at Trullo, forbade clergymen or laymen to enter a Jewish synagogue to pray or to take oil on a feast day, on pain of excommunication.[118]

The seventh "ecumenical" council (II Nicea), which met in 787, required that, in order to be received as genuine Christians, Jewish converts must abandon all semblance of Jewish customs and ordinances.

The fourth council of Toledo (c. 631) was presided over by the well known medieval scholar, Isidore of Seville. After affirming its disapproval of forced baptism, the Council decreed what punishments should be meted out on Jews who had accepted Christian baptism but had subsequently lapsed. Some of these were quite severe. For example, children of the lapsed, if they had been subsequently circumcised, were to be taken away from

---

[115] NPNF ss 14: 504.
[116] Canon XIV, *ibid.*, p. 278.
[117] Canon XI, *ibid.*, p. 370.
[118] Canons LXIV & LXXI, *ibid.*, p. 598.

their parents. In a mixed marriage the non-Christian partner had the choice of separation or accepting Christianity. Children of mixed marriages were to be brought up as Christians. A worse fate was in store for Jews who had never accepted baptism. Such Jews could not hold office and were to be deprived of their children.[119]

It is clear that by now Jews were, for all practical purposes, denied the privileges of citizenship. They were forced to live in what amounted to a social and legal ghetto, long before the appearance of the material Jewish ghetto.[120]

Anti-Jewish legislation was advanced still further by the fourth Lateran Council in 1215. The Council began by sharpening previous anti-Jewish legislation, including the authorisation of Crusaders to not pay their debts to Jewish money lenders. New canon laws passed included: prohibiting Christians from having commerce with usurious Jews (67), requiring Jews to wear a distinctive badge or dress to mark them off from Christians, forbidding them to appear in public in Holy Week, to avoid the risk of insult to Christians at that time (68), and denying them any public function involving the exercise of power over Christians (69).[121]

D. Conclusion

The requirement to wear a distinctive badge or dress stigmatised the Jewish community as nothing else had done. It showed that there was no place for the nation which had refused to accept Jesus as the promised Messiah and which doggedly awaited a

---

[119] Parkes, *Conflict.*, pp. 356-357.

[120] A more direct foundation for the Jewish ghetto was laid in 1179 by the III Lateran Council, which forbade true believers to lodge amongst infidels. The Venetian Republic was one of the first civil governments to order, in 1516, the segregation of the Jews in a special quarter. This example would soon be followed elsewhere in Italy, in southern France, Germany and Poland (Roth, *A short History*, pp. 210-211, 297).

[121] *New Catholic Encyclopedia*, 15 vols, New York: McGraw Hill Book Company, 1967, 8:409.

different manifestation of God's kingdom. However it is more significant for Christian theology that some anti-Jewish canons were formulated in the context of Councils, such as the Council of Chalcedon (451), which live in the Church's memory as occasions in which orthodoxy was defined. Thus we can speak of a parallel development of Orthodox theology on the one hand and an official anti-Judaic stance on the other. Why is this?

I believe that the clue to this unlikely association is to be found in what we have called *replacement theology*. Our findings lead us to conclude that this concept was not the product of careful reflection on Scripture; rather Scripture was interpreted allegorically in such a way as to convalidate it. This is particularly evident in the way Origen sought to legitimise the categories of *carnal* and *spiritual* Israelites, to indicate historical Israel and the Church.

The echo of Origen's use of these concepts was still clearly discernible in the writings of Rupert of Deutz (c. 1070-1129). He has the following to say concerning such Old Testament passages as Zechariah 8, Isaiah 2:2-3 and Micah 4:1-2, which refer specifically to the Jews, Jerusalem and the land of Israel:

> These things which are promised are spiritual, and they are appropriate for spiritual people and desired by them. Those however to whom the Word came were carnal, and desired carnal things... Condescending to the carnal, therefore, like an old man with children, lisping in order to amuse them, the divine Word says, "Old men and old women shall again dwell in the streets of Jerusalem".[122]

Such allegorical interpretation of the Old Testament effectively disinherited Israel of their Scriptures. James Parkes makes this general statement concerning the Church's reading of the Hebrew Scriptures:

---

[122] Rupert of Deutz, *Commentary on the Twelve Minor Prophets*, PL 168:756-757. David E. Timmer ("Biblical Exegesis and the Jewish-Christian Controversy in the Early Twelfth Century," *CH* 58 [1989]: 319) notes that Rupert also invokes the Christological principle of interpretation. Accordingly, with reference to Jewish, literal interpretation of these passages, this Benedictine Abbot wrote, "Once this carnal and puerile interpretation was permitted; now, however, it has been emptied of meaning by Christ, and the error is inexcusable" (PL 168:811).

For the Gentile Church the Old Testament no longer meant a way of life, a conception of the relation of a whole community to God, but a mine from which proof texts could be extracted. Instead of being the history of a single community, and the record of its successes and failures, it became the record of two communities, the pre-Incarnation Church symbolised by the 'Hebrews', and the temporary and rejected people of the Jews. Out of this artificial separation of history into two parts, on the simple principle that what was good belonged to one group and what was bad to the other, grew the caricature of the Jew with which patristic literature is filled.[123]

Among the various effects of *replacement theology,* three might be mentioned at this point: First, the Church tended to establish its own identity in anti-Judaic terms: *the Church is what the Jews are no longer or never have been.*[124] Secondly, Christendom's way of interpreting the Old Testament, based on prejudice, has made it very difficult for Jews to take seriously the claim that Jesus of Nazareth is the Messiah of Israel.[125] Thirdly, Christian writers have tended to talk about Israel in the past tense, as may be seen in the convention of terminating histories of Israel with the advent of Christianity or with the fall of the second temple in A.D. 70.[126]

---

[123] Parkes, *Conflict,* p. 374.
[124] See Williamson, *Guest,* , pp. 112-114.
[125] Cf. Parkes, *Conflict,* p. 373.
[126] The following works, though not in themselves anti-Judaic, follow this convention: John Bright, *A History of Israel,* London: SCM Press, 1960; F.F. Bruce, *Israel and the Nations,* Exeter: The Paternoster Press, 1963.

Chapter Four

REPLACEMENT THEOLOGY AND ECCLESIOLOGY

A. Introduction

According to Origen *corporeal* Israelites were mere types of *spiritual* Israelites. Origen identified the latter in the Church, which he understood in transcendental terms and as already in existence at the time of Adam.[1] Clearly there is a link between Origen's concept of physical Israel and his concept of the Church. The purpose of the present chapter is to determine whether this connection is peculiar to the theology of Origen or whether there was a more general link between the pattern of Christian understanding concerning Israel and the developing pattern of ecclesiology.

The problem we face, in pursuing this objective, is the spontaneous nature of ecclesiastical developments in the early centuries.[2] However, as J.N.D. Kelly observes, despite the lack of "consciously formulated ecclesiology", there was, in fact, considerable development in ecclesiology in the second and third centuries, particularly in the area of the sacraments and in the concepts of catholicity and unity of the Church.[3] Apparently the question was not put as to whether New Testament teaching concerning the nature of the gospel and the Church justified these developments. However the question remains: What *was* the cause of these apparently spontaneous developments? Is it possible that,

[1] Origen, *Princ.* bk IV, 1:21. (ANF 4:370-371).
[2] Cf. Alister McGrath *(Christian Theology: An Introduction.* London: Blackwell, 1994, p. 405): "ecclesiology was not a major issue in the early church". McGrath comments further, "The eastern church showed no awareness of the potential importance of the issue. Most Greek patristic writers contented themselves with describing the church using recognizably scriptural images, without choosing to probe further."
[3] J.N.D. Kelly, *Early Christian Doctrines,* 3d ed., London: Adam & Charles Black, 1965, pp. 189 220.

in the absence of a conscious formulation of ecclesiology, the disinheriting of Israel by the Church had repercussions on the development of the Christian ministry and church structure?

As a basis for evaluating these developments, we will consider briefly what the New Testament teaches concerning church structure and the nature of the Christian ministry and various attempts to explain subsequent developments. We will then examine the patristic writings in order to discover whether there is a discernible relationship between post-apostolic *replacement theology* and the developing concepts of Christian ministry and hierarchical Church structure. Our survey will extend to the time of Constantine.

B. New Testament Teaching Concerning Church Structure and the Nature of the Christian Ministry

Jesus prophesied that he would build a church that would withstand all opposing forces (Mt 16:18; cf. Jn 10:16). On the other hand his disciples dreamed of the restoration of the kingdom to Israel in a context of apocalyptic glory, hoping that their close relationship with Jesus would procure them positions of prestige and power in this kingdom (Mk 10:35-41; cf. Lk 19:11; Ac 1:6-8). When James and John, the sons of Zebedee, formulated a specific request in this sense, Jesus used the circumstance to affirm that such positions did not reflect the true nature of Christian discipleship:

> You know that those who are regarded as rulers of the Gentiles lord it over them, and their high officials exercise authority over them. Not so with you. Instead, whoever wants to become great among you must be your servant, and whoever wants to be first must be slave of all. For even the Son of Man did not come to be served, but to serve, and to give his life as a ransom for many (Mk 10:42-45).

The role of Jesus' disciples was to be that of special witnesses to his earthly ministry and resurrection and heralds of the gospel to the whole world (Ac 1:8, 21-22; Mk 16:15-16).

Ultimately they would be instrumental in multiplying the number of his disciples (Mt 28:18-20; cf. Ac 6:7; 11:26).

For a fuller idea of what Jesus envisaged for the community of his disciples, we need to consider what the Holy Spirit revealed after the ascension of Jesus (Jn 16:12-15). So far as church structure is concerned, the role of elders, who had been part of Israel's national life from the time of Moses (Ex 4:29), was confirmed almost at once in the apostolic church (Ac 11:30; 15:2,22-23). Moreover Paul and Barnabas introduced government by a college of elders into the new Gentile churches (Ac 14:23; cf. 20:17; Tit 1:5; 1 Ti 4:14). The same concept of leadership was later reaffirmed by Peter (1 Pe 5:1-3). The function of the body of elders or "presbyters" (πρεσβύτεροι), is to *oversee* God's people, hence their office is described as that of "overseers" or "bishops" (ἐπίσκοποι) in several New Testament passages (Ac 20:17,28; Php 1:1; 1 Ti 3:1). The New Testament also refers to the ministry of "deacons" whose function is more circumscribed than that of elders (Ro 16:1; 1 Ti 3:8-13; cf. Ac 6:1-6).

Although the New Testament uses a variety of terms to describe church leaders (cf. Ac 13:1; Gal 2:8-10; 1 Th 5:12), it is clear that "presbyter" refers to the same person as "bishop"[4] and that only a two-tier ministry, of elders/bishops and deacons, was envisaged. Furthermore, the role of bishops or overseers was limited to one local church (Php 1:1-2; 1 Pe 5:1-4). That which appears significant, in the light of subsequent developments, is the absence of a *three-tier* ministry consisting of a bishop as a distinct figure, a college of local elders, and deacons.

The most important ministries envisaged for church leaders were teaching and pastoral care (Ac 20:28-31; 1 Pe 5:1-4) while

---

[4] This is recognised by Jerome in his commentary on Titus (quoted by Eric G. Jay, *The Church: its changing image through twenty centuries,* Atlanta, GA: John Knox Press, 1978, p. 93). Jerome affirms that initially each church was governed by a council of presbyters and that the election of one of the presbyters to the office of Bishop was an expedient used to overcome the kind of problem mentioned in 1 Co 1:12. However it should be noted that the most systematic presentations of the two-tier concept of the Christian ministry – elders/bishops and deacons – are found in New Testament writings which date from after Paul wrote 1 Corinthians (see Ac 20:17-31; Php 1:1; 1 Tim 2:1-13; Tit 1:5-9)

deacons were commonly responsible to meet practical needs. However the concept of ministry was not limited to the roles of elders/bishops and deacons. Both Peter and Paul conceive of the Church as a society in which *every member* has his or her function and is called to serve according to the particular χάρισμα ("gift of grace") received (1 Pe 4:10-11; Ro 12:4-8; 1 Co 12:7-30). In the light of later developments it is strikng that nowhere in the New Testament are elders invested with a priestly function which sets them apart from the rest of the church. Moreover no list of spiritual gifts includes a particular χάρισμα for performing priestly functions. The purpose of all the gifts was the edification of the Church, not mediation between God and other church members. Nor did the distribution of gifts entail the conferment of special prerogatives for the dispensing of divine grace. Both Peter and the writer to the Hebrews make it clear that priesthood is a prerogative of all members of the spiritual house which Christ is building and over which he presides (1 Pe 2:1-10; Heb 3:1-6; 4:14-16; 7:11-10:23). The only distinctive priestly function in the context of the new covenant is the *high* priesthood of Christ which is described as permanent and as being "over the house of God" (Heb 7:23-25; 8:1-2; 10:19-22).[5] As for Peter and Paul, they understood their apostleship as involving witnessing and teaching but not in terms of a special *priestly* function (1Pe 5:1; 2Pe 1:12-13; 1 Co 1:17; 1 Ti 2:7).

When Paul elaborated on what it means to be ministers of the new covenant (2 Co 3:4-11), he was careful to distinguish this ministry from what pertained to the Mosaic covenant. While both are glorious, ministry pertaining to the new covenant is more glorious first because it is peculiarly the *ministry of the Spirit* and thus life-giving (vv. 6, 8), and secondly because it has to do with what is permanent (v. 11). The purpose of this ministry is

---

[5] Nothing in the New Testament writings contradicts what is taught explicitly in 1 Peter and Hebrews (cf. Jn 14:6; 1Ti 2:5-6), rather the opposite (Jn 4:19-24; Ac 11:19-23; 15:7-11; Ro 12:1-2; Heb 13:15); cf. Dunn (*Partings*, p. 92), "In all the references to Christian worship and Christian community within the NT *there is simply no allusion to any order of priesthood within the Christian congregations*"(emphasis his).

reconciliation – "as though God were making his appeal through us". Such reconciliation is made possible by the saving work of Christ on the cross (2 Co 5:18-21). It is clear from the superiority and permanency of the ministry pertaining to the new covenant that the forms of the Mosaic covenant are incompatible with it (2 Co 3:7,11; Heb 10:1-23). This is confirmed by the commemorative, rather than sacrificial, nature of the Lord's Supper (Lk 22:14-21; 1 Co 11:23-26).

C. Various Opinions Concerning the Reasons for Subsequent Developments in Ecclesiology

According to two Roman Catholic scholars who write concerning ecclesiology and ecclesiastical institutions in the early church,[6] the attenuation of collegial leadership in the churches, after the close of the apostolic era, depended partly on persecution and partly on the absence of bishops on which the function of the presbyters depended.[7] They affirm that from the time of Ignatius *(Smyrn.* VIII): "The bishop is head of the community in all of its manifestations".[8] For our purposes it is significant that, according to these scholars, certain elements in the developing Christian liturgy were patterned on aspects of Jewish liturgy.[9]

In the Cunningham Lectures of 1902[10] Thomas Lindsay observed that, by the end of the second century, Ignatius' dream of church life and order being based on the office of the bishop had become a reality. By the third century, "every Christian community had at its head a single president who is almost always

---

[6] Vittorino Grossi & Angelo Di Berardino, *La chiesa antica: ecclesioogia e istituzioni,* Roma: Borla, 1984.

[7] *Ibid.,* p. 102.

[8] *Ibid.,* p. 100.

[9] *Ibid.,* "Le matrici giudaiche" (pp. 257-263), where mention is made of the liturgy of the synagogue, the sanctification of the Sabbath and the Passover.

[10] Thomas M. Lindsay, *The Church and the Ministry in the Early Centuries,* The 18th series of the Cunningham Lectures, 1902, London: Hodder & Stoughton, 1907³.

called the bishop."[11] According to Lindsay, among the causes for this, besides persecution and what he calls natural development, were the requisites for the celebration of the Lord's Supper. Already in the writings of Ignatius, this celebration had been associated with an "altar" (θυσιαστήριον), a concept derived from the Levitical tradition.[12]

Concerning the change in the concept of Christian ministry which occurred during the same period, Lindsay writes:

> Without any apostolic sanction, in virtue of the power lying within the community and given to it by the Master, the Church of the second century effected a change in its ministry quite as radical if not more so, as that made by the Reformed Church in the sixteenth century...[13]

For the purposes of our study it is important to understand the grounds for this radical change. Philip Schaff makes the following general statement:

> Judaism, with its religion and its sacred writings, and Graeco-Roman heathenism, with its secular culture, its science, and its art, were destined to pass into Christianity to be transformed and sanctified.[14]

According to this Church historian, Judaism, as a religion, helped to shape Christianity. Panfilo Gentile also attributes certain developments in second century Christianity to a takeover of aspects of Judaism.[15] Dunn considers this takeover a retrograde step:

> Rabbinic Judaism was able to survive the loss of a cult centre (the Temple), and so also the loss of the possibility and need for sacrifice and priesthood, by reorganizing itself round the Torah. *In rabbinic Judaism priest was replaced by teacher.* In contrast, and somewhat surprisingly, *it was*

---

[11] *Ibid.,* p. 204.

[12] *Ibid.,* p. 208.

[13] *Ibid.,* p. 210.

[14] Philip Schaff, *History of the Christian Church,* 2:428.

[15] Panfilo Gentile, *Il Cristianesimo Dalle Origini a Costantino,* Collana di Studi storici e Filosofici, Carlo Antoni (ed.), Firenze: Le Monnier, 1946, p. 193. According to Gentile, Christianity began to consider itself exactly as the Jews considered themselves, with the only difference that Christianity dispensed with nationalistic requisites, conceding to anyone the rights of citizenship in the new and true Israel.

Christianity which found it necessary to revert to OT categories of sacrifice and priesthood, at first in a spiritual or allegorical way, as a means to expressing continuity with the ideal of OT spirituality, but then in an increasingly literal way.[16]

According to Dunn, the way Christianity appropriated some central features of Old Testament religious practice had negative effects not only upon the concept of Christian ministry but also upon the concept of the Church as the body of Christ.[17]

D. Replacement Theology and Developments in Concepts of Church Structure and Ministry

1. *At the close of the first century*

The letter known as *1 Clement,*[18] written in the name of the Roman church to its sister church in Corinth (A.D. 90 - 100), contains a surprising anticipation of some future developments. In order to explain what it means to be "made partakers in the blessings of His elect", the author quotes Deuteronomy 32:8-9, where it is stated that "his people Jacob became the portion of the Lord, and Israel the lot of His inheritance".[19] This is followed, later in the letter, by a definition of church order and ministry in which free use is made of Old Testament Levitical terminology. For example the author mentions three levels of ministry, High Priest, other priests and levites, all of which are distinguished from the role of the laity. Church members are exhorted not to go beyond the boundaries of each one's own particular ministry, that is: "beyond the rule of the ministry prescribed to him".[20]

Thus a simple form of *replacement theology* – the Church identified as Israel – is followed by the application of the Levitical model to ecclesiastical order and the concept of Christian ministry.

[16] Dunn, *Partings*, pp. 254-255.
[17] *Ibid.*, pp. 257-258.
[18] PG 1:122-178.
[19] 1 Clement, 29 (ANF 1:12-13/PG 1:151).
[20] *Ibid.*, 40-41 (ANF 1:16/PG 1:158-160).

2. In the *Epistles of Ignatius*

In his *Epistle to the Philadelphians,* Ignatius orders his readers not to listen to anyone who preaches the law (VI,1). Moreover he links Abraham with the Church, making his acceptance with God depend upon Jesus' role as High Priest (IX, 1-2). Other elements in this letter which point in the direction of a simple form of *replacement theology* are its three-tier concept of the Christian ministry and the use of the term "altar" to qualify the Eucharist.[21] When Ignatius refers to the "one Eucharist", he also speaks of:

> one altar; as there is one bishop, along with the presbytery and deacons" (IV, 1).

The dominant theme in these letters is solidarity with the bishop as the secret of Christian unity.[22] The passage just quoted suggests that behind the crucial role attributed to the bishop may be the Levitical model of ministry now presumed to pertain to the Church. The direction in which the new concept of ecclesiastical structure would take the Church is further suggested by the way Ignatius greets the church of Rome which is said to "preside over the region of the Romans", and even more significantly, to "preside over love" (προκαθήμενη τῆς ἀγάπης).[23] These expressions may bear witness to the beginning of the concept

---

[21] Cf. the pattern of thought observed in *1 Clement* where a simple form of *replacement theology* is followed by the use of priestly categories in relation to a three-tier concept of the Christian ministry.

[22] The errors combatted by Ignatius of Antioch have been variously understood as one composite Judaeo-Christian-Docetic error or as two distinct errors: those of the Docetists and the Judaisers. Christine Trevett suggests that Ignatius might have been combatting three errors, the third being the opposition of those gifted as prophets to office bearers who lacked this *charisma* (Christine Trevett, "Prophecy and Anti-Episcopal Activity: a Third Error Combatted by Ignatius?" *JEH* 34/1 (1983):1-18. Whatever the analysis of the errors which Ignatius set himself to combat, there is little doubt that he saw the key to its/their solution in the general acceptance of monarchical episcopacy, perhaps a relatively novel institution.

[23] These expressions appear in both the shorter and longer forms of Ignatius' *Epistle to the Romans* (ANF 1:73/PG 5:801).

of the primacy of Rome, which certainly was to take root in the thought of later Church Fathers.[24]

3. In pseudonymous *2 Clement*

In *2 Clement* for the first time we meet the idea of the Church being pre-existent[25] and essentially spiritual in nature (XIV, 1). As well as considering the Church to exist from eternity past, the writer of *2 Clement* uses Old and New Testament writings indiscriminately. For instance he makes belonging to the Church and obtaining final salvation depend upon observing the law of purity and doing works of righteousness (XV-XIX). Thus we see that disregard for the essential link between the Old Testament and Israel and failure to consider the specificity of the Church in God's plan, can lead to neglect of the gospel of grace on which membership in the true church depends (see Ac 15:1-11).

4. In Justin Martyr's *Dialogue with Trypho, a Jew*[26]

Justin was convinced that the Church occupied the place which the Jews believed was reserved for them. After listening to the Christian apologist freely apply to the Church promises originally addressed to Israel, his Jewish interlocutor exclaimed, "What then? are you Israel? and does He [God] speak such things [Isa 19:24-25; Eze 34:12] to you?"[27]

For Justin, the presupposition that the Church has replaced Israel meant that Old Testament concepts could be applied indiscriminately to the Church. This is evident when he speaks of the priesthood in chapter CXVI:

> We are the true high priestly race of God, as even God Himself bears witness, saying that in every place among the Gentiles sacrifices are presented to Him well-pleasing and pure. Now God receives sacrifices from no one, except through His priests.

[24] J.N.D. Kelly, *Early Christian Doctrines*, p. 191.
[25] Cf. the figure of an old woman by which the Church is represented in *Hermas (Visions*, 2,4,1/PG 1:1317-1318).
[26] PG 6:471-800.
[27] *Tryph. Jud.* CXXIII (ANF 1:261/PG 6:764).

113

This theme is further developed in chapter CXVII, where Justin builds on Malachi 1:10-12, in order to prove the unacceptable nature of the sacrifices offered by the priests of Israel.[28] According to Justin the passage refers to the "sacrifices" of the bread and the cup of the Eucharist. He denies that there was a Jewish dispersion at the time when Malachi was written and claims that by his own time there were "Christians in all places throughout the world". He was mistaken on both counts, yet his exegesis of the Malachi passage became part of presuppositional *replacement theology.* For example in his *Tract Against the Jews,* written almost three centuries later, Augustine uses Malachi 1:10-11 to show that the Jews have been dismissed while Christians offer acceptable sacrifices everywhere on earth and in heaven![29]

The most questionable aspects of Justin's exposition of the Malachi passage are, first, his complete neglect of what the prophet's words would have meant for readers of his time and, secondly, the definition of the memorial meal instituted by Jesus in terms analogous to the Levitical sacrifices.[30] Justin's reasoning has important implications for the concept of Christian ministry, which he understands as being essentially that of offering sacrifices which replace those offered by unworthy Jewish priests.

5. In Irenaeus' *Against Heresies*[31]

In our last chapter we saw that Irenaeus read the Old Testament in the light of *replacement theology.* We now turn to his teaching concerning church structure and the Christian ministry. Irenaeus appealed to an uninterrupted succession of bishops, from the apostles to his own time, as a guarantee of orthodoxy. Where no bishop standing in this line of succession was present, meetings were to be considered unauthorized and could be occasions for the dissemination of the perverse opinions of men.[32] According to Irenaeus, the importance of

[28] The same use is made of Mal 1:10-12 in *Tryph. Jud.* XLI (PG 6:564).
[29] PL 42:60-63.
[30] This understanding of the Lord's Supper is already evident in the *Didache,* XIV, 1-3 *(Collana di testi patristici,* 5:38).
[31] PG 7:433-1224.

being able to trace the succession of bishops increases in the case of the church of Rome, because it is supremely this church, founded by the apostles Peter and Paul, which guarantees the faithful transmission of the apostolic tradition. He writes:

> For it is a matter of necessity that every Church should agree with this Church, on account of its preeminent authority.[33]

It is clear that Irenaeus' primary concern here is the preservation of apostolic truth. However it is significant that a Church Father who set himself to defend orthodoxy and stressed the canonicity of certain writings, also stressed the office of the episcopate, thus considering a three-tier concept of church leadership an essential part of Christian orthodoxy.

Irenaeus' treatment of sacrifices raises the question of the nature of the Christian ministry. He uses a catena of Old Testament quotations to show that God did not desire sacrifices and holocausts for himself but instituted these for Israel, whereas God sought faith, obedience and righteousness in view of Israel's salvation.[34] Irenaeus then proceeds to use Malachi 1:10-11 as a basis for asserting that the sacrifice that God seeks is what Jesus' disciples offer to him in every place among the nations. According to Irenaeus, Malachi 1:11 indicates "in the plainest manner... that the former people [the Jews] shall indeed cease to make offerings to God, but that in every place sacrifice shall be offered to Him... among the Gentiles."[35] The whole of chapter 18 of book IV is dedicated to a discussion of the Eucharist which Irenaeus describes variously as "the oblation of the Church" and a "sacrifice".[36]

The parallelism which Irenaeus creates between Levitical sacrifices and what he considers the "sacrifice" consisting in the bread and wine of the Eucharist, ignores the unique and final value of

---

[32] *Haer.* III, 3, 1-2 (PG 7:848-849).
[33] *Ibid.* III, 3, 2, (ANF 1:415-416/PG 7:849).
[34] *Haer.* IV, 17,1-4 (PG 7:1019-1023).
[35] *Ibid.*, 7, 5 (ANF 1:484/PG 7:1024).
[36] *Ibid.*, IV, 18,2 (ANF 1:484-485/PG 7:1025).

Christ's sacrifice (Heb 10:10-18). He also neglects the specificity of Old Testament Scripture in its relationship to Israel and shows gratuitous contempt for Israelites whom he describes as slaves.[37] This neglect of the specificity of Israel and its institutions in the divine plan leads him to confuse Christ's unique sacrifice (Heb 9:1-10:19), of which the Lord's Supper was intended to be a commemoration (Lk 22:19), with Levitical sacrifices. Thus the Eucharist is seen to be similar to, but better than, the Levitical sacrifices and as having salvific value in and of itself:

> For as the bread, which is produced from the earth, when it receives the invocation of God, is no longer common bread, but the Eucharist, consisting of two realities, earthly and heavenly; so also our bodies, when they receive the Eucharist, are no longer corruptible, having the hope of the resurrection to eternity.[38]

In terms of the development of the Christian ministry, the most significant word here is "invocation" (ἐπικλήσις). Moreover it is noteworthy that the transformation of the bread into a heavenly as well as an earthly reality, is said to infuse incorruptibility into the bodies of those who receive it. Ignatius had already taught that the bread, when received in a context of obedience to the bishop and the presbytery is "the medicine of immortality".[39] Irenaeus adds that the transformation of the bread into this special substance is caused by the *invocation*. A study of the theme of invocation (ἐπικλήσις) in early Christian writings and liturgies[40] shows that it was understood to be a priestly function performed by the bishop. It is possible that the origin of this *invocation* is to be traced to Jewish synagogue practice and ultimately to the

---

[37] Cf. the following statements:
Inasmuch, then, as the Church offers with single-mindedness, her gift is justly reckoned a pure sacrifice with God...
But the Jews do not offer thus: for their hands are full of blood... *Haer* IV, 18,4 (ANF 1:485-486/PG 7:1026).

[38] *Ibid.*, 18,5 (ANF 1:486/PG 7:1028-1029).

[39] Ignatius, *Eph*, XX, φάρμακην ἀθανασίας, ἀντίδοτος τοῦ μή ἀποθανεῖν (PG 5:661).

[40] Cf. "Development of epiclesis in the liturgy," by Zechariah Schariah, an unpublished paper presented at the Evangelische Theologische Faculteit, Heverlee (Louvain), Belgium, September 1992.

concept of the divine "Shekhina" which filled the Tabernacle (Ex 40:34-35).[41] Irenaeus' expression "the invocation of God" harmonises well with this view. Eventually the invocation would become the prayer for the coming of the Holy Spirit and for the transformation of the bread and wine into the body and blood of Christ.[42] According to the *Apostolic Constitutions* "such sacred offices are conferred by the laying on of the hands of the bishop".[43]

Irenaeus' teaching concerning the Eucharist marks a significant development in the understanding of Christian ministry. Inasmuch as the practice of the invocation of God can be traced to Old Testament influence,[44] it is another instance of how the Church appropriated Old Testament liturgical practice indiscrimately. It is striking that an ecclesiastic of the stature of Irenaeus should develop a Christian doctrine of *invocation* without regard for what the New Testament teaches concerning the nature of authentic Christian worship and its attendant privileges (Jn 4:23-24; Heb 10:19-23; 13:15; 1 Pe 2:4-5). The fact that his teaching on the Eucharist was accompanied by an attitude of contempt for the Jews further illustrates the relationship between *replacement theology* and the tendency to confuse aspects of Levitical practice with Christian ministry.

6. *In the writings of Tertullian*

In our last chapter we saw that Tertullian shared Justin Martyr's conviction concerning circumcision, that it was given to Israel to mark her out as a "contumacious people". Furthermore, on

---

[41] *Ibid.*, pp. 17-22.

[42] See the following fourth century witnesses: *Apostolic Constitutions* bk VIII, 2 (PG 1:553-555); Cyril of Jerusalem, *Catechetical Letures* XIX, Mystagogica I, 7 (PG 33:1072).

[43] *Apostolic Constitutions* III, 10. "Neither do we permit the laity to perform any of the offices belonging to the priesthood; as, for instance, neither the sacrifice, nor baptism, nor the laying on of hands, nor the blessing, whether the smaller or the greater: for 'no one taketh this honour to himself, but he that is called of God' [Heb 5:4]. for such sacred offices are conferred by the laying on of the hands of the bishop" (ANF 7:429/PG 1:432). Only Bishops are allowed to ordain new ministers of the Church (ANF 7:430./PG 1:433).

[44] Schariah, "Development of epiclesis", p. 22.

the basis of Genesis 25:23, he considered Israel to be the servant of the Church. Because such exegesis ignores the clear meaning of the biblical text (cf. Ro 9:11-12), it would appear that Tertullian's understanding of Israel's place in the divine economy depended primarily on the *Adversus Judaeos* tradition.[45] This may also be seen in his *An Answer to the Jews,* where he writes, "The 'less' — that is the posterior — *people* attains the grace of divine favor from which Israel has been divorced".[46]

We noticed in the last chapter that Tertullian coined a number of theological terms which are still in use today. One of these, which he introduced while still a member of the Catholic Church, is *domina mater ecclesia,* which characterises the Church as the mother of Christians.[47] Moreover in his *Prescription against heretics,* written in the same period,[48] Tertullian claimed that faith, in order to be apostolic, must descend from the apostles, through apostolic churches.[49] At the time of making this assertion, Tertullian held to the organic unity of the catholic, apostolic church. In this early period he also introduced the term *summus sacerdos* in his work *On baptism.* This term defined the bishop, understood to stand above elders and deacons.[50] At the same time Tertullian excluded that the laity, without special authorisation from the bishop, could perform functions reserved for the latter because the bishop, and to a more limited extent the elders and deacons, were presumed to have special powers.[51] This concept of special "powers" has much in common with the prerogatives of Levitical priests (Lev chs 1-9,16,21) but little in common with the New Testament teaching concerning the Christian ministry. Tertullian considered baptism to be one of the higher functions

---

[45] The most important of these works are listed in ch. 3, n. 13.

[46] Tertullian, *Adv. Jud.*. I (ANF 3:152/PL 2:598).

[47] *On Martyrs,* I (ANF 3:693/PL 1:619). D. F. Wright considers this one of Tertullian's first writings, dating from 197 *(NIDCC,* s.v. "Tertullian").

[48] *NIDCC,* s.v. "Tertullian"

[49] *Prescription against heretics, XX.*

[50] *bap.* XVII, PL 1:1218 "Dandi quidem habit jus summus sacerdos, qui est episcopus. Deinde presbyteri et diaconi, non tamen sine episcopi auctoritate, propter Ecclesiae honorem."

[51] *Ibid.*

which properly belonged to the bishop *(summus sacerdos)*. For Paul, on the other hand, preaching belonged to a higher order of ministry than did baptising converts (1 Co 1:14,17), a conviction shared by Peter (cf. Ac 15:7-11 with 10:36-48).

The assimilation of Jewish titles such as "high priest" tended to give pre-eminence to Christian *rites* over faith and discipleship. Tertullian himself became dissatisfied with a church characterised by such religious forms, to the extent that he eventually left the official church around A.D. 205. Some interesting changes are discernible in the writings which follow Tertullian's disenchantment with the official church. In his *On the veiling of virgins* he criticises the idea of an hierarchical church:

> They [the churches founded by apostles or by apostolic men] and we have one faith, one God, the same Christ, the same hope, the same baptismal sacraments; let me say it once for all, we are one church. Thus, whatever belongs to our brethren is ours: only, the body divides us.[52]

Tertullian no longer sees apostolic succession in terms of a human catena or of structural solidarity with the Roman hierarchy, rather he identifies it in five of the elements listed by Paul in Ephesians 4:1-6. The omission of the *one Spirit and the one body* (1 Co 12:12-13), is not accidental. In fact Tertullian states openly that "the body divides us". Furthermore, in a previous chapter he had spoken of the Paraclete's administrative office as including, among other things, "the direction of discipline," something he saw sadly lacking in the hierarchical church where custom was put before truth. Tertullian takes up his polemic again with what he calls the "Psychic Church" in chapter XXI of his *On Modesty*, where he reasons that the keys entrusted by Christ to Peter concerned supremely entrance into the kingdom and "had nothing to do with the capital sins of believers".

When describing the kind of church which is authorised to administer discipline and the forgiveness of sins, Tertullian distances himself even further from the *hierarchical* church by asserting the concept of the *gathered* church:

[52] *On the veiling of virgins*, 2.

> For the very Church itself is, properly and principally, the Spirit Himself, in whom is the Trinity of the One Divinity – Father, Son, and Holy Spirit.... And thus, from that time forward, every number (of persons) who may have combined together into this faith is accounted "a church," from the Author and Consecrator (of the Church).[53]

Although Tertullian makes a substantial move here towards the New Testament concept of the Church, his concept of Christian ministry proved to be less flexible. Thus, in the chapter from which we have just quoted, he continues to use Levitical language, as when he writes of "the ministry of a priest ordained" to a sacred office.[54] Even so, it appears significant that the attenuation of the concept of *replacement theology* in his later writings coincided with a critical stance towards the conception of a monolithic, hierarchical church.

7. *In the writings of Origen*

We saw that Origen's *replacement theology* went beyond that taught by Justin Martyr and Irenaeus. It is perhaps more appropriate to speak of the disinheriting of *all* "corporeal" Israelites, including those who lived before Christ. His prowess as a biblical exegete helped to make this version of *replacement theology* a standard presupposition of Christian theology. Thus, as we have seen, churchmen such as Ambrose of Milan, Cyril of Alexandria and John Chrysostom of Antioch, had in common with Augustine of Hippo and Pope Gregory the Great that they regarded *replacement theology* as a fact.

Immediately after presenting *corporeal* Israelites as mere types of *spiritual* Israelites in Book IV of his *On First Principles*, Origen describes the Church as a transcendent reality, from which even Adam descended.[55] He thus asserts that physical Israel, as such,

---

[53] ANF 4:99-100/PL 2:1026 "Nam et Ecclesia proprie et principaliter ipse est Spiritus in quo est trinitas unius divinitatis, Pater et filius et Spiritus Sanctus. Illam Ecclesiam congregat, quam Dominus in tribus posuit. Atque ita eximde etiam numerus omnis qui in hanc fidum conspiraverint, Ecclesia ad autore et consacratore censetur.

[54] *Exhortation to Chastity,* XI (ANF 4:56/PL 2:926-927).

[55] Origen, *Princ.* bk IV, 1, 21.

never did occupy the place in God's plan that a *literal* reading of the Old Testament would suggest. The real members of God's people are *spiritual*Israelites, that is to say, the Church, understood to be something quite distinct from *corporeal* Israelites.

The question we now have to consider is whether Origen's *replacement theology* influenced his understanding of church structure and Christian ministry in a similar way that it influenced the ecclesiology of the Church Fathers that we have already examined. Given Origen's predilection for heavenly realities and his belief that earthly realities have merely typological or allegorical value, we might well expect that he would dispense with the literal use of Levitical categories. However, as Hanson observes,

> [Origen] always intended to interpret the Bible as the Church interpreted it. He was a loyal churchman....
> The whole life, custom and practice of the Church was very dear to him.[56]

In order to know Origen's view concerning the relevance of Levitical categories to Christian ministry, we will examine some of his *Homilies* on Leviticus and on the Song of Songs.

In the introduction to his *Homilies on Leviticus,* Origen establishes the principle that, as the Word of God had taken the form of flesh, just so the written Word of God is covered by the letter. Accordingly, the interpreter's goal is to perceive the hidden, spiritual meaning contained in the "letter".[57] Later on in these *Homilies,* he teaches that the references to Christ's flesh and blood in John 6:53,55 are to be understood as referring to Jesus' Word.[58] Moreover, in discussing the eucharistic doctrine, while allowing "the more usual interpretation concerning the Eucharist" for the simpler folk, he adds, "but to those who have learnt to hear deeper things, let it be understood also according to the more divine promise about the nourishing word of truth".[59] According to Origen, the efficacy of the eucharistic bread depends partly on the words pronounced by the one who prays over it and partly

---

[56] Hanson, *Allegory and Event,* pp. 371-372.
[57] *Hom. on Lev.* 1 (PG 12:405-411).
[58] *Hom.. on Lev.* VII,5 (PG 12:486-489).
[59] *Comm. on Jn* XXXII, 24, cited by Hanson (*Allegory and Event,* p. 325).

on the state of worthiness of those who receive it.[60] The importance which Origen attributes here to the words pronounced over the eucharistic bread raises an important question: Did he follow others in understanding the Christian ministry in Levitical terms?

While recognising that Christ conferred the privilege of priesthood upon *all* members of the Church,[61] this Alexandrian father insists that the forms of the Levitical ministry *are* pertinent to Christian ministry. Thus Leviticus 8:13 teaches us to distinguish between lesser and greater priestly ministries in the Church, while the role of "pontiff" or bishop is similar to that of Moses and Aaron.[62] Moreover, according to Origen, Paul's teaching concerning church leaders serves to confirm the validity of the instructions given to the priests in Leviticus 9:7; 10:8-9 and Numbers 18:20. Thus the precepts contained in 1 Timothy 3:2-3 and Titus 1:7-8 are addressed to "the priests" and "the princes of the priests".[63] Similarly, commenting on the limitations of entrance into the Jewish tabernacle, Origen divides humanity into priests who can enter the holy place, the pontiff who alone can penetrate the most holy place, the "children of Israel, that is the laymen", and the foreigners who have not yet been numbered in the Lord's Church.[64] Origen seems to have forgotten that, by prescribing the divisions of the tabernacle and restrictions of entry,

> The Holy Spirit was showing... that the way into the Most Holy Place had not yet been disclosed... (Heb 9:8).

The clear implication of Hebrews 9:1-8 is that the division of humanity into the categories of high priest, priests, laymen and foreigners was temporary. Both the writer to the Hebrews and the apostle Paul teach that the finished work of Christ made it possible for those who had been excluded from covenant blessings to gain full access to God's presence (Heb 10:10-23; Eph 2:11-22).

[60] *Comm. on Mt* XI,14 (PG 13:952).
[61] *Hom. on Lev.* (PG 12:440,451,489,508-509,521-523).
[62] PG 12:450-453.
[63] PG 12:475-478.
[64] PG 12:452.

Because of the prevalence of allegorism, Origen's preferred hermeneutical method, in his *Homilies* of the Song of Songs, we may consider opinions expressed here particularly indicative of his *own* thought. This is confirmed in the Prologue. The Song of Songs, writes Origen, is not to be interpreted according to its "carnal" sense; even the author of the work is to be regarded not as the son of David or the king of Israel, but as a symbolic "Solomon".[65] Yet even in this work Origen reverts to transposing Old Testament hierarchical distinctions into the context of the Church. For example the things contemplated by the queen of Sheba (1 Kgs 10:5) would indicate the ecclesiastical order made up of the episcopate and the presbytery, while the attending servants would indicate the deacons who assist the divine office.[66] Elsewhere Origen suggests that we are to understand the Levites to be superior to the twelve tribes of Israel because they were not counted in the census (Nu 2:32-33), while the priests are to be considered superior to the Levites (Nu 3:5); thus also the true Church is superior to the physical Israelites.[67]

Among the influences which determined Origen's use of Old Testament forms, the platonic concept of the Church propounded by Clement, his predecessor at the School of Alexandria, stands out as particularly prominent. According to Clement, "the grades here in the Church, of bishops, presbyters, deacons, are imitations of the angelic glory".[68] This three-tier concept of ministry has the following ancestry: first Israel, as God's elect people and heir of the promises, is disinherited, then the instructions which the God of Israel gave to the Levites are applied to the Church. Allegorical interpretation of the Scriptures gave the Church free rein in applying indiscriminately to herself what had pertained to Israel under the Mosaic covenant.

How far can this process be taken without losing sight of the specificity of the Church and the terms of the new covenant, as

---

[65] Origen, *Cant..* Prologue (PG 13:81).
[66] *Cant.,* bk II (PG 13:104).
[67] *Ibid.* (PG 13:81).
[68] Clement, *Strom.* VI, 13 (ANF 2:504/PG 9:328-329).

taught by the apostles? It is evident from the writings of Origen that, once *replacement theology* becomes an axiom of Christian hermeneutics, nothing can prevent the wholesale appropriation of Old Testament cultic practice into Church life.

E. The Eclipse of the Old Catholic Church

1. *Cyprian* (c. 200 - 258)

Some four decades after Tertullian's death, another churchman of Carthage left his mark on the developing Christian Tradition. Cyprian, bishop of Carthage from 248 until his death in 258, is significant for the theme of our present chapter because, as well as writing *Three Books of Testimonies against the Jews,*[69] he also made a distinctive contribution to ecclesiology.[70] This contribution has been evaluated in very different ways. On the one hand Vatican Council II made repeated use of his writings, in expounding Roman Catholic ecclesiology.[71] On the other hand D. F. Wright assesses Cyprian's contribution to ecclesiology in substantially negative terms:

> His rigid correlation of Church and episcopate and his application of OT sacrificial and priestly categories to Christian ministers and sacraments constituted an unhappy legacy.[72]

Our main task will be to establish whether or not there is a relationship between Cyprian's *replacement theology* and the ecclesiological elements to which Wright draws attention. This

[69] Cyprian, *Testimonies* (PL 4:703-802).

[70] According to Eric Jay (*The Church*, p. 72), Cyprian's concept of the Church "prevailed in the West throughout the middle ages".

[71] I refer to the first three chapters of *Lumen Gentium* (21-11-1964): I The mystery of the Church, II The People of God, & III The hierarchical constitution of the Church and in particular of the episcopate. Eleven references to Cyprian's writings are to his Epistles: Ep.11,48,55,56,63,64,66,69(twice), one gen. ref. is to his Epistles with regard to the role of bishops, as priests and governors of the Church) and one is to his *On the Lord's Prayer*, 23 (*Tutti i documenti del Concilio*, pp. 1-41).

[72] *NIDCC*, s.v. "Cyprian".

will help determine the extent to which *replacement theology* contributed to what became standard Christian ecclesiology for over one thousand years.

The logical place to begin this survey is with Cyprian's explicit statement of *replacement theology* in his introduction to *Three Books of Testimonies against the Jews.* He writes:

> I have endeavoured to show that the Jews, according to what had before been foretold, had departed from God, and had *lost* God's favour, which had been given them in past time, *and had been promised them for the future;* while *the Christians had succeeded to their place,* deserving well of the Lord by faith, and coming out of all nations and from the whole world.[73]

Cyprian's *replacement theology* concerns both the past and the future. A sampling of chapter headings of *Three Books of Testimonies against the Jews* shows the extent to which his thought was impregnated with *replacement theology.* Moreover it is evident that while assimilating certain Old Testament sacrificial and priestly categories into the context of the new covenant, he also projected certain Christian terms back into the Old Testament economy. Here is the sampling:

12. That the old baptism should cease, and a new one should begin [Isa 43:18-21; 48:21; Mt 3:11; Jn 3:5-6].
16. That the ancient sacrifice should be made void, and a new one should be celebrated [Isa 1:11-12; Ps 50:13-15,23; 4:5; Mal 1:10-11].
19. That two peoples were foretold, the elder and the younger; that is, the old people of the Jews, and new one which should consist of us [Ge 25:23; Hos 2:23; 1:10].
20. That the Church which before had been barren should have more children from among the Gentiles than what the synagogue had had before [1sa 54:1-4; 1 Sa 2:5].
22. That the Jews would lose while we should receive the bread and the cup of Christ and all His grace, and that the new name of Christians should be blessed in the earth [Isa 65:13-15; 5:26-27; 3:1-2; Ps 34:8-10; Jn 6:35; 7:37-38; 6:53].[74]

[73] ANF 5:507/PL 4:704 (emphasis mine).
[74] ANF 5:512-514/PL 4:723-724.

In no case does a straightforward reading of the passages mentioned above lead to the conclusions suggested in the chapter headings.

In the third book of *Testimonies,* Cyprian affirms "that the Eucharist is to be received with fear and honour".[75] The biblical passages on which this consideration is based are Leviticus 7:20 and 1 Corinthians 11:27. The first of these speaks of sacrifice, literally a "fellowship offering belonging to the Lord", which was not to be eaten in the case of it becoming ceremonially unclean, on pain of death. The second is related to the Lord's Supper which Jesus' disciples are commanded to celebrate (1 Co 11:27; cf. Lk 22:19). The only logical link between the two passages is the requirement to act according to God's instructions with an accompanying warning concerning the consequences of disobedience. For the rest the differences are profound. The reference in Leviticus is to a *sacrifice* which could be offered any number of times and which had to be *taken to a priest* who offered it to the Lord (Lev 7:14-19). On the other hand, the Lord's Supper has to do with the *giving of thanks* (εὐχαριστία) and the *commemoration* and *proclamation* of the *once-for-all sacrifice* which Christ offered to God, thus putting an end to all sacrifices (1 Co 11:23-26; cf. Heb 7:27; chs 9-10).

It is significant that Romans chapters 9-11 are virtually ignored in the *Three Books of Testimonies against the Jews.* In particular no part of these chapters is quoted in which reference is made to the present status or future prospect of unbelieving Israel.[76] The choice to ignore these passages shows that Cyprian's conviction that Israel has irretrievably lost what *had been given them in past time* and what *had been promised them for the future,* was based on a selective use of Scripture.

Cyprian's contribution to ecclesiology was tied to the course of events. As bishop of Carthage, he had to face the problem of how to treat baptised Christians who, after having denied their

[75] ANF 5:554/PL 4:804.
[76] The only passages quoted in Cyprian's *Testimonies* from Ro 9-11 are 9:3-5, 11:20-21 and 11:33-36.

faith in Christ during the persecution decreed by emperor Decius (250-251), repented and sought re-entry into the Church. The different positions propounded regarding the possibility of re-admitting these people caused some serious divisions in the church of Carthage. Following two Synods of African bishops, Cyprian took an intermediate position between the inflexible stance of Novatus and the more liberal attitude of those who opposed him. However the Church remained divided and this caused Cyprian to meditate on the whole question of Christian unity. This led to the writing of his most famous treatise: *On the Unity of the Church.*[77]

According to Cyprian, the unity of the Church has its origin in the apostle Peter, understood to be the source of the episcopate and the foundation of the Church.[78] Furthermore he identified in the succession of Roman bishops "the throne of Peter," understood in terms of primacy, not supremacy.[79] Consequently the true church is that which maintains fellowship with the petrine bishop of Rome and submits itself to legitimately ordained bishops who replace their predecessors in the same See. Where cohesion between the local See and the legitimate bishop of Rome is lacking, the Church does not exist and all religious functions, including baptism and the Eucharist, are null and void.[80]

Cyprian's ecclesiology is summed up in the memorable phrase: *He can no longer have God for his Father who has not the Church for his mother.*[81] The word "Church" here refers to those parts of Christendom whose unity with Christ is mediated by the apostolic See of Rome.

A second characteristic of Cyprian's ecclesiology is his use of the term "catholic". Whereas previously this term had been used with reference to the worldwide church[82] and to those holding

---

[77] Cyprian, *Unit. eccl.* (PL 4:509-536).

[78] *Ibid.,* 4-5 (PL 4:512-518); cf. *Ep.* LIV, 7; (ANF 5:341/PL 4:358).

[79] *Ep.* LIV, 14; LXXIV, 15-17 (ANF 5:344,394-395/PL 4:358, 425-426).

[80] *Unit. eccl.,* para. 4-6 (ANF 5:422-423/PL 4:512-520).

[81] "Habere jam non potest Deum patrem qui Ecclesiam non habet matrem" (PL 4:519).

[82] See the greeting in *The Encyclical Epistle of the Church at Smyrna concerning the Martyrdom of the Holy Polycarp* (PG 5.1023).

to orthodox doctrine,[83] it is now associated with Cyprian's more limited concept of the true church,[84] according to which catholicity depends on the "sacrament of unity, this bond of a concord inseparably cohering [with the Roman See]."[85] Outside of *this* unity, which he calls the *Catholic* church, the sacrifices offered by priestly rivals are thought to be invalid.[86]

A reader of the New Testament may well ask: What do the *offering of sacrifices* and *priestly rivals* have to do with Christianity? Such talk has much more to do with Levitical categories than anything the New Testament has to say about Christian ministry. The following passage taken from Cyprian's tractate on Christian unity, illustrates well the extent to which his ecclesiology was organised in Levitical categories:

> Does he think that he has Christ, who acts in opposition to Christ's *priests,* who separates himself from the company of His *clergy* and *people?...* An enemy of the *altar,* a rebel against Christ's *sacrifice...* a hostile brother, despising the *bishops,* and forsaking God's *priests,* he dares to set up another *altar...* to profane the truth of the Lord's offering by *false sacrifices.*[87]

Cyprian's concept of Christian unity, based on a combination of apostolic succession and priestly ordination, produced episcopal exclusivism. This new principle replaced the apostolic concept of Christian unity *based on the gospel* (see Ac 15:1-14; Ro 15:7). Cyprian's contribution turned out to be a watershed in the history of ecclesiology. With him the *Catholic* church ceased being the universal church and became the *Roman* Catholic church, while *orthodoxy* came to mean obedience to the ecclesiastical institution thought to mediate God's grace through the sacraments. All of this presupposes the conviction that the Church now occupies the place which was once Israel's and that its ministers possess the same prerogatives as the Levitical priesthood.

---

[83] Irenaeus, *Haer.,* III, 4 (PG 7:855-857).

[84] *Ep.* LXIX, 1 (PL 4:413).

[85] *Unit. eccl.* 7 (ANF 5:423/PL 4:521).

[86] *Ibid.,* 13 (ANF 5:425/PL 4:525-526; cf. *Ep.* LXIX (ANF 5:375/PL 4:413-420).

[87] *Unit. eccl.* 17 (ANF 5:427/PL 4:529), italics mine.

2. Emperor Constantine

a. *Constantine's contribution to the development of Christian antisemitism.*

The edict of toleration promulgated by emperor Galerio in A.D. 311 and the ecclesiastical politics of Constantine, which began with the publication of the edict of Milan (313), inaugurated a new era for the Church. With imperial persecution virtually a thing of the past, it was reasonable to expect that members of the Church would be free to live according to their Christian conscience. In actual fact, freedom from persecution was immediately followed by interference in the affairs of the Church on the part of the secular power, in the person of the emperor himself.[88] Moreover Constantine reorganised the Church, using as his model the administrative structures of the Roman empire. This factor, wedded to the hierarchical structure inherited from the School of Alexandria and from Cyprian, radically changed the concept of the Church from that of a body whose leaders were servants, to that of "a fixed order where some were permanently set over others."[89] In order to understand the nature of Constantine's relationship with the Church, this must be kept in mind. The "people" were counted as part of the Church only through their link with the bishop who incarnated the Church's true substance.[90]

Constantine believed that his religious role as "pontifex maximus" (supreme priest) included being high priest of the Christian church as well as of pagan religion. Hence he felt it his

---

[88] This came to be known as *Cesare-papism,* a term used to define the situation in which the Church is effectively conditioned or controlled by the secular power.

[89] See Giles, *Church*, pp. 214-215.

[90] This had been the teaching of Cyprian *(Ep.* LXIX,8/PL 4:418-419); cf. Joseph Ratzinger, *Popolo e casa di Dio in Sant'Agostino,* Già e non ancora, n. 36, Milano: Cooperativa Edizioni Jaca Books, 1978, pp. 99-100. Eusebius' account of how Constantine was able to enquire quickly concerning the meaning of his famous vision of a cross of light, suggests that when Constantine moved with his Gallic army to impose his dominion over Italy, some bishops travelled with him *(The Life of Constantine,* I,32 (PG 20:948).

duty to maintain order in the Church, for example by convening Councils to resolve doctrinal disputes.[91] By such interference,[92] and by the creation of ecclesiastical regions, he left an indelible mark on the life of the Church. In what follows, we will first notice how Constantine set in motion what was to become standard practice in Church-Israel relations. We will then consider some long term effects of his religious politics on ecclesiology itself.

The main concern of the Council of Nicea (A.D. 325), convened and presided over by the emperor himself, was to overthrow Arianism by defining orthodox Christology. However a number of less important matters were also discussed. Among these there was the question concerning the date of Easter. Constantine treated this in a letter he sent to those not present at Nicea. At a certain point of this letter, he writes:

> It was declared to be particularly unworthy for this [Easter], the holiest of all festivals, to follow the custom [the calculation] of the Jews, who had soiled their hands with the most fearful of crimes, and whose minds were blinded... We ought not therefore, to have anything in common with the Jews... we desire, dearest brethren, to separate ourselves from the detestable company of the Jews... [even if their deliberations were not wrong] it would still be your duty not to tarnish your soul by communications with such wicked people."[93]

For the first time the Church's theological understanding concerning Israel dictated official policy, albeit indirectly. It may appear paradoxical that while the Church felt free to take over cultic forms and sacrifical language from the Jewish Scriptures, she scrupulously avoided any identification of the Christian Easter with the Jewish Passover, despite the fact that New Testament

---

[91] For a good introduction to this period, see Frend, "The Constantinian Revolution 305-30", *Rise of Christianity*, pp. 474-517.

[92] The Church historian, Eusebius, a contemporary of Constantine, did not consider Constantine's involvement in ecclesiastical affairs as interference, but rather as being the fruit of providence (Eusebius Pamphilus, *Oration in Praise of the Emperor Constantine* [NPNF ss 1:581-610]).

[93] Eusebius, *The Life of Constantine*, III, 18-20 (PG 20:1074-1080).

terminology establishes a close link between Jewish practice and Christian faith at this point (Lk 22:14-16; 1 Co 5:7). A possible explanation is that the Church felt free to assimilate elements of Levitical cultic practice into the pattern of Christian worship because the sacrificial system and all that went with it were no longer a part of contemporary Jewish life. On the other hand, the Passover celebration *did* continue to occupy an important place on the Jewish religious calendar,[94] as indeed it still does today. Hence the Church, in its desire to disassociate with physical Israel, felt the need to hold its own Easter celebration on a different date from that of the Jewish Passover.

Constantine's letter established a precedent for the practice of making official statements which discriminated against the Jews.[95] James Parkes makes this general comment:

> There is no other adequate foundation [for modern antisemitism] than the theological conceptions built up in the first three centuries. But upon these foundations an awful superstructure has been reared, and first stones of that superstructure were laid, the very moment the Church had power to do so, in the legistlation of Constantine and his successors.[96]

b. *Constantine's influence on the development of ecclesiology*

The link established between the Church and the secular State was to have a profound effect both on the concept and the perceived role of the Church. In the Eastern part of the Roman Empire the practice of the State exercising power over the Church became normative after Constantine, in A.D. 330, shifted his capital to Byzantium, renaming it Constantinople. Meanwhile the West, accustomed to there being a powerful political head in Rome, increasingly attributed to its bishop a unifying political role. Thus the Roman bishop grew in prestige to the point of eventually gaining ascendancy over secular powers.

[94] For almost nineteen centuries the Passover celebration was the occasion in which the Jews dispersed throughout the world expressed the wish: "Next year in Jerusalem!"

[95] See Parkes, *Conflict*, pp. 381-391. A recurring theme in the long list of ecclesiastical sanctions against the Jews was the contempt in which Christians were to hold all Jewish customs and practices.

[96] *Ibid.*, p. 375, see chap. 3, C. 5, in the present work.

Constantine's religious policies had three further effects. They favoured the concept of the territorial Church; they consolidated the division between clergy and laity; and they contributed to the development of medieval theocracy. Here we will consider the first and second of these aspects, leaving the development of the medieval theocracy to the next chapter.

In order to understand the import of Constantine's policy of favouring the Christian religion throughout the Roman empire, it is necessary to remember that, in the Roman world, religion was generally subservient to the State. Thus Constantine's decision to favour Christianity over paganism in effect turned Christianity into a State church whose dimensions corresponded to a given territory. All those living in this territory were expected to be Christians. This goal was facilitated by a sacramental understanding of baptism, according to which this Christian ordinance confers divine grace on those baptised and introduces them into the Church.

The sacramental understanding of baptism had developed gradually but was already well advanced by the time Tertullian wrote his treatise *On Baptism* (c. A.D. 200). There is a certain tension in Tertullian's doctrine of baptism which both affirms the sacramental value of the rite and teaches that entrance into the Church implies living a holy life. The first of these elements is present in the opening phrase of his treatise:

> Happy is our sacrament of water, in that, by washing away the sins of our early blindness, we are set free *and admitted* into eternal life![97]

Towards the end of the same work Tertullian recommends that baptism be delayed in the case of small children and the unwedded in order to lessen the probability of grave sins being committed after baptism.[98]

Half a century after Tertullian wrote his treatise, Cyprian counselled Fidus *not* to wait to baptise infants until the eighth day, because "the mercy and grace of God is not to be refused to

---

[97] *bap.* I, emphasis his (ANF 3:669/PL 1:1197).
[98] *bap.* XIX (ANF 3:678/PL 1:1222).

any one born of man".[99] It is clear from this advice that baptism had, by Cyprian's time, come to be understood as effecting forgiveness of sins and entrance into the Church. The preference Fidus had expressed,[100] to baptise infants on the eighth day, rested on the conviction that Christian baptism took the place of circumcision. However, because baptism was thought to be an efficacious means of communicating God's mercy and grace, Cyprian deemed it advisable to over-ride the symbolism of the eighth day.

The practice of baptising the newly-born was part of a general tendency linked with a priestly understanding of the Christian ministry. In Constantine's day, this sacramental understanding of ministry facilitated the formal conversion of the Roman empire to Christianity. But are there grounds for considering baptism analogous to the rite of circumcision and the chief means whereby lost sinners receive saving grace?

The issue of circumcision and of how God administers salvation were the two interrelated questions discussed at the Jerusalem Conference during the apostolic era. Many modern scholars regard this meeting, of which the proceedings are summarised in Acts 15:1-29, as the first Church Council.[101] It is significant that no-one in this important meeting, not even Peter (vv. 7-11), suggested that baptism had replaced physical circumcision. More significant still, in the light of later teaching concerning baptismal regeneration, is the lack of any suggestion that baptism is a means whereby sin is forgiven and salvation is applied. The fact that the deliberations of the Jerusalem meeting were substantially ignored by Christian leaders in subsequent centuries, while *priestly*

---

[99] Cyprian, *Ep.* LVIII, 3,6 (ANF 5:353-354, not in PL).

[100] *Ibid.*

[101] For a guide to the vast literature on Acts ch. 15, see Ernst Haenchen, *The Acts of the Apostles*, 14th ed., trans. from the German by Basil Backwell, Philadelphia, PA: Westminster Press, 1971, pp. 441-442; for a helpful treatment of the "Council" which treats Ac 15 as a factual account, see Gregory Dix, *Jew and Greek*, Glasgow: University Press, 1963, pp. 39-60. If the Jerusalem meeting can be regarded as a Church Council, it is the only such gathering during the early Christian centuries in which soteriology was the main subject of discussion.

administration of both baptism and the Eucharist became the chief functions of Christian ministers, testifies to the far-reaching effects of confusing the Church with Israel and its institutions.

The other, largely neglected, effect of the Constantinian revolution concerned the order of Christian worship. Justo Gonzàlez sums it up well: "…the congregation came to have a less active role in worship."[102] Gonzàlez also describes some formal changes:

> Incense, which was used as a sign of respect for the emperor, began appearing in Christian churches. Officiating ministers, who until then had worn everyday clothes, began dressing in more luxurious garments. Likewise, a number of gestures indicating respect, which were normally made before the emperor, now became part of Christian worship. The custom was also introduced of beginning services with a processional.[103]

Constantine's religious policies favoured the building of basilicas such as the one dedicated to the Most Holy Saviour, now known as St. John Lateran. The design of these buildings reflected and consolidated the ecclesiological developments which we have been considering: In the atrium there was a fountain where the faithful could perform ritual washings, next there were naves for the people, with a pulpit on either side for the reading and exposition of Scripture. At the end of the central nave, on a higher level, there was the sanctuary with an altar at its centre. There was space on this elevated area for the officiating ministers, as it was here that communion was celebrated. If it was the bishop's main church, there was a special chair or "cathedra"[104] for the bishop.[105]

Constantine gave architectural expression to the separation of the clergy from the laity. He also rendered the idea that the main function of the clergy was the administration of the sacraments, in particular of the Eucharist, on an *altar of sacrifice*, in *the most holy place*. Baptistries were usually built separately.

---

[102] Justo L. Gonzàlez, *The Story of Christianity*, 2 vols, New York: HarperCollins, 1984, 1:125.
[103] *Ibid.*
[104] "Cathedral", that is to say, the "seat" of the bishop, derives from the lat. *cathedra*.
[105] Gonzàlez, *Story of Cristianity*, I:125-128.

While proclamation was still important, it was shown not to be central. From this point on, in the popular understanding, the basilica with its officiating ministers, would be perceived as *the church* while the laity, who received the ministrations offered by the hierarchical church, became the *faithful* who *attended* church.

Inasmuch as the general structure and functions of the basilica are comparable to those of the Jewish tabernacle and temple, it is no exageration to say that such forms and functions were the practical consequence of the assimilation of Levitical cultic forms and priestly ministrations into Christianity, a practice which was facilitated by presuppositional *replacement theology*.

F. Replacement Theology in the *Catechetical Lectures* of Cyril of Jerusalem

The fact that Cyril (c. 310-386) was familiar with the condition of the so-called "Holy Places" before Constantine began adorning them,[106] suggests that he spent some of his early years in Jerusalem. He was ordained deacon sometime before the death of bishop Macarius in 334 or 335 and bishop about fifteen years later.[107] His role as defender of orthodoxy, his personal concern for the poor and the fact that he was bishop of the Apostolic See considered to be "the Mother of all the Churches", where the Jewish temple had once stood, all make Cyril's pronouncements particularly significant.

In his seventeenth lecture, Cyril explains that because of the existence of "a *Church of evil doers,…* of the heretics," it was necessary to use the formula "the one Holy Catholic Church" to describe "the Church of us Christians."[108] This church replaced the former one:

---

[106] *Cat.*. XIV,9 (NPNF ss 7:96/PG 33:929).

[107] This can be deduced from a letter written to emperor Constantius on May 7, 351 in which he refers to his consecration as bishop as a recent event (See Edwin Hamilton Gifford, "The Life of Cyril," (NPNF ss 7, pp. i-xi) and *NIDCC* s.v. "Cyril of Jerusalem").

[108] *Cyril of Jerusalem, Cat..*, XVIII, 25 (NPNF ss 7:140/PG 33:1043,1045).

But after the Jews for the plots which they made against the Saviour were cast away from His grace, the Saviour built out of the Gentiles a second Holy Church, the Church of us Christians, concerning which he said to Peter, *And upon this rock I will build My Church, and the gates of hell shall not prevail against it.*[109]

In teaching that the Churches of Christ throughout the world replace the "one Church in Judea [which] is cast off",[110] Cyril failed to take into account the vital role that the Jewish Christian church played in apostolic times. Paul gave recognition to this role when he gathered, from the Gentiles who "shared the Jews' spiritual blessings", a collection for the poor among the saints in Jerusalem (Ro 15:25-27). Not only was the first Christian church Jewish but it was from the Jewish church in Jerusalem that the Christian gospel was taken first to Samaria, later to Syrian Antioch and thence to the rest of the world. Cyril, on the other hand, used the expression "Church in Judea" as a synonym for unbelieving Israel which he identified as "the Congregation of evil doers" abhorred by David (Ps 26:5). Moreover he followed the tradition of applying God's words through the prophet Malachi: "I am not pleased with you" (Mal 1:10) to the Jews as a whole, who had been cast off, while applying to the Holy Catholic Church, which has replaced the Jews, the prophecy of God being known and worshipped among the nations (v. 11).[111]

The effects of such *replacement theology* are evident in the immediate context of these declarations. After linking the idea of the Church with priesthood,[112] Cyril describes the Holy Catholic Church as the sphere in which, "receiving instruction and behaving ourselves virtuously, we shall attain the kingdom of heaven, and inherit eternal life; for which also we endure all toils, that we may be made partakers thereof from the Lord."[113] Such behaviour means to go *"from Baptism to the Holy Altar of*

[109] *Ibid.*, PG 33:1045.
[110] *Ibid.*
[111] *Ibid.*
[112] *Ibid.*, 24 (NPNF ss 7:141/PG 33:1044-1050).
[113] *Ibid.*, 28 (NPNF ss 7:141/PG 33:1050).

God, and enjoy its spiritual and heavenly mysteries."[114] Here again a sacramental understanding of Christian ministry and of the duties of Christians take precedence over the proclamation of the gospel and the response of faith.

This brief survey of the ecclesiology of Cyril of Jerusalem gives further grounds for concluding that *replacement theology* favours a "Christian ministry" understood in terms of a new Levitical priesthood. Moreover it shows that returning to the logic of the Levitical covenant, the Church lost sight of the "better things" which spring from Christ's victorious redemptive work.

G. In Post-Reformation Times

The logic of presuppositional *replacement theology* continued to influence ecclesiology even after the eclipse of the monolithic power of the papacy in the West. This may be seen in the debate on Church government which took place in Puritan England over one thousand years after the time of Cyril. In *The Answer of the Assembly of Divines to the Reasons of the dissenting Brethren,* the Presbyterians who stressed "the continuity between old and new Israel", wrote the following:

> The JEWISH *subordinations,* being no *Temple Ordinances,* nor *Typicall* or *Ceremoniall,* doe in the *morall equity* of them concern Us, as well as Them: at least we may, with much more reason urge an Argument, *à pari ratione,* from Subordinations in the *Jewish Church* to prove a subordination *still...* there should be Subordinations *now* in the Christian Church, that was *then* in the *Jewish.*[115]

In other words Israel's Levitical order is seen to constitute a model for the Church. Even in our day *replacement theology* can be seen to influence some protestant ecclesiology. For example Edmund Clowney writes:

---

[114] *Ibid.,* 32 (NPNF ss 7:141-142/PG 33:1054).

[115] *The Answer of the Assembly of Divines to the Reasons of the dissenting Brethren,* London, 1648, p.147, quoted by David Walker, "Thomas Goodwin and the Debate on Church Government", *JEH* 34/1 (1983): p. 94, emphases theirs.

137

In the history of revelation, the Old Testament people of God become the Church of the Messiah.[116]

Clowney, who identifies Peter as the foundation of the new form of God's people,[117] affirms that the Church was renewed, and not founded, at Pentecost.[118] When speaking of ethnic Israel, Clowney accentuates all that was negative in her national life, and affirms that her significance ended with Christ.[119] On the other hand, the Church is "the new and true Israel in Christ and it is this which must inspire our mission in the contemporary world".[120]

While this concept of the Church may conceivably serve to inspire some aspects of the Church's mission in the contemporary world, as Clowney suggests, it also creates a serious obstacle for mission to the Jewish people. In fact *replacement theology* and its corollary: the Church's self-understanding as *the true Israel,* are historically linked with overt contempt for Israel. This is evident both in the *Adversus Judaeos* tradition and in the antisemitic thought and practice of Post-Reformation Europe.

H. Conclusion

Various reasons are given for the changes in church structure and for the transformation of Christian ministry in the early centuries.[121] Persecution and the influence of Greco-Roman culture are among the external influences widely recognised as significant factors. So far as internal influences are concerned, it is thought that the dearth of competent bishops and the requisites for the celebration of the Lord's Supper played a significant part.

---

[116] Edmund P. Clowney, *The Church,* Contours of Christian Theology, Gerald Bray (ed.), Downers Grove, IL: InterVarsity Press, 1995, p. 29.
[117] *Ibid.*
[118] *Ibid.*, p. 53; cf. Christ's statement in Mt 16:18: "I *will* build my church...".
[119] *Ibid.*, p. 35.
[120] *Ibid.*, p. 163.
[121] See section C. of this chapter.

According to Philip Schaff and James Dunn this list would not be complete without mentioning the gradual assimilation and adaptation of Judaism and a return to Old Testament categories of sacrifice and priesthood. Our purpose in examining the post-apostolic literature and later patristic writings has been to see whether this return to Levitical categories depended in some way on *replacement theology*. We have found considerable evidence that presuppositional *replacement theology* did in fact facilitate the normalisation of Levitical categories in the Church. A striking case of this is the way Malachi 1:10-12 was interpreted by Justin Martyr, Irenaeus, Augustine and Cyril of Jerusalem, all of whom understood this passage to mean that, while the Jews have been dismissed, Christians offer sacrifices which are acceptable to God. Thus, on the assumption that the Old Testament is a thoroughly Christian book, it became a standard practice for the Lord's Supper and the Christian ministry to be described in Levitical terms.

This had many ramifications for ecclesiology. In particular it led to the virtual eclipse of the apostolic concept of the Church as a charismatic body, the abandonment of the doctrine of the priesthood of all believers and the neglect of gospel preaching. Moreover it facilitated the development of a new concept of Christian unity which was no longer conceived of as being based on the gospel of the grace of God but rather on cohesion with the bishop of Rome.

So far as liturgical developments are concerned, the use of Levitical terminology such as "sacrifice" and "altar" in the context of the Lord's Supper obscured the memorial nature of the ordinance and the unique value of Christ's once-for-all sacrifice.

What emerges from the data we have examined is that the radical transformation of the Christian ministry, during the second and third centuries, was to a large extent the result of the Church taking over Levitical practice on the assumption that such instruction was intended for the Church. This assumption was a fruit of *replacement theology*, according to which the Church, and not Israel, was the true subject of the Law and the Prophets.

The Roman Catholic "Jubilee" witnesses to the continuing influence of such thinking on ecclesiastical practice. The Old Testament Jubilee had in view the restitution of property to rightful owners, the emancipation of slaves and the recognition that the people of Israel are God's servants (Lev 25). It was to *follow* the Day of Atonement and so was not concerned with the problem of sin. On the other hand the central feature of the Roman Catholic "Jubilee", announced for the first time by Pope Boniface VIII on February 22, 1300, and which reached its twenty-third edition in the year 2000, is the promise of plenary indulgences.

The Roman Catholic "Jubilee", which corresponds neither to the Old Testament institution nor to New Testament teaching concerning the grounds for forgiveness, illustrates well both the theological and practical effects of *replacement theology.*

Chapter Five

REPLACEMENT THEOLOGY AND ESCHATOLOGY

Israel is the church's eschatological goad and it is no accident that the church has lost the sense of eschatological tension; this happened as the church increasingly lost sight of the mystery of the permanence of Israel.[1]

A. The Importance of Eschatology

According to Peter Beyerhaus, failure to observe the distinctions between the different stages in which the redemptive economy of God is unfolded, has the effect of "changing the *Kingdom of Heaven,* as promised and given to God's sons and daughters, into a *Kingdom on Earth* which is to be constructed solely by the autonomous efforts of man himself".[2] Thus in World Council of Churches circles loss of eschatological precision has been followed by the demise of mission.[3] This is not the first time that a substantial change in eschatologial orientation has impinged on the way in which the Church has perceived its role in history.[4] According to Archibald Robertson, the eclipse of millenarianism[5] in the early Christian centuries produced an earth-bound "medieval theocracy".[6] My purpose in this chapter is to determine

[1] "This statement was made on Nov. 28, 1987 by the Roman Catholic scholar, Enzo Bianchi, at a seminar on the theme: "Twenty years after Nostra Aetate", Bologna (Enzo Bianchi, "Israele e la chiesa", *Storia cristiana,* 10 [1989]: 93).

[2] Peter P. J. Beyerhaus, *God's Kingdom and the Utopian Error,* Wheaton, IL: Good News Publishers, 1992, p. ix.

[3] *Ibid.*

[4] See Archibald Robertson, *Regnum Dei,* Eight lectures on the Kingdom of God in the history of Christian Thought, The Bampton Lectures 1901, London: Methuen & Co., 1901.

[5] The term "millenarianism" is used as a synonym of *premillennialism,* while a similar term, "millennialism" is a synonym of *postmillennilism.* (See Grant Underwood, "early Mormon Millenarianism: Another Look", *CH* 54 [1985]: 216).

[6] Robertson, *Regnum Dei,* pp. 119-240. The "medieval theocracy" included the illusion of a Christian empire and the concept of the Kingdom of God as an omnipotent church.

whether there is a cause-effect relationship between *replacement theology* and what Robertson calls "medieval theocracy".

Before returning to the patristic writings, we need to consider a fundamental issue: *Is the complete assimilation of the promised messianic kingdom into the present life of the Church justified by the New Testament evidence?* If it is, there is no point in investigating the matter further. We must simply accept the verdict of the New Testament. However if the process of assimilation alluded to above cannot be justified by the New Testament evidence, then it is at least possible that presuppositional *replacement theology* contributed to the development of medieval theocracy.

There are very different opinions on this matter. For example Hans LaRondelle claims that Old Testament Kingdom promises have been completely fulfilled in Christ's saving work and in the Church.[7] He writes, "The Church, as the eschatological Israel, with its new covenant in the blood of Christ, is the fulfillment of God's plan with ancient Israel".[8] To support this position LaRondelle considers Christ and the Church as anti-types of all the institutions, as well as the people, of Israel. This analysis of type and anti-type is based on the following trajectory:

> Among all the nations of the Oriental world, only Israel developed an eschatology, a hope in which God gradually unfolded His promise, corrected false, nationalistic hopes, and constantly transcended Israel's concepts of His kingdom by pointing to a future fulfillment that would exceed all Israel's earthly expectations (Isa 64:4; cf. 1 Co 2:9).[9]

This trajectory neglects the fact that both Jewish particularism and universal purpose are evident in God's dealings with Israel throughout the *whole* of the Old Testament, from the call of Abraham (Ge 12:1-3) to the prophetic predictions made by exilic and post-exilic prophets (Eze 36-40; Zec 12-14).

---

[7] Hans K. LaRondelle, *The Israel of God in Prophecy,* Berrien Springs, MI: The Seventh-Day Adventist Andrews University Press, 1983.

[8] Hans K. LaRondelle, *The Israel of God,* p. 40. LaRondelle does not consider the possibility of the relation between Israel and the Church being characterised by partial continuity and partial discontinuity.

[9] *Ibid.,* p. 35.

In order to make statements such as "Jesus *is* Israel, and in His resurrection Israel's restoration is accomplished,"[10] LaRondelle builds on some tenuous exegesis. For example, he takes Hosea 6:2 as a veiled prediction of Christ's resurrection[11] and uses Romans 9-11 selectively.[12] Furthermore his assimilation of the messianic kingdom into the present implies that the consummation will be limited to judgment.[13]

Jewish opinion concerning the realisation of kingdom promises[14] is summarised by the Roman Catholic scholar Rosemary Ruether:

> For Judaism, however, there is no possibility of talking about the Messiah having already come, much less of having come two thousand years ago, with all the evil history that has reigned from that time to this (much of it having been done in Christ's name!), when the Reign of God has not come. For Israel, the coming of the Messiah and the coming of the Messianic Age are inseparable.[15]

Pinchas Lapide, a Jewish New Testament scholar, open to dialogue with Christians,[16] focuses on what he considers the false claims of realised eschatology according to which the kingdom of God is being fulfilled in the Church. He writes:

> A realized eschatology, which basks in a salvation which it supposes to be already attained, produces a triumphalism which transforms the kingdom

[10] *Ibid.*, p. 68.

[11] *Ibid.*

[12] *Ibid.*, 124-134. LaRondelle fails to take into consideration the *a fortiori* statements of Ro 11:12,15, the temporal references in vv. 24-25 and Paul's statement in v. 28 regarding unbelieving Israel's present status as an elect nation.

[13] *Ibid.*, p. 44.

[14] There are also leading Christian scholars, such as Peter Beyerhaus, who reject the position propounded by LaRondelle. Beyerhaus asks "Why do I believe that the millennium is an intervening period between the return of Christ and the creation of a new heaven and a new earth? It is because of the specific role which the OT has assigned to the people of Israel within the messianic Kingdom. These prophecies have not yet been fulfilled, nor have they been nullified by the creation of the Church as the new spiritual Israel (Acts 1:6). Paul in Rom 11:29 very definitely states that the gifts and the call of God to Israel are irrevocable" (Beyerhaus, *God's Kingdom*, p. 35).

[15] Rosemary Ruether, *Fratricide*, pp. 246-247.

[16] Lapide's openness to dialogue was shown by his willingness to participate, with Walter C. Kaiser Jr., in the John Ankerberg Show, in 1984, in a series of discussions on the Messianic prophecies.

of God into the church and relegates Christ the king to the far heavens. Such eschatology is like a painting in nothing but black and white: the one indicating the obstinate Jewish people, the other the ecclesiatical people which is already redeemed.[17]

A series of essays entitled *Continuity and Discontinuity,*[18] has set a new standard for debating such subjects as the relationship between Israel and the Church and the mode of realisation of the Kingdom of God.[19] In his Preface, John Feinberg observes that all contributors "see both continuity and discontinuity between the Testaments," although they represent opposing sides in the debate.[20] One of the reasons for this attenuation of extreme positions is the attention given in these essays to the New Testament evidence. It is generally agreed that the way the New Testament writers interpret the Old Testament must set the pattern for all Christian interpretation.[21] This principle implies that we must listen to what the New Testament says concerning the present and future status of Israel in God's overall plan. H.L. Ellison, a twentieth century biblical scholar, also involved in the Jewish-Christian dialogue, observed:

> To ignore the New Testament picture of the Jews in our formulation of its theology is surely as foolish as to foretell the future of Israel using purely Old Testament evidence.[22]

---

[17] Pinchas Lapide & Jürgen Moltmann, "Israele e chiesa: camminare insieme? un dialogo," *Giornale di teologia,* 140, Rosino Gibellini (ed.), Brescia: Queriniana, 1982, p. 63.

[18] John S. Feinberg (ed.), *Continuity and Discontinuity,* Essays in Honor of S. Lewis Johnson, Jr., Westchester: Crossway books/Good News Publishers, 1988.

[19] Other topics discussed in this volume are: The Hermeneutics of Continuity and Discontinuity, The Biblical Method of Salvation, The Law of Moses and the Law of Christ, and The Kingdom Promises as Spiritual/The Kingdom Promises as Spiritual and National.

[20] John Feinberg, *Continuity and Discontinuity,* p. 12; cf. Robert Saucy ("Israel and the Church: A Case for Discontinuty," *ibid.,* pp. 239-259) who writes, "In our understanding, the scriptural concept of the people of God supports both a certain continuity and discontinuity" (p. 240).

[21] S. Lewis Johnson, Jr., *The Old Testament in the New,* Grand Rapids, MI: Zondervan, 1980, p. 23.

[22] H.L. Ellison, *The Mystery of Israel,* Exeter: The Paternoster Press, 1966, p 13. Ellison was first a member of the International Missionary Council's Committee on

B. The New Testament Evidence

1. *General evidence*

It is convenient to begin our survey with the words spoken by the angel Gabriel concerning Jesus, the son of David:

...and he will reign over the house of Jacob forever; his kingdom will never end (Lk 1:33).

Some understand these words to apply to the inauguration of the messianic kingdom through the death and resurrection of Christ and the coming of the Holy Spirit at Pentecost.[23] On the other hand, for Walter Kaiser they relate primarily to the kingdom of God understood as "a domain and a realm."[24] In evaluating the eschatological significance of Jesus, it is helpful to remember that, according to Jesus himself, two advents were necessary for the completion of his ministry (Lk 4:14-21; 19:11-27; Jn 14:1-3; Mt 13:36-43). These two advents were to be divided by an unspecified period of time, hence Jesus spent much time preparing human (Jewish) instruments for their crucial role in the building of his Church (Mk 3:13-19; Mt 9:35-10:42; 16:18-19; 28:18-20). Moreover Jesus categorically excluded that the realisation of an earthly kingdom or the judgment of the nations belonged to his first advent; insisting rather that he had come to accomplish salvation (Jn 6:1-21; 12:47, cf. 5:24-30).

Many Old Testament predictions relating to the accomplishment of salvation found fulfillment during Messiah's first advent. Others find fulfillment in the Church's relationship with God and in its mission to the world.[25] Many would agree with Kaiser

the Christian Approach to the Jews and later of the WCC Committee on the Church and the Jewish People.

[23] Fred H. Klooster, "The Biblical Method of Salvation: A Case for Continuity," Feinberg, *Continuity and Discontinuity,* pp. 156-157.

[24] Walter C. Kaiser, Jr. "Kingdom Promises as Spiritual and National," Feinberg, *Continuity and Discontinuity,,* p. 304. Kaiser associates the words of the angel Gabriel with Dan 2:44; 7:13-14.

[25] Mt 5:17-18; Lk 24:25-27,44-47; Heb 8:1-13 [cf. Lk 22:19]; 11:39-40; Isa 49:5-6, Mk 16:15-16; Ac 13:46-48; 15:14-18.

when he affirms that what Christ accomplished in his first advent inaugurated the spiritual dimension of God's kingdom.[26] They would also agree with Robert Saucy when he recognises that the people that God is now gathering up out of all nations has much in common with God's Old Testament people Israel.[27] This is why the experiences of Israel contain important lessons for the Church (1 Co 10:1-13) and why Israel and the Church can figure together as a complex unity in the apocalyptic vision of the new Jerusalem (Ap 21:12-14). These elements of continuity have led some to believe that the Old Testament teaching concerning a messianic kingdom finds expression in the Church.

However there remain some stubborn passages across the whole spectrum of New Testament literature which envisage a futuristic realisation of kingdom promises as well as a distinctive future for physical Israel. While it would be a mistake to use these passages to detract from what the Church has in common with Israel, it would be equally erroneous to ignore their witness to a futuristic manifestation of the kingdom and to Israel's distinctive hope.

Three affirmations made by Jesus are significant. The first of these is presented in the form of a parable. In an introductory statement, Luke explains that the purpose of the parable was to correct the erroneous idea that the kingdom of God was to "appear" (ἀναφαίνεσθαι) at once (Lk 19:11). The parable itself makes it plain that the visible manifestation of the kingdom will follow a long absence of the appointed king (vv. 12-27).[28]

---

[26] Kaiser, "Kingdom Promises", in Feinberg, *Continuity and Discontinuity*, pp. 303,306-307; cf. Ac 2:14-21; Mt 13:1-52; 28:18; Mk 9:1; Ac 28:28-31; Ro 14:17.

[27] Saucy ("Israel and the Church: A Case for Discontinuity," Feinberg, *Continuity and Discontinuity*, p. 241) observes that a number of references used in the OT for Israel as the people of God are now applied to the Church which includes both Jews and Gentiles. He cites the following examples: Tit 2:14; Ro 9:25-26; 2 Co 6:16; 1 P 2:9-10.

[28] Cf. the following observation: "Both Hebrew and Christian thought have their specificity in the expectation of a future redemption through the full manifestation of the majesty of God" (Daniele Garrone, "Il regno di Dio nell'antico e nel nuovo testamento", *Certezze*, n. 150, Feb. 1996, p. 7).

The second affirmation concerns the relationship of the Jews and the city of Jerusalem to what Jesus calls "the times of the Gentiles":

> They will fall by the sword and will be taken as prisoners to all the nations. Jerusalem will be trampled on by the Gentiles until the times of the Gentiles are fulfilled (Lk 21:24).

The use of the adverb "until" (ἄχρι) does not, in itself, prove that there will be a period of historical time following "the times of the Gentiles." However, it is clear that the idea of fixed periods of time is present. I. Howard Marshall suggests that the reference is to one of the "allotted times" of prophetic scripture[29] and he links Jesus' statement with early church teaching reflected in Romans 11:25-27.[30] With reference to Romans 11:25, Cranfield writes:

> The temporal conjunction ἄχρις οὖ must here mean "until": though it sometimes means "while" (e.g. in Heb 3.13), it cannot have that sense here in view of the aorist subjunctive εἰσέλθῃ. Paul's meaning is... that the hardening will last until the fullness of the Gentiles comes in.[31]

In the same way "...Jerusalem will be trampled on by the Gentiles *until* the times of the Gentiles are fulfilled" (Lk 21:24).

Jesus' third statement is also prophetic. Speaking to unbelieving Israel, he warned, "Look, your house is left to you desolate. For I tell you, you will not see me again until you say, *Blessed is he who comes in the name of the Lord*"(Mt 23:38-39). This statement implies that the people of Israel will see Jesus again and will pronounce this benediction upon him. Furthermore it reveals that this occasion will coincide with the end of the prophesied state of desolation of the house of Israel.

Such statements as these may have contributed to convincing Jesus' disciples that the period of world mission, into which

---

[29] See the juxtapposition of ἄχρι χρόνων... in Ac 3:21 where a distinction between present and future time is clearly intended.

[30] I. Howard Marshall, *The Gospel of Luke,* The New International Greek Testament Commentary, I. Howard Marshall and W. Ward Gasque (eds.), Exeter: The Paternoster Press, 1978, pp.773-774; cf. Hodge (*Romans,* pp. 372-373) who compares the use of ἄχρις οὖ in Ro 11:25 with its use in Rev 15: 8 and 17:17.

[31] Cranfield, *Romans,* 2:575.

they had been introduced by the coming of the Holy Spirit at Pentecost (Ac 1:5-8; 2:1-36; cf. Mt 28:18-20; Mk 16:15-16; Lk 24:44-47; Jn 20:21), was to be followed by the realisation of another dimension of kingdom promises. The following statement made by Peter denotes such a prospect: "[Jesus] must remain in heaven until the time comes for God to restore everything, *as he promised long ago through his holy prophets"* (Ac 3:21). Evidently this future prospect was felt to be compatible with the disciples' awareness that the kingdom had been inaugurated by Christ's triumph over sin and death. The growth of the kingdom in a veiled form flowed from Christ's first advent and from the coming of the Spirit at Pentecost, but Jesus has made no secret of the fact that only with his return will the devil and all who do evil be finally overthrown (Mt 13:36-43; cf. Ro 16:20 and Rev 19:11-20:10).

The apostle Paul sounded a similar futuristic note in some significant historical and literary contexts. When he revisited Lystra, Iconium and Antioch, "strengthening the disciples and encouraging them to remain true to the faith," he cautioned, "We must go though many hardships to enter the kingdom of God" (Ac 14:22). We may conclude from this warning that, in his preaching concerning the kingdom of God, Paul distinguished between its present aspects – "righteousness, peace and joy in the Holy Spirit" – and a future, universal manifestation of the kingdom (Ac 20:25-27; 28:28-31; Ro 14:17).

Paul makes his most general eschatological statement in the course of a discussion concerning resurrection (1 Co 15:22-28). In this passage Paul describes a sequence of events which begin with Christ's resurrection (15:23a). The second major event listed, which is to occur at Christ's return, is the resurrection of those who belong to him (v. 23b, ἔπειτα οἱ τοῦ Χριστοῦ ἐν τῇ παρουσίᾳ αὐτοῦ). This, in turn, will be followed by "the end, "when Christ will hand over the kingdom to the father (v. 24, εἶτα τὸ τέλος, ὅταν παραδιδῷ τὴν βασιλείαν τῷ θεῷ καὶ πατρί) *after having* subdued "all dominion, authority and power". The two Greek adverbs used in this passage, ἔπειτα and εἶτα, refer to time sequence ("then... next")[32] and thus link the process of subduing "all dominion, authority and power" with the period which goes from Christ's second coming until "the end". Paul quotes Psalm 110:1 in order to emphasise the necessity of Christ reigning *until he has overcome* all of his enemies (1 Co 15:25).[32]

Before considering the eschatological content of Romans 11:25-27, we will note briefly some further New Testament passages which support what Archibald Robertson calls a "realistic eschatology".[34] In 2 Timothy 2:12 we read, "If we endure, we will also reign with him". The same idea is repeated three times, in more explicit terms, in the book of Revelation. The first of these occurrences is in the letter to the church in Thyatira: *To him who overcomes and does my will to the end, I will give authority over the nations* (2:26). The quotation of Psalm 2:9 in conjunction with this promise suggests that, although referring to the future, this promise does not have in view the eternal state. Secondly, in relation to those purchased by Christ from every tribe, language, people and nation, it is said: *You have made them to be a kingdom and priests to serve our God, and they will reign on the earth* (5:10). Finally we learn from Revelation 19:11-20:6 that, following the appearance of the King of kings and Lord of lords, the judgment of the beast and the false prophet and the confinement of Satan, those who have received authority to judge will experience resurrection and will reign with Christ for one thousand years.[35]

---

[32] See Zerwick & Grosvenor, *Analysis of the Greek NT*, pp. 528-529. According to Garrone ("Il regno di Dio", p. 5), 1 Co 15:24-26 offers an outline of intermediate time between the coming of Christ and the full establishment of the Lordship of God over the world.

[33] In the light of this sequence of events described by Paul, I disagree with Archibald Robertson (*Regnum Dei*, p. 120) when he states that "[Paul's] belief as to the kingdom of Christ is so formulated as to positively exclude the supposition that a millennium of any kind was part of it." On the contrary, elements in his teaching, such as those reviewed above, appear to be quite compatible with it.

[34] With this expression Robertson intends some form of "millenarianism" (*Regnum Dei*, pp. 119-120).

[35] The formula καὶ εἶδον recurs in Ap 19:11,17: 20:1,4,11;21:1. The fact that the final judgment of the beast and the false prophet is assumed in 20:10, and the binding and loosing of Satan are taught in 20:1-3,7, strongly suggest that the events referred to here are sequential.

While the term "millennium" is often associated with this prophecy, the earlier references in Revelation to the saints reigning with Christ in an earthly kingdom show that the prospect of a messianic kingdom does not depend upon a knowledge of its duration.

2. *The future of Israel according Romans 11*

Towards the end of his long discussion concerning the present and future relationship of Israel with history of salvation, Paul unveils a "mystery" (μυστήριον) so that his Gentile readers "may not be conceited" (11:25; cf. v. 13). In the parable of the olive tree he had expressed a similar concern (vv. 17-21). He now strengthens the grounds for avoiding arrogance and conceit by giving more information concerning the future of Israel (cf. vv. 15,24). Here is the text of the mystery[36] passage:

> I do not want you to be ignorant of this mystery, brothers, so that you may not be conceited: Israel has experienced a hardening in part until the full number of the Gentiles has come in. And so all Israel will be saved, as it is written, "The deliverer will come from Zion; he will turn godlessness away from Jacob. And this is my covenant with them when I take away their sins" (vv. 25-27).

Readers of the Old Testament already knew that non-Israelites were to be blessed through the seed of Abraham (Ge 12:3; Isa 49:5-6; cf. Ro 11:12,15), that God, when provoked by the Israelites, would harden them (see Dt 29:4; Isa 29:10; Ps 69:22-23, cf. Ro 11:8-9), that Israel will return to seek the Lord "in the last days" and that, sooner or later, she would enter into the blessing of the new covenant (Isa 59:20; Hos 3:4-5; Jer 31:31-37; cf. Mt 23:39; Ro 11:11-24). What is *new* in this mystery passage concerns

---

[36] According to G. Bornkamm *(TDNT* 4:822), "everywhere in the NT μυστήριον has an eschatological sense." Concerning the use of the term in Ro 11:25, he writes: "Paul unfolds the final destiny of Israel as a specific mystery. In so doing Paul disclaims personal cleverness (ἵνα μὴ ἦτε ἐν ἑαυτοῖς φρόνιμοι). To his own intelligence the hardening of Israel would be either a pure enigma or a temptation to arbitrary rational conclusions."

the order of the events. "*All* Israel will be saved" after "the full number of the Gentiles has come in" and thus after the partial hardening of Israel[37] has ended.[38] What emerges is a clear contrast between the salvation of a *remnant* of Israel ("at the present time", v. 5) and that of *all* Israel as an eschatological event (v. 26).

Our knowledge of when and how the national conversion of Israel will take place is enriched by the quotation of some Old Testament prophetic passages. The first of these is part of a messianic prophecy tied to the Davidic covenant (Isa 59:20), *The deliverer will come from Zion; he will turn godlessness away from Jacob* (Ro 11:26b-27a). Part of the following phrase, *And this is my covenant with them...,* appears for the first time in Genesis 17:4, as the introduction to the covenant God made with Abraham. It recurs in Isaiah 59:21, immediately after the prophecy quoted in Romans 11:26, and again, in a slightly different form, in Jeremiah's prophecy concerning the new covenant (Jer 31:33). The words: *...when I take away their sins* (Ro 11:27b), makes clear that Paul is thinking about Israel's entrance into the new covenant as envisaged by Jeremiah (31:34). This event will be marked by the forgiveness of their sins. The possibility of this forgiveness is based on the redemptive work of Christ and will occur, at a national level, when the messianic deliverer reveals himself to Israel and the nation repents (cf. Jer 31:34;

---

[37] Steve Motyer *(Israel in the plan of God,* Leicester, Inter-Varsity Press, 1989, p. 55) understands this *hardening* to mean "doing nothing, or rather nothing beyond issuing appeals for repentance which fall on deaf ears, and simply produce an ever greater unwillingness to hear God speak. Romans 2:4-5 sums it up perfectly."

[38] According to C.F.D. Moule *(An Idiom Book of New Testament Greek,* Cambridge: Cambridge University Press, 2d ed., 1959, 7th reprint, p. 82), the meaning of ἄχρις οὗ, in Rom 11:25 as elsewhere, is to be considered strictly prepositional = ἄχρις ἐκείνου χρόνου ἐν ᾧ. Thus Hodge *(Romans,* pp. 372-373); Cranfield *(Romans,* 2:575); cf. the NIV "until." Contra Calvin, who asserts *(Romans,* p. 255) that ἄχρις does not suggest the course or order of time but rather expresses purpose with reference to the full number of the Gentiles. The way ἄχρις is used elsewhere in the NT (see Ro 1:13; 5:13; 8:22) favours a temporal sense. It may be significant that Calvin avoids commenting on v. 24, where the re-admission into their own "olive tree" of the branches that have been broken off, is presented in the future indicative tense.

Lk 22:20).[39] He will "turn godlessness from Jacob" (cf. Zec 12:10-13:1).[40] The repentance of *some* Israelites during the period between Christ's two advents is an anticipation of this national event, however the attention which Paul gives in this passage to time sequence and in particular to the eschatological nature of the salvation of all Israel, shows that the apostle is thinking here of a new stage in salvation history (cf. vv.13-15; Ac 3:19-21).[41]

According to LaRondelle, Paul's failure to mention Israel's restoration to the land in Romans 11 implies that, with the advent of the new covenant, the land of Israel has become theologically insignificant.[42] However there is in fact an allusion to the land in v. 26.[43] The form of the original prophecy, "The Redeemer will come *to* Zion" (Isa 59:20) finds an echo in the prediction that the Messiah will reveal himself to the inhabitants of Jerusalem who will respond by mourning for "the one they have pierced" (Zec 12:10-14). The preposition "from", in Paul's phrase "the deliverer will come from Zion" (Ro 11:26), suggests that the deliverer will turn away the "wickedness" (ἀσεβείας) of "all Israel," *beginning* from Jerusalem. What is common to both forms of the prophecy is the centrality of Zion – Jerusalem – in the work of the deliverer. The temporal reference in v. 25 implies that this

---

[39] Johnson (*The OT in the New*, pp. 215-216) notes that the blend of texts quoted by Paul relate to all the unconditional covenants which God has made with Israel; moreover: "the same passages that declare a future for ethnic Israel also speak of Israel's preeminence among the nations in the kingdom of God."

[40] In the light of the temporal references contained in these passages and the fact that "the deliverer" is indicated as the cause of Israel's repentance, we cannot accept Munck's suggestion that Paul conceived of his own apostleship as the determining factor in all Israel entering into the new covenant (see Munck, *Paul and the Salvation of Mankind*, pp. 40-41). Munck's thesis presupposes that the τὸ κατέχον (2 Th 2:5-6) refers to Paul's apostolic ministry. Paul clearly distinguishes between his hope that *some* of his own people would be saved as a result of his own ministry (Ro 11:14) and the salvation of *all* Israel, v. 26.

[41] Contra Luz, *Paulus*, pp. 288-295. According to Luz, Paul attached more importance to *how* Israel will be converted than to the order of events.

[42] LaRondelle, *The Israel of God*, p. 132.

[43] There is no doubt that Paul's primary purpose in Romans 9-11 is to define the relationship of Israel to the "gospel of God" which has been expounded in the first eight chapters of the letter. For the OT prophets also, the question of Israel's relationship to God is more important than her relationship to the land.

work will be accomplished in the context of Messiah's second advent.[44] That being the case, the reference to Zion establishes a link between the prospect of Israel's national conversion and the ultimate fulfillment of Old Testament prophiecies concerning the land (see Zec 14:1-21). Moreover the *a fortiori* statements of Romans 11:12,15 suggest that the realisation of Israel's fullness will produce great blessing for the rest of the world.

C. Israel and Eschatology in Early Christian Theology

1. *Millenarianism*

According to Robertson, the Church's conception of the kingdom of God includes one constant element and two variables. That which remains constant is "the perfect reign of God in heaven after the Last Judgment." The variables are: the understanding of Christ's reign in the visible church between his two comings and the conviction that he will reign on earth between his second coming and the final judgment.[45] Our concern here is with the variable elements.

Because "the history of the conception of the Kingdom of God…in the early church is the history of the prevalence and decline of Millenarianism"[46] it will be convenient for us to follow this trajectory. Our purpose will be to determine whether the eventual decline of millenarianism was in any way related to the Church's understanding of Israel.

During the period to be considered, millenarianism did not exclude the conviction that Christ already reigned in his Church. On the contrary, the development of doctrine in this period took for granted that the age of fulfillment had dawned and that the

---

[44] LaRondelle (*The Israel of God*) follows R.C.H. Lenski (*The Interpretation of St. Paul's Epistle to the Romans*, Columbus, Ohio: Wartburg Press, 1945, p. 729) in taking the phrase "Out of Zion" to refer to Christ's first advent.

[45] Robertson, *Regnum Dei*, p. 119.

[46] *Ibid.*, p. 169.

Church was already feasting at the eschatological banquet.[47] The early Christian philosophy of history required both the presence of the kingdom and the hope of its more general manifestation in relation to the second coming of Christ.[48]

Teaching concerning a millennial reign of Christ was, in general, closely associated with Revelation 20:1-10.[49] However, the millennial hope also had roots in Jewish eschatology.[50] In fact millenarianism fitted naturally into the Old Testament world view which envisages a literal messianic kingdom in which unrighteousness will be banished and all nations will worship the God of Israel (Isa 2:1-5; Eze 37:15-28; Mic 4; Zec 14). A sampling of second century exposition of millenarianism will illustrate the above remarks.

Papias (c.60-c.130), bishop of Hierapolis, is the first post-apostolic writer whose millenarianism is documented. Knowledge of it reaches us by way of Irenaeus[51] and Eusebius. The latter, alluding to certain things which Papias is said to have gathered from unwritten traditions, writes:

> To these belong his statement that there will be a period of some thousand years after the resurrection of the dead, and that the kingdom of Christ will be set up in material form on this very earth...

According to Eusebius, these things "were spoken mystically in figures... But it was due to him [Papias] that so many of the

---

[47] J.N.D. Kelly, *Early Christian Doctrines*, pp. 461-462.

[48] Robertson, *Regnum Dei*, p. 119

[49] See Justin, *Tryph. Jud.*, LXXXI (PG 6:669); Irenaeus, *Haer.*, V, 33,4; 34,2 (PG 3:1214,1216).

[50] Pelikan, *Tradition*, 1:124.

[51] ANF 1:563/PG 6:1214. The material to which Papias bears witness is said to have derived from the teaching of the Lord himself and to have been communicated to Papias by John. The passage quoted by Irenaeus begins, "The days will come, in which vines shall grow, each having ten thousand branches, and in each branch ten thousand twigs, and in each true twig ten thousand shoots, and in each one of the shoots ten thousand clusters, and on every one of the clusters ten thousand grapes, and every grape when pressed will give five and twenty metretes of wine" (*ibid.*). This quotation was taken from a work entitled *Exposition of Dominical Oracles*, in 5 books written by Papias around A.D. 110 of which only fragments survive (*NIDCC*, s.v. "Papias").

Church Fathers after him adopted a like opinion."[52] However the evidence would seem to suggest that Papias simply drew together threads from Old Testament messianic prophecies and Christ's own words, linking them with the particular contribution of Revelation 20:1-6.

In the *Epistle of Barnabas* the thousand year reign is taken to be the ideal sabbath rest which corresponds to the seventh day of creation, while the beginning of the eighth day is thought to be prefigured by Christ's resurrection. The writer of *Barnabas* quotes Isaiah 1:13 as proof that the Jewish Sabbaths are unacceptable to God.[53] Having disqualified Israel the writer of *Barnabas* transfers her hope of a messianic kingdom to the sphere of Christian eschatological hope.

Justin Martyr considers Christian millenarianism, in which the eschatological hope of Israel is fully assimilated, an essential part of orthodox faith. He writes:

> But I and others, who are right-minded (Gk ὀρθογνῶμονες) Christians on all points, are assured that there will be a resurrection of the dead, and a thousand years in Jerusalem, which will then be built, adorned, and enlarged [as] the prophets Ezekiel and Isaiah and others declare.[54]

Later in his *Dialogue with Trypho*, Justin makes explicit mention of "John, one of the apostles of Christ," as the source of this teaching,[55] and affirms that "those who believed in *our* Christ would dwell a thousand years *in Jerusalem*."[56] The expression *"our* Christ," said in the context of Justin's dialogue with Trypho the Jew, is obviously polemical. Like *Barnabas,* Justin freely assimilates into the visions of Revelation 20:1-6 material taken from such Hebrew prophets as Ezekiel and Isaiah.

In a similar way Irenaeus uses the Old Testament to describe what Papias is reputed to have heard from John, insisting in particular on the literal fulfillment of Isaiah 11:6-9. He quotes

---

[52] Eusebius, *Hist. eccl.* II, 39,12-13 (NPNF ss, 1:172).
[53] *Barn.* XV, (PG 1:1224).
[54] *Tryph. Jud.* LXXX (PG 6:668).
[55] The reference is evidently to Rev. 20:1-5.
[56] Justin, *Tryph. Jud.*, LXXXI (PG 6:669), emphasis mine.

the beatitude of Revelation 20:6 to confirm such Old Testament kingdom prophecies.[57] However his adherence to the literal interpretation of kingdom prophecies appears tenuous as he freely applies to the Church part of another prophecy (Jer 31:10-14) concerning the regathering of Israel in their own land where they will enjoy material blessings from the Lord's hand.[58]

Christian appropriation of the Jewish hope is also apparent in Tertullian's confession of faith in a thousand year reign before the final state. In his *Against Marcion,* Tertullian states that the Jewish hope of the restoration of Judea "is spiritually applicable to Christ and His church, and to the character and fruits thereof."[59] Tertullian informs us that he has dealt more fully with the matter in his work *De Spe Fidelium,* no longer extant. However his tract *Against Marcion,* does contain the following comment:

> ...we do confess that a kingdom is promised to us upon the earth, although before heaven, only in another state of existence; inasmuch as it will be after the resurrection for a thousand years in the divinely-built city of Jerusalem, "let down from heaven..."[60]

We have seen that early Christian apologists and theologians expected a literal millennial reign of Christ, following his return to earth in glory and before the beginning of the eternal state. One feature of this expectation was the transferral of Israel's hope of a messianic kingdom to the Church. In some of the writings we have examined, it is very clear that this is a fruit of *replacement theology.* This transferral of Israel's kingdom hope to the Church did not immediately cause radical changes in the understanding of general eschatology. This may be due to the fact that the general eschatological vision of the New Testament strongly resembles that of the Hebrew Scriptures. Jesus himself had taught that the final manifestation of the kingdom was

---

[57] *Haer,* V, 33,3-4; 34,2 (PG 7:1213-1217).

[58] *Haer,* V, 34,3-4 (PG 7:1217). The literal nature of the messianic reign is further stressed by citing Isa 31:9; 32:1.

[59] Tertullian, *Marc.* III, 25 (ANF, 3:342-343; in PL 2 *Marc.* bk III concludes with ch. 24).

[60] *Marc.* III, 25.

future (Mt 13; Lk 19:11-27) while the apostles had taught that at the appointed time God would restore everything through Christ "as he promised long ago through his holy prophets" (Ac 3:20-21; cf. 1 Co 15:23-28). Moreover the visions of Revelation 19:11-20:6 both confirmed and enriched the expectation of a future messianic kingdom.

Hippolytus, a Roman churchman who died around A.D. 236, is known as the first Christian scholar to have calculated the date of Easter without considering the date of the Jewish Passover.[61] By so doing Hippolytus introduced a further element of separation between the Christian faith and Judaism. However we learn from his treatise *On Antichrist* that Hippolytus continued to teach a future reign of Christ in which the saints are destined to participate.[62] While not making specific mention of the millennium in this work, his allusion to Revelation 20:6 suggests that it was not foreign to his thought. Hippolytus does not speculate on how unfulfilled biblical prophecies are to be fulfilled; he simply affirms that they will be fulfilled.[63] This is significant in the light of developments at Alexandria to which we now turn.

2. Origen's eschatology

Clement of Alexandria (c.155 - c.220)[64] was unashamedly a Christian platonist and as such he quoted from Plato, and indeed from other philosophers, with the same ease as he quoted from the Hebrew Scriptures and the New Testament. Moreover he interpreted the Bible in the light of Platonic concepts. This is evident in the following passage in which Clement speaks of the perfect man's relation with the world:

---

[61] *NIDCC*, s.v. "Hippolytus".

[62] Hippolytus, *Antichr.* V (PG 10:735) cf. XXIX (PG 10:749).

[63] *Ibid., passim.* In treating the Antichrist, the great harlot of Rev. 17-18 and the overthrow of earthly kingdoms by Christ, Hippolytus makes repeated reference to Daniel and Revelation and mentions the predictions of other OT prophets, Christ and other NT writers.

[64] Clement succeeded Pantaenus as head of the Catechetical School at Alexandria in 190. Although he saw faith to be the means by which mankind arrives at true

But I shall pray the Spirit of Christ to wing me to my Jerusalem. For the Stoics say that heaven is properly a city, but places here on earth are not cities; for they are called so, but are not. For a city is an important thing, and the people a decorous body, and a multitude of men regulated by law as the church by the word – a city on earth impregnable – free from tyranny; a product of the divine will on earth as in heaven. Images of this city the poets create with their pen.... And we know Plato's city placed as a pattern in heaven.[65]

Clement quotes also from Plato's *Phaedo* when speaking of future rewards and punishment.[66] His dependence on Plato is further evident in a speculative passage in which the Jews feature as "helpers" while the Christians are considered "fit to rule".[67]

Origen continued the Alexandrian tradition of interpreting the Bible in a way which harmonised with Greek philosophy. For example, in his *On First Principles* Origen affirms the total impassibility of God to the point of excluding the objective reality of his wrath. He applies this principle to the parable of Ten Minas (Lk 19:11-27) which refers to the future manifestation of Christ's kingdom and the judgment which will accompany it. Origen writes: "we do not take such expressions literally, but seek in them a spiritual meaning, that we may think of God as He deserves to be thought of."[68] Origen also denies the reality of God's wrath in his *Homilies on Ezekiel* where God's interventions are said to be dictated by necessity and not by passion. God is compared with a doctor and father who administer chastisements in order to heal the wicked or educate them.[69] But his wrath is only apparent. Consequently, when the Bible speaks of eternal punishment, such

---

γνῶσις, he understood that it is γνῶσις which leads them to freedom from sin and to immortality and righteousness *(NIDCC,* s.v. "Clement of Alexandria").

[65] *Strom.,* IV, 24 (ANF, 2:441/PG 8:1382).

[66] *Strom.,* IV, 22 (PG 8:1353).

[67] *Strom.,* V, 14 (ANF 2:467/PG 9:141,144-145). τὴν χρυσήν is supplied by the translator, according to a very probable conjecture.

[68] *Princ.* II, 4 (ANF, 4:277-278); cf. *Cels.* IV,72 (PG 11:1141 "Rursus iram non esse Dei affectum, sed cam in se quemque peccatis derivare").

[69] *Hom. Eze.* (PG 13:667-669). For further examples, see Origen's *Comm. on Mt.* XIV,9 PG 13:202-203).

teaching has only nominal value. It serves, as do the manifestations of God's wrath in history, to correct the wicked[70] while spiritual death is not to be understood as eternal.[71]

Hanson observes that, "in rationalizing and spiritualizing the biblical doctrine of God's wrath and God's punishment, Origen was obviously moving with the tide of contemporary sentiment."[72] Origen reduces the concept of eternal punishment even further when he states that the judgments of God will not require "times" but rather will happen "in the twinkling of an eye." Similarly he discounts the literal meaning of such phrases as "take charge of ten cities" (Lk 19:17,19), with which Jesus describes how his faithful servants will be rewarded.[73]

An eschatology which envisages all the wicked being eventually purified and understands divine judgment as being unrelated to time, has no place for a millennial reign of Christ which is to be ushered in by a series of judgments and is to be followed by other judgments (see Rev 19:11-20:15). So it is not surprising that Origen opposed millenarianism. In his opinion those who understand such a prospect in literal terms, do not understand the meaning of the apostle's teaching which is spiritual.[74] Hanson observes:

> The contrast between Justin, who regards a literal interpretation of the millennial kingdom as part of Christian orthodoxy, and Origen, who regards in precisely the same light an allegorical interpretation of the same subject, is striking.[75]

Just as Origen's concept of the heavenly church excludes ethnic Israel as a subject of theological reflection, so his mystical understanding of the kingdom of God excludes the typically Jewish hope of an earthly kingdom. It is interesting that thirteen

[70] Origen, *Cels.*, IV, 13 (PG 11:1043).

[71] *Comm. on Ro.* V,2 (PG 14:1021-1026).

[72] Hanson, *op. cit.*, p. 341. For a useful introduction to the complex theme of divine punishment in Origen, see Hanson, *Allegory and Event*, p. 341.

[73] *Comm. on Mt.* XIV,9 (PG 13:1205).

[74] *Comm. on Mt.* XVII, 35 (PG 13:1593) and *Comm. on Ro.* X,1 (PG 14:1249-1251).

[75] Hanson, *Allegory and Event*, p. 345.

centuries after Origen the drafters of the Augsburg Confession defined as *Jewish* those opinions "which are even now making an appearance and which teach that, before the resurrection of the dead, saints and godly men will possess a worldly kingdom…"[76]

While some aspects of Origen's eschatology, in particular his doctrine of resurrection and his Restorationism (the teaching that ultimately all will be saved) were later called into question,[77] his largely mystical concept of the kingdom and his rejection of millenarianism were not similarly denounced. Why? One way of explaining this would be to say that Justin Martyr had erred when he made the millennial hope an essential point of Christian orthodoxy. Another possible explanation could be a waning of interest in this doctrine as the Christian era advanced. A third possibility is that, following the general acceptance of *replacement theology,* the world view intrinsic to Jewish eschatology was perceived as obsolete.[78]

3. *Millenarianism after Origen*

Despite his erudition, Origen's mystical teaching concerning the kingdom of God did not convince all of his contemporaries. This may be seen in the fact that Commodianus, a North-African bishop, preserved a simple form of the doctrine of the millennial reign of Christ. Concerning the beginning of this age he writes:

[76] The Augsburg Confession, Art. XVII, in Mark A. Noll (ed), Grand Rapids, MI: Baker Book House, 1991, p. 93. Moreover, in the first edition of the Anglican Articles, drawn up by Thomas Cramner, in 1553, the second to last of the Forty-Two Articles described millenarianism as "a fable of Jewish dotage" (Philip Schaff, *History of the Christian Church,* 8 vols, Charles Schribner's Sons, 1910; Reprint, Grand Rapids: Eerdmans, 1967, 2:619).

[77] *NIDCC,* s.v. "Origenism." Following a letter written by emperor Justinian 1 (483-565), a synod at Constantinople issued, in 543, an edict anathemizing Origen's errors concerning the pre-existence of souls, the Incarnation, the resurrection body and Restorationism.

[78] The overthrow of "chiliasm", a term based on the Greek term χιλιάς ("one thousand"), was also facilitated by the widespread assimilation of Greek philosophical categories into Christian theology. It is significant in this regard that Tertullian, a supporter of chiliasm, is also author of the rhetorical question: "What has Athens to do with Jerusalem?" *Prescription of Heretics* VII,9 (PL 2:20).

the dead who have been devoted to Christ will experience "the first resurrection," being raised incorruptible, while those who have overcome the Antichrist "will live for the whole time, and receive blessings because they have suffered evil things. They will marry and beget children for a thousand years." For the duration of the thousand year period, God will keep all evil at bay. There will follow "the day of judgment" for the unbelievers who are destined to experience a second death.[79]

Besides the writings of Commodianus, there are other witnesses to the failure of Origen's realised eschatology to influence the thinking of North African bishops. Even Cyprian's eschatology was essentially futurist. This may be seen in the following statement regarding the Church's prospect of reigning with Christ: "he cannot attain unto the kingdom who forsakes... [the Church] which shall reign there."[80]

Millenarianism also continued to have supporters elsewhere. For example, Methodius (died c. 312), bishop of Olympus and a critic of Origen, describes as "miserable men" those who "deal with figures of the future as if they were already things of the past".[81] Moreover he speaks of a seventh period of one thousand years.[82] Lactantius, c. 240-c.320, was a gifted rhetorician who, after his conversion, became a Christian apologist and an historian of the last season of imperial persecutions of the Church.[83] In his major work he writes polemically of the dead who: ...*will rise*

---

[79] *Instructions of Commodianus*, 43-45 (ANF, 4:211/PL 5:254-256). Little is known concerning Commodianus, save what we learn from the fragments of his writings which remain. He is thought to have been a North-African bishop who was active around A.D. 240 (ANF, 4:201).

[80] Cyprian, *Unit. eccl.* 14 (ANF, 5:425-426/PL 4:526).

[81] *The Banquet of the Ten Virgins,* IX, 1 (PG 18:177).

[82] *Ibid.* Methodius differs from Commodianus in some details, as when he excludes begetting in the thousand years. However he has in common with Commodianus that he envisages the millenium being a part of history.

[83] *NIDCC,* s.v. "Lactantius." A. Cleveland Coxe writes, "Lactantius was doubtless the instrument of Providence in bearing the testimony of Jesus, 'even before kings', in language which promised to Roman letters the new and commanding development imparted to its language by Christianity, which has made it imperishable, and more truly 'eternal' than Rome itself" (ANF, 7:5).

again, not after a thousand years from their death, but that, when again restored to life, they may reign with God a thousand years.[84]

The millenarianism of Lactantius is presented more systematically in an *Epitome* of his former work. In chapter seventy-one he enlarges on the statement: "When the last end shall begin to approach to the world, wickedness will increase," and treats the career of the Antichrist, in terms similar to those found in Revelation 13. In chapter seventy-two he follows the sequence of events described in Revelation 19:11-20:15, stating emphatically that Christ

> will deliver all nations into subjection to the righteous who are alive, and will raise the *righteous* dead to eternal life, and will Himself reign with them on the earth, and will build the holy city, and this kingdom of the righteous shall be for a thousand years.[85]

Lactantius's defense of future corporeal punishment, involving a post-millennial resurrection of the unrighteous and eternal punishment, is in striking contrast to Origen's teaching on these subjects and would seem to confirm that a futuristic understanding of eschatology, including millenarianism, was still widespread in the fourth century. Pelikan makes the point that even the polemical attacks against this doctrine, such as that of Victorinus, "is evidence more for the continuation of millenarianism than for its disappearance."[86]

A futuristic concept of the kingdom is also witnessed to in the *Apostolic Constitutions,* which are thought to have been compiled by an eastern Arian in the late fourth century.[87] The *Constitutions* contain the following prayer: "Gather us all together into Thy kingdom which Thou hast prepared. Let this Thy kingdom come."[88]

---

[84] *The Divine Institutes,* VII, 22 (ANF, 7:218/PL 6:804).

[85] *The Epitome of the Divine Institutes,* 72 (ANF, 7:255/PL 6:1091).

[86] Pelikan, *Tradition,* 1:125. Pelikan refers to a commentary on the Apocalypse (20:1-3) written by Victorinus in which he states that the "thousand years" is a mode of speaking, signifying the whole.

[87] *NIDCC,* s.v. "Apostolic Constitutions."

[88] *Apostolic Constitutions* VII.26.5 (ANF, 7:470); cf. Pelikan, *Tradition,* 1:126.

About this time there was a new development in biblical interpretation associated with Antioch. In the latter half of the fourth century Diodore of Tarsus (d. c. 391, bishop from 378) strongly opposed the allegorism which was so prominent in the writings of Origen and upon which his eschatology depended. According to Diodore, allegorism is the ruin of the text because it destitutes it of its historical foundation, while history is the primary foundation on which any higher meanings must rest. Prophecy, inasmuch as it is the word of God, applies to the past, present and future.[89]

In his prologue to Psalm 118, Diodore identifies the origin of allegorism as being pagan and its purpose as being to suppress the literal sense of what is narrated in the text.[90] Diodore was acquainted with the use which Julian the Apostate[91] and Salustius made of allegorical interpretation in their anti-Christian apologetics at Antioch, in order to salvage pagan myths. For these arch-enemies of Christianity, allegorical interpretation included the negation of the historical worth of the text. Clearly the historicity of the biblical text could not be dismissed in so cavalier a manner, given its infinitely greater value than the texts containing pagan myths.[92]

In the light of the popularity of allegorical interpretation at Alexandria, it is not surprising that Cyril opposed Antiochene

---

[89] This criterion of interpretation is expounded by Diodore in his Preface to his Commentary on the Psalms (Giancarlo Rinaldi, "Diodoro di Tarso, Antiochia e le ragioni della polemica antiallegorista," *Augustinianum* 33 [1993], pp. 416-430).

[90] Rinaldi, *Diodore*, p. 418. Rinaldi writes:

Renouncing the historicity of the facts narrated in the myths was for Salustius, and indeed for all neo-platonists who sought to defend paganism, the only way to confer philosophical validity to the myths, to find justification for ancient feasts and cultic practices, to defend themselves from the attacks of Christians and to develop a theology which could be presented as a substitute to Christian theology.... (p. 426).

[91] Julian, who had earlier apostatised from Christianity while studying under the philosopher Libanius, sought to restore the old religions during his brief reign as sole ruler of the Roman empire (A.D. 361-363).

[92] Rinaldi, *Diodore*, pp. 426-429. Opposition to allegorism was consolidated by Theodore of Mopsuestia (c. 350-428), one of Diodore's disciples and a leading exponent of the Antiochene School of biblical interpretation. In his *Against the*

teachers who insisted on the primacy of literal interpretation of the biblical text.[93] Yet, for the moment, the increasing popularity of allegorical method[94] was insufficient to overthrow the Christian hope of a literal thousand year reign of the saints with Christ. We may presume that Origen's attacks on millenarianism failed because he did not offer a viable alternative.[95]

In summary, millenarianism remained a normative doctrine during the first four centuries of the Christian era. It was not overthrown until Augustine brought together the concepts of the Church and the kingdom of Christ in such a way as to almost identify the two. However two important factors had already set the stage for the transformation of the *eschatological* hope of a messianic kingdom into an *ecclesiastical* theocracy.[96] Since the time of Justin, the prospect of an earthly messianic kingdom had become an altogether *Christian* hope, to the exclusion of *ethnic Israel's eschatological hope.* The other, related, factor was the widespread use made of allegorical interpretation.

D. Augustine's Teaching on Israel, the Church and the Kingdom of Christ

1. *Augustine's teaching concerning ethnic Israel*

We will limit our survey of Augustine's thought concerning ethnic Israel and the kingdom of Christ to relevant parts of his

---

Allegorists, of which an almost integral copy is preserved in the Cambridge University library, Or. 1318,F 17v-21Or., Theodore distinguishes between the biblical use of allegory and pagan allegorism which was developed in order to rid myths of all historical foundation (Rinaldi, *Diodore,* p. 429).

[93] *NIDCC,* s.v. "Antiochene theology," and "Ephesus, council of (431)."

[94] Augustine wrote in his treatise concerning biblical interpretation, "Now it is surely a miserable slavery of the soul to take signs for things, and to be unable to lift the eye of the mind above what is corporeal and created, that it may drink in eternal light" *(On Christian Doctrine,* III, 5 (NPNF, fs, 2:559/PL 34:69); cf. *On Christian Doctrine,* III,5-8 (PL 34:69-70).

[95] According to Robertson (*Regnum Dei,* p. 174), the disappearance of chiliasm "left unsatisfied a genuine Christian instinct, the demand for a tangible interpretation of the Kingdom of GOD as an object of present effort and as a now living fact."

[96] *Ibid.,* p. 178.

famous work *The City of God*. The writing of this work spanned most of the latter period of Augustine's life (c.413-27), therefore the ideas expressed in it can be taken as representative of his mature thought.

Two circumstances stimulated Augustine to meditate on the nature of the Church in the more general contexts of history and Christian theology. The first of these was the sack of Rome in 410, followed by the attempt to attribute this calamity to Christian influence. The second was the century-old Donatist controversary which continued to trouble the North African church and concerning which, as bishop of Hippo, Augustine found himself compelled to take position. *The City of God* was Augustine's answer to the first of these challenges.[97]

It is convenient to begin our survey by noticing Augustine's treatment of ethnic Israel in *The City of God*. In book XV he associates the people descended from Abraham through Isaac with the earthly city spoken of in Galatians 4:21-31. Of this city he writes: it *was founded not for its own sake, but to prefigure another city*.[98] Thus ethnic Israel, consisting of the children of promise, features in Augustine's thought as but a type of the heavenly Jersualem. In similar vein he suggests, in book XVI, that the phrase "the older shall serve the younger" used by Paul in Romans 9:13, finds its ultimate fulfilment not in the physical descendants of Esau and Jacob but rather "in some greater thing… in the Jews and the Christians." Augustine thus concurs with the almost universal consensus of Christian interpreters in the early centuries, according to whom the phrase "the older

---

[97] The occasion which led Augustine to embark on his major work, *The City of God*, is well known. Augustine himself writes of it:

Rome having been stormed and sacked by the Goths under Alaric their king the worshippers of false gods, or pagans, as we commonly call them, made an attempt to attribute this calamity to the Christian religion, and began to blaspheme the true God with even more than their wonted bitterness and acerbity. It was this which kindled my zeal for the house of God, and prompted me to undertake the defence of the city of God against the charges and misrepresentations of its assailants *(Retractations*, II, 43, cited by Marcus Dods, NPNF fs 2: xi/PL 32:647-648).

[98] *Civ.* XV,2 (NPNF fs 2:285/PL 41:438-439).

shall serve the younger" means "that the elder people, the Jews, shall serve the younger people, the Christians."[99]

In book XVII Augustine characterises the Jews, in terms of the wish expressed by David in Psalm 69:22-23, as incapable of contemplating heavenly things because perennially bowed down with their faces towards the earth.[100] The Jews, as a whole, are seen by Augustine as being trapped by divine decree in a mental attitude which excludes them from the blessings reserved for those belonging to the *real* heavenly Jerusalem. This theme is continued in book XVIII, where Augustine meditates on the prayer and song of Habakkuk. He writes:

> For when many people are troubled, he saw the threatening tribulation of the Church, and at once acknowledged himself a member of it... "That I may ascend," he says, "among the people of my pilgrimage," departing quite from the wicked people of his carnal kinship, who are not pilgrims in this earth, and do not seek the country above....
> He sees that nation which was to slay Christ about to lose the abundance of spiritual supplies, which, in prophetic fashion, he has set forth by the figure of earthly plenty.[101]

There is no reason, in the book of Habakkuk, for introducing the idea of the disinheriting of Israel into the prophet's prayer.[102] Moreover Augustine makes this disinheriting of the nation coincide with the transformation of the Old Testament moral *and* material concept of the kingdom into something purely

---

[99] *Civ.*, XVI, 35 (NPNF fs 2:331/PL 41:514).

[100] *Civ.*, XVII, 19 (NPNF fs 2:356-357/PL 41:553-554). Augustine comments on the Jews' failure to accept the evidence of Ps 68:20 which he quotes as: "Our God is the God of salvation: even of the Lord the exit was by death." Cf. the Hebrew: Adonay weleYHWH lemoshaot ellanu hael tosaot lemmawet, meaning: "The Lord YHWH is the God of our salvation; [to him belong] the exits of death."

[101] *Civ.*, XVIII, 32 (NPNF fs 2:379/PL 41:591). The passage continues, "And because that nation was to suffer such wrath of God, because, being ignorant of the righteousness of God, it wished to establish its own, he immediately says, 'Yet will I rejoice in the Lord; ...'." In chapter xix of the same book (NPNF fs 2:379-380) Augustine affirms that only the believing remnant of the nation will inherit the promises made through such prophets as Isaiah and Jeremiah, including the prophecy of the new covenant (Jer 31:31, but cf. vv. 35-37).

[102] Cf. Hab 3:12-13.

spiritual in nature. The liberty which Augustine takes with this Old Testament passage is paralleled by his approach to the *locus classicus* of millenarianism: Revelation 20:1-6.

2. *From a future millennium to the reign of Christ in the Church*

Augustine explains why he gave up belief in a future millennial reign of Christ. Concerning the opinion that the first resurrection of Revelation 20:4-6 refers to the saints who will reign with Christ for one thousand years on earth, he writes:

> ...this opinion would not be objectionable, if it were believed that the joys of the saints in that Sabbath shall be spiritual, and consequent on the presence of God; for I myself, too, once held this opinion.[103] But, as they assert that those who then rise again shall enjoy the leisure of immoderate carnal banquets, furnished with an amount of meat and drink such as not only to shock the feeling of the temperate, but even to surpass the measure of credulity itself, such assertions can be believed only by the carnal.[104]

Augustine proceeds to give what he believes to be the correct interpretation of Revelation 20:1-6 and by so doing circumscribes the future debate concerning a future messianic reign on earth to this one New Testament passage. According to Augustine, the term "one thousand years" indicates a period which reaches to the end of time. This interpretation neglects the evidence of vv. 7-8, according to which, after the termination of the *thousand years,* Satan will regain the ability to deceive those whom he was formerly incapable of deceiving.[105] Other problems with Augustine's exegesis are the presupposition that entire nations belong to Christ and that the *abyss,* where Satan is confined, refers to "the countless multitude of the wicked whose hearts are unfathomably deep in malignity against the Church of God". A further difficulty is that the ban on Satanic seduction is seen to extend only to those who believe.

---

[103] Serm. 259, (PL 38:1197).
[104] *Civ.* XX, 7 (NPNF fs 2:426/PL 41:666-667).
[105] *Civ.,* XX, 7-8 (NPNF fs 2:426-429/PL 41:666-672).

Augustine's change of mind rested on a threefold foundation: the conviction that the images of earthly plenty contained in Israel's eschatological hope were figurative, that this hope was now the exclusive inheritance of the Church and his disgust at the material emphasis in much millenarianism with which he was acquainted.

However the real novelty contained in Augustine's proposal was his alternative, ecclesiastical conception of the Kingdom of Christ. In his application of Jesus' explanation of the parable of the tares and the wheat (Mt 13:36-43) to true and false elements in the Church, he cautiously identifies the kingdom with the Church:

> Must we think that in this kingdom there are no scandals? Therefore, from this his [Christ's] kingdom, which here is the Church, they [the zizzania] are collected out.[106]

Particularly important, in view of future developments, is Augustine's teaching concerning those who govern the kingdom during the present age. Concerning Revelation 20:4a: "I saw thrones on which were seated those who had been given authority to judge...", he writes:

> It is not to be supposed that this refers to the last judgment, but to the seats of the rulers and to the rulers themselves by whom the Church is now governed.[107]

Although he allows that Christ's reign does not extend to the disobedient members of the Church whom he likens to "tares," Augustine does not hesitate to identify all who are regularly ordained to ecclesiastical positions as the "wheat" in Jesus' parable." It is through these in particular that Christ, the Head of the Church, exercises his reign.

It was perhaps inevitable that the crucial role which Augustine attributed to the ecclesiastical hierarchy, as principal agents of

---

[106] "Numquid de regno illo, ubi nulla sunt scandala? De isto ergo regno eius, quod est hic Ecclesia, colligentur" (*Civ.*, XX, 9/PL 41:672).

[107] *Civ.* XX,9 (NPNF fs 2:430/PL 41:675). Augustine links this interpretation with Mt 18:18 (*ibid.*).

Christ's kingdom, would be accentuated in subsequent Church history, to the neglect of other elements of his teaching. But this was not the only aspect of his interpretation of Revelation 20:1-6 to influence Christian practice. His exegesis of this passage also tended to legitimise the cult of the martyrs. Beginning with the assumption that the first resurrection (v. 5) refers to regeneration, he reflects on the present status of those "who had been beheaded" and subsequently "came to life and reigned with Christ a thousand years" (v. 4). According to Augustine,

> ...the souls of the pious dead are not separated from the Church, which even now is the kingdom of Christ....
> The Church, then, begins its reign with Christ now in the living and in the dead....[108]

The medieval church understood the part which the martyrs have in ruling the Church as a special mediatorial role. Pelikan makes this general comment on the phrase "the communion of saints" in the so-called Apostles' Creed:

> The close identification between Christ and his saints made it possibile, and even mandatory, for believers who prayed to God to invoke the saints also, since the saints prayed for them in turn.[109]

E. Some Effects of Augustine's Ecclesiastical Conception of the Kingdom of Christ

1. *A triumphant medieval theocracy*

Augustine considered ethnic Israel but an image of the city of God and believed that all talk of divine blessing in the Scripture

---

[108] *Civ.*, XX, 9 (NPNF fs 2:430-431/PL 41:676).

[109] Pelikan, *Tradition,* 3:176. Pelikan cites in particular Peter the Venerable (c. 1092-1156), *Against the Hardness of the Jews,* 2, (PL 189:521) and Alain of Lille (1125-c.1203), *On the Catholic Faith against the heretics of His Time* 1.73 (PL 210:374). As late as 1522 the former Augustinian Monk Martin Luther continued to attribute a special mediatorial role to the saints (Martin Luther, Epistel... von den Heiligen du die Kirche zu Erfurt, July 10, 1522, in Luthers Werke, Weimar, 1883-, vol. 10, II, pp. 164-166; Zwei Sermone aufs Fest Allerheiligen... und Wie dei Heiligen zu ehzen, 1522, Luthers Werke, 10, III, pp. 400-419).

is to be understood in spiritual terms. Hence he abandoned the hope of an earthly messianic kingdom, as taught in both the Old and New Testaments. According to this African Church Father, the Church embodies the kingdom of Christ imperfectly, because the visible church contains elements which have no part in the true, invisible Body of Christ. However those who occupy positions of government in the Church are "rulers" in Christ's kingdom.

Augustine's conviction that the hierarchical church embodies the kingdom of Christ had important implications for the future relationship of Church and State. Previously realistic eschatology had provided the Church with a workable philosophy of history, the focal point of which was "the expectation of the imminence of the second Advent with the earthly reign of Christ in its train."[110] In the *ecclesiastical* concept of the kingdom of Christ proposed by Augustine, all this was transferred to the present.

Augustine left no precise teaching concerning the form of the hierarchy which would make his concept of the kingdom into a workable reality. However Leo I, elected as bishop of Rome just ten years after Augustine's death, made a decisive contribution in this regard. An able diplomat, Leo I also made a vital contribution to orthodoxy in the occasion of the Council of Chalcedon (451).[111] From this time the Western Church began to credit the bishop of Rome with being the arbitrator of orthodoxy. Thus it is hardly surprising that almost canonical value were given to Leo's teaching concerning the unique authority of the bishop of Rome, as the heir of Peter and universal Pastor. His most famous pronouncements to this effect are contained in a sermon delivered on the anniversary of his elevation to the Pontificate, when he declared that through him Peter "still today…

---

[110] Robertson, *Regnum Dei*, pp. 225-226.

[111] See Leo I's Letter XXVII, addressed to Flavian, commonly called "The Tome of Leo." Bishop Dioscurus of Alexandria refused to have this letter read at the so-called "Robber's Council" (Ephesus, 449). However at the Council of Chalcedon two years later, section 4 of the letter, in which Leo treats "the properties of the twofold nativity and nature of Christ," became the basis of the Symbol of Chalcedon (NPNF ss, 12:38-43/PL 54:751-756).

more fully and effectually performs what is entrusted to him."
Furthermore Leo called on his hearers to:

> celebrate to-day's festival by such methods, that in my humble person he
> may be recognized and honoured, in who abides the care of all the
> shepherds, together with the charge of the sheep commended to him,
> and whose dignity is not abated even in so unworthy an heir.[112]

The role of the medieval popes was consolidated by Gregory
the Great (590-604) who effectively laid the foundation of the
temporal power of the Roman Catholic church.[113] His greatness
lay primarily in his ability to administrate but he is also
remembered as populariser of Augustine's teachings.[114] From the
time of Gregory it became quite normal to speak of the *reign of*
the pope, even though this *reign* was not accepted in the East
where the emperor maintained the Constantinian role of
supremacy over the ecclesiastical patriarchs.

The claim of the Roman bishop to wield supreme authority
over an omnipotent church gave tangible form to Augustine's
ecclesiastical concept of the kingdom of Christ. What this claim
led to, in the history of the medieval church, is well known. The
phenomenon of nepotism and political maneuvering are only
two of the fruits of a papacy which believed itself the instrument
of divine rule over all secular kingdoms. Papal power reached its
zenith with the reigns of Innocent III (1160-1216) and Boniface
VIII (1294-1303). The latter issued a papal Bull, "Unam
Sanctam", which spoke of two swords, one representative of
temporal and the other of spiritual authority. The following words
sum up well the philosophy behind this Bull:

---

[112] Leo I, *serm.* III (NPNF ss, 12:117/PL 54:147).

[113] James Barmby, 'Prolegomena" (NPNF ss, 12: vi-xvii).

[114] Many are of the opinion that, in popularizing Augustine's thought, Gregory
lost sight of its original meaning. R.R. Atwell cites Reinhold Seeberg's phrase: "Almost
everything in him has its roots in Augustine and yet almost nothing is genuinely
Augustinian" and B.J. Kidd's summary statement: "Gregory «erected speculation into
a certainty»" (R.R. Atwell, "From Augustine to Gregory the Great: an Evaluation of
the Emergence of the Doctrine of Purgatory", *JEH* 38/2 [1987]: 173). Atwell shows
that these evalutations are particularly apt when applied to Gregory's elaboration of
Augustine's ideas about purification in the afterlife (pp. 173-186).

> One sword must be under the other, and temporal authority must be subject to the spiritual... Therefore, if earthly power strays from the right path it is to be judged by the spiritual... But if the supreme spiritual authority strays, it can only be judged by God, and not by humans... We further declare, affirm, and define that it is absolutely necessary for salvation that all human creatures be under the Roman pontiff.[115]

Augustine cannot be held responsibile for the abuses of power and the repeated instances of conscious fraud used to consolidate and preserve the temporal power of the Church.[116] At the same time the concept of the "triumphant church" was an elaboration of Augustinian thought which presupposed the logic of *replacement theology.* There is little question that the abuses of power by the "triumphant church" were very damaging to the cause of Christ. Of particular interest to our study are the Crusades, called for by Pope Urban II on Christmas day 1095, which led to the massacre of many communities of Jews, particularly during the first and second crusades (1096-1103 and 1146-1147). Similarly the various inquisitions authorised by Pope Gregory IX during the years 1231-1235 and by Sixtus IV in 1478 led to great suffering for the Jews.

2. *The defeat of the iconoclasts*

The Jews did *not* disappear as a clearly recognisable entity, despite anti-Jewish legislation. At the same time, the claim to have completely replaced Israel in God's plan or, more often, to be the *reality* of which Israel had only been the *type,* led the Church to discriminate against all things Jewish, except those things that she herself had taken over. Among the latter were the sacred

---

[115] Corpus of canon Law 2.1245, quoted by Justo L. Gonzàlez, *Story of Christianity*, 1:311.

[116] Robertson (*op. cit.*, p. 238) lists nine conscious frauds, of which the most famous are: the (false) Donation of Constantine, probably written in the VIII century (*NIDCC*, s.v. "Donation of Constantine"), and the False Decretals, which originated in the mid-IX century and were interpolated into an earlier genuine collection of Conciliar Acts (*NIDCC*, s.v. "False Decretals"). Both of these forgeries were used to increase the temporal possessions and power of the papacy until they were proved false, by Lorenzo Valla and Nicholas of Cusa, in the period of the Renaissance.

Writings which God had entrusted to Israel (Ro 3:1-2). We have seen that the practice of allegorical interpretation permitted the Church to neglect the clear teaching of Scripture when this did not agree with current theological opinion. This could explain why the Medieval Church ignored the prohibition of icons in the books of Moses, the Hebrew prophets and Paul's letter to the Romans. The authorised use of images came to be so common that those who opposed the practice were thought to be guilty of grave error while those supporting them were considered orthodox! Pelikan attributed this reversal of clear Scriptural teaching to prejudice against all things Jewish. He writes:

> To the orthodox, therefore, an iconoclast was simply "one with a Jewish mind ['Ιουδαιοφρῶν]," and an iconoclastic synod was not a church council but "Caiphas's Sanhedrin."[117]

In the light of such flagrant disobedience of God's revealed will, it would have been extremely difficult for Jewish observers to accept the claim of the medieval church to be the *true* Israel of God.[118]

F. Conclusion

The literature examined in this chapter suggests that the abandonment of the hope of a future messianic kingdom in favour of the conviction that the Church itself embodies this kingdom now, was a logical development stemming from *replacement theology*. We saw that neither Jesus nor the writers of the New Testament linked the prospect of a universal kingdom of peace and righteousness with the present age, rather they associated it

---

[117] Pelikan, *Tradition*, 2:201. Pelikan alludes to John V of Jerusalem, *Against Constantinus Cabalinus on the Images*, 3 (PG 95:313) and Nicephorous of Constantinople, *Greater Apology for the Holy Images*, 7 (PG 100:549).

[118] Peter Toon ("Iconoclastic Controversy", *NIDCC*, p. 498), calls attention to three elements of theologial significance in this controversy and its outcome: "it caused a development of thinking about the use of icons and of sacramental theology; it emphasized the importance of tradition in the church; and (in the West) it strengthened the papacy."

with Messiah' *second* advent. Moreover we saw that the realised eschatology developed by Augustine, which makes the Church the normative form of the messianic kingdom, required the allegorisation of both Old and New Testament teaching concerning the kingdom.

It is a fact of history that the Augustinian concept of a Christian theocracy is closely linked with the anti-Jewish attitudes of the Medieval church and unbelievably harsh treatment of the Jewish people. Thus it is not surprising that the traditional claim of Christendom to embody the promised messianic kingdom is an embarrassment to Christians involved in dialogue with the Jewish people. Hans Ucko, executive secretary for Christian-Jewish relations in the World Council of Churches' Office on Inter-religious Relations, addresses this issue:

> Christians are obliged to answer the questions of the Jews: "Where is the messianic kingdom? Where is the redeemed world? Where is the unending peace? How can Jesus possibly be the Messiah we are waiting for?"[119]

If the view according to which the Church incarnates the promised messianic kingdom is a corollary of *replacement theology*, it follows that the widespread repudiation of this view should lead Christian theologians to also re-examine the grounds for realised eschatology.

[119] Hans Ucko, *Common Roots New Horizons,* Geneva: WCC Publications, 1994, p. 8. Charlotte Klein, of "The Sisters of Sion," makes the same point: "According to the Jewish religious experience there is no sign that the Messiah has already come. Jews have continued to suffer oppression and persecution in the centuries since Jesus Christ; the messianic prophecies of the Bible still await fulfilment" (Charlotte Klein, "From conversion to dialogue- The Sisters of Sion and the Jews: A paradigm of Catholic-Jewish Relations?" *JES* 18/3, Summer 1981, pp. 398-399).

Chapter Six

LESSONS FOR CHRISTIAN THEOLOGY

A. A Summary of our Findings

We began with a survey of Israel's uniqueness. Besides examining the evidence contained in the Old and New Testaments, we considered briefly the witness of history from A.D. 70 to the present. Considering the institutional uniqueness of this people among the nations of the world, the scant attention given to Israel by Christian theologians is puzzling.

We saw that in the early centuries of the Christian era this neglect was linked with what has become known as *replacement theology*. According to this concept all that formerly pertained to ethnic Israel now pertains to the Church. In spite of the fact that Israel's status as an elect people was confirmed by Paul in Romans 9-11, the view that the Church had completely replaced Israel in God's plan became the dominant opinion in post-apostolic Christendom. Some Church Fathers went further when they affirmed that the Church had always been the *true* Israel of which physical Israelites were but the visible sign.

The logic of *replacement theology* required that much of the Old Testament be allegorised. Only in this way could the Church be made the subject of passages in which Israel is addressed. This led to the virtual abandonment of the Hebrew world view and concept of God, in favour of a framework of thought which had its roots in Greek philosophy. All of this fostered an attitude of contempt towards ethnic Israel and led to the exclusion of Israel as a subject of theological reflection.

The disinheriting of Israel did not remain an isolated element in the development of Christian thought. One area of theology influenced by it in the early Christian centuries was ecclesiology. For example, in what became the standard interpretation of Malachi 1:10-12, the idea that the Church had replaced Israel was linked with the reinterpretation of the Lord's Supper in the Levitical terms of sacrifice. Once the Hebrew Bible was thought to be a thoroughly Christian book, there developed a more general use of Levitical forms and terminology in the context of the Church. Thus instead of being called "elders", local church leaders began to be called "priests", while the concept of the Christian ministry was now thought of primarily in priestly terms. At the same time important characteristics of the new covenant, such as the priesthood of all believers, the sufficiency of Christ's once-for-all sacrifice and the crucial importance of faith in Christ for personal salvation, were neglected.

Eschatology was another area of theology to be influenced by the logic of *replacement theology*. The presumed repudiation of Israel as an elect people permitted the Church to consider itself the normative expression of the long awaited messianic kingdom. However, instead of promoting peace and righteousness, as might have been expected of an institution claiming to mediate the universal kingdom of Christ, the Triumphant Church of the Middle Ages proved to be arrogant and self-serving. From the time of Constantine the disinheriting of Israel was supported by ecclesiastical legislation while violence against the Jews was common.

There were of course a number of other influences which contributed to the transformation of ecclesiology and eschatology in the ways just mentioned. However the documentary evidence bears testimony to the fact that they were also the logical out-working of *replacement theology*. This calls for reflection.

B. Principles Emerging from our Study

1. *Failure to reflect seriously on Israel, in the light of all the relevant biblical data, has serious consequences for the entire enterprise of Christian theology.* It was the neglect of the relevant biblical data concerning the place of Israel in God's plan which permitted *replacement theology* to develop during the early centuries of the Christian era. Once *replacement theology* had

become a presupposition of theological reflection, it required that much of the Old Testament be interpreted allegorically. This involved the loss of the Hebrew world view and influenced the direction of theological reflection in areas such as ecclesiology and eschatology. The widespread repudiation of *replacement theology,* following the *Shoah,* confirms that more attention should have been given to the biblical data concerning the institutional uniqueness of Israel during the early Christian centuries.

The development of a new majority view, following the *Shoah,* according to which the Jewish people have their own covenant and are thus exonerated from the need to believe in Jesus in order to be saved, has also been marked by a selective use of Scripture. For example repeated use is made of Romans chapter 11 while chapter 10, which addresses the question of the salvation of Jews in the present, is completely ignored. Because of this selective use of Scripture the new majority view represents a similar threat to Christology, soteriology and missiology, as *replacement theology* posed to the areas of theology considered in chapters 4-5.[1]

2. *Christian theology must be based on sound hermeneutical principles which presuppose the Church's essential relationship with Israel.* These include: taking into account the whole of the biblical canon, taking seriously the Jewishness of Jesus and of much of the New Testament, recognising the institutional distinctions between Israel and the Church, avoiding gratuitous allegorisation of Scripture and giving normative value to what the New Testament teaches concerning both the first *and* second advents of Christ. In the early Christian centuries neglect of these five principles favoured the development of a theology of the Church and of the Christian ministry in which apostolic teaching was

---

[1] I treat the development and effects of the new majority view in the final section of my dissertation (see p. x). For a brief summary, see my article: "Jewish-Christian Dialogue and Soteriology", *Trinity Journal* 20 NS (1999): 23-37.

subordinated to Old Testament cultic practice. It also favoured a medieval ecclesiastical theocracy in which the qualities of the messianic kingdom described in the Old Testament were notably absent.

C. Implications for the Enterprise of Christian Theology

Christian theology cannot afford to ignore the momentous events of the twentieth century which first threatened the very existence of the Jewish people and subsequently secured a homeland for them. The response of Christian theology to these developments has been mixed. While there have been some proposals for a post-Holocaust theology, *replacement theology* and/or its effects continue to influence much systematic theology.

Post-Holocaust theologies characterised by a selective use of Scripture are not enough. What is needed is reflection on Israel in standard works of systematic theology and biblical doctrine *which takes into consideration all the relevant biblical data.* Likewise the teaching of systematic theology, whether in schools or in local churches, should include reflection on Israel just as it includes reflection on the Church. Both the similarities and institutional distinctives of Israel and the Church need to be emphasised. Theologians also need to weed out those elements in Christian theology which are the fruit of *replacement theology.*

Moreover biblical reflection on Israel's place in God's plan must be seen to inform other aspects of theology such as ecclesiology and eschatology and must itself be informed by New Testament Christology and soteriology. When one or more of the foundational, component parts of Christian thought are neglected, the product of theological reflection no longer corresponds to "the whole counsel of God" but rather to the intellectual climate of the moment.

BIBLIOGRAPHY

1. Ancient Works

Ambrose
> *Sermons*
> *Apostolic Constitutions*

Augustine
> *City of God*
> *Sermons*
> *Tract Against the Jews*
> *Barnabas, Epistle of*

Clement of Alexandria
> *Stromata*

Commodianus
> *Instructions*

Cyprian
> *Epistles*
> *On the Unity of the Church*
> *Three Books of Testimonies Against the Jews*

Cyril of Alexandria
> *Commentary on Romans*

Cyril of Jerusalem
> *Catechetical Lectures*
> *Didache*
> *Diognetus, Epistle to*

Eusebius of Cesarea
> *Ecclesiastical History*
> *Life of Constantine*

Hippolytus
> *On Antichrist*
> *Expository Treatise Against the Jews*

Ignatius of Antioch
> *Epistles*

Irenaeus
> *Against Heresies*

John Chrysostom
> *Demonstrations to the Jews and Gentiles that Christ is God*
> *Eight Orations Against the Jews*
> *Sermons*

Bibliography

John Damascene
> *On the Orthodox Faith*

Josephus, Flavius
> *The Life of Josephus*

Justin Martyr
> *Dialogue with Trypho*
> *First Apology*

Lactantius
> *Divine Institutes*
> *The Epitome of the Divine Institutes*

Methodius of Olympus
> *The Banquet of the Ten Virgins*

Origen
> *Against Celsus*
> *On First Principles*
> *Homilies*
> *Commentaries on Matthew and Romans*

Tertullian
> *To Martyrs*
> *Against the Jews*
> *Against Marcion*
> *On Baptism*
> *Exhortation to Chastity*
> *On Modesty*
> *Prescription of Heretics*

2. Collections

Classici delle religioni. Turin: U.T.E.T., 1969-

Collana di testi patristici. Directed by Antonio Quacquarelli. Rome: Città nuova editrice, 1975-

Ante-Nicene Christian Library. Alexander Roberts & James Donaldson, eds. 24 vols. Edinburgh: T. & T. Clark, 1867-1872.

Ante-Nicene Fathers. Alexander Roberts & James Donaldson, eds. American reprint, A. Cleveland Coxe & Allan Menzies, eds. 10 vols. Grand Rapids, MI: Eerdmans, 1986.

Luther's Works. vols 1-30, Jaroslav Pelikan, ed. Saint Louis, Concordia 1958-1967; vols 31-55, Helmut T. Lehmann, ed. Philadelphia: Fortress, 1957-1986.

Nicene & Post-Nicene Fathers. First Series, Philip Schaff, ed. 14 vols. Reprint, Grand Rapids, MI: Eerdmans,1979-1987.

Nicene & Post-Nicene Fathers. Second Series, Philip Schaff & Henry Wace, eds. 14 vols. Reprint, Grand Rapids, MI: Eerdmans, 1983.

Patrologia Graeca. 162 vols. Paris: J.P. Migne, 1856-1866.

Patrologia Latina. 221 vols. Paris: J.P. Migne, 1862-1865. Reprint, Turnbolti, Belgium: Typographi Brepols Editores Pontifichi, n.d.

Pauluskommentare aus der Griechischen Kirche, Karl Staab, ed. 1933. Reprint Münster, Westfalen: Aschendorff, 1984.

The Greek New Testament. Kurt Aland, Matthew Black, Carlo M. Martini, Bruce M. Metzger & Allen Wikgren, eds. Germany: United Bible Societies, 1975³.

The Holy Bible. New International Version. Grand Rapids, MI: Zondervan, 1985.

3. Biblical Commentaries

Abbott, T.K. *The Epistles to the Ephesians and to the Colossians.* ICC. S.R. Driver, A. Plummer, C.A. Briggs, eds. Edinburgh: T. & T. Clark, 1897. 5th reprint, 1956.

Barrett, C.K. *The Epistle to the Romans.* Black's New Testament commentaries. London: Adam & Charles Black, 1957. 2d reprint, 1967.

Barth, Karl. *Der Römerbrief.* Zürich: Evangelischer Verlag Zollikon, 1954.

Barth, Markus. *Ephesians 1-3.* The Anchor Bible. New York: Doubleday & Co., 1974.

Best, Ernest. *The Letter of Paul to the Romans.* The Cambridge Bible Commentary. P.R. Ackroyd, A.R.C. Leaney & J.W. Packer, eds. Cambridge: Cambridge University Press, 1967.

Betz, H.D. *Galatians.* Philadelphia, PA: Fortress Press, 1979

Bruce, F.F. *The Epistle of Paul to the Romans.* Tyndale New Testament Commentaries. London: The Tyndale Press, 1965. 2d ed., 1985.

———. *The Gospel of John.* Grand Rapids, MI: Eerdmans, 1983.

———. *Commentary on Galatians.* New International Greek Testament Commentary. I. Howard Marshall & W. Ward Gasque eds. Grand Rapids, MI: Eerdmans, 1982.

———. *The Epistle to the Hebrews.* The New International commentary on the New Testament, F.F. Bruce, ed. Grand Rapids, MI: Eerdmans, 1964. Reprint, 1981.

Burton, E.D. *The Epistle to the Galatians.* ICC. S.R. Driver, A. Plummer, C.A. Briggs (eds.). 1921. Reprint, Edimburgh: T. & T. Clark, 1957.

Calvin, John. *Romans.* Calvin's Commentaries. Translated and edited by John Owen. Grand Rapids: Eerdmans, 1947. Reprint, *Epistles of Paul the Apostle, to the Romans and to the Thessalonians.* Calvin's Commentaries. Edinburgh: The Saint Andrew Press, 1961.

Carson, D. A. *Matthew.* The Expositor's Bible Commentary. Frank E. Gaebelein, ed. Grand Rapids, MI: Zondervan, 1984.

_____. *The Gospel According to John.* Grand Rapids, MI: Eerdmans, 1991.

Cranfield, C.E.B. *The Epistle to the Romans.* 2 vols. ICC. J.A. Emerton, ed. Edinburgh: T. & T. Clark, 1975-1979.

Davids, Peter H. *The First Epistle of Peter.* The New International Commentary on the New Testament. F.F. Bruce, ed. Grand Rapids, MI: Eerdmans, 1990.

Dunn, James D.G. *Romans 9-16.* Word Biblical Commentary. Dallas: Word Books, 1988.

Delitzsch, Franz. *Isaiah.* Translated by James Martin. Vol. 7 in Commentary on the Old Testament by C.F. Keil and F. Delitzsch. 10 vols. Reprint, Grand Rapids, MI: Eerdmans, 1980.

Godet, F. *St. Paul's Epistle to the Romans.* 2 vols. Edinburgh: T. & T. Clark 1880-1881.

Grudem, Wayne. *1 Peter.* Tyndale New Testament Commentaries. Downers Grove, MI: InterVarsity Press, 1988.

Haldane, Robert. *The Epistle to the Romans.* 1835-1839. Reprint, London: Banner of Truth, 1958.

Hill, David. *The Gospel of Matthew.* The New Century Bible Commentary. Matthew Black, NT ed. Grand Rapids, MI: Eerdmans, 1972.

Hodge Charles. *Commentary on the Epistle to the Romans.* Revised ed. 1886. 6th reprint, Grand Rapids, MI: Eerdmans, 1965.

Huby, Giuseppe S. J. *San Paolo, Epistola ai Romani.* P. Stanislao Lyonnet S.J., ed. Rome: Editrice Studium, 1961.

Leenhardt, Franz J. *L'Épître du saint Paul aux Romains.* Commentaire du Nouveau Testament. Vol. VI. Genéve: Labor et Fides, 1957.

Lenski, R.C.H. *The Interpretation of St. Paul's Epistle to the Romans.* Columbus: Wartburg Press, 1945. Reprint, 1960.

Lightfoot, J.B. *The Epistle of St. Paul to the Galatians.* 1865. 20th reprint, Grand Rapids, MI: Zondervan, 1957, 1982.

Luther, Martin. *Commentary on the Epistle to the Romans.* Translation by J. Theodore Mueller. Grand Rapids, MI: Kregel, 1976.

Marshall, I. Howard. *The Gospel of Luke.* The New International Greek Testament Commentary. I. Howard Marshall and W. Ward Gasque, eds. Exeter: The Paternoster Press, 1978.

————. *The Acts of the Apostles.* Tyndale New Testament Commentaries. R.V.G. Tasker, ed. Grand Rapids, MI: Eerdmans, 1980.

Moffatt, James. *Epistle to the Hebrews.* ICC. S.R Driver, A. Plummer, C.A. Briggs, eds., Edinburgh: T. & T. Clark, 1924. 3d reprint, 1957.

Moo, Douglas J. *The Epistle to the Romans.* The New International Commentary on the New Testament, Gordon Fee, ed. Grand Rapids; MI: Eerdmans, 1996.

Morris, Leon. *The Epistle to the Romans.* Leicester: Inter-Varsity Press, 1988.

Murray, John. *Epistle to the Romans.* The New international Commentary on the New Testament. F.F. Bruce, ed. Grand Rapids, MI: Eerdmans, 1968.

Nygren, Anders. *Commentary on Romans.* 4th ed., Philadelphia: Fortress, 1978.

Sanday, William and Arthur C. Headlam. *The Epistle to the Romans.* The International Critical Commentary. S.R. Driver, A. Plummer and C.A. Briggs, eds. Edinburgh: T. & T. Clark, 1895.

Schlier, von Heinrich. *Der Römerbrief.* Freiburg im Breisgau: Verlag Herder, 1977.

Vine, W.E. *The Epistle to the Romans.* 2d ed., London: Oliphants, 1948.

Perkins, William. *A Commentary on Galatians.* Gerald T. Sheppard, ed. The Pilgrim Classic Commentaries. New York: The Pilgrim Press, 1989.

Vermigli, Pietro Martire. *Most Fruitfull and Learned Commentaries of Doctor Peter Martir Vermil Florentine.* London: John Day, 1564.

4. Historical and Systematic Theology

Aquinas, Thomas. *Somma contro i Gentili.* Tito S. Centi, ed. Torino: U.T.E.T., 1975.

Ball, Bryan W. *A Great Expectation: Eschatological Thought in English Protestantism to 1660.* Leiden: E. J. Brill, 1975.

Barth, Karl. *Dei Kirchliche Dogmati.* Zweiter Band, Dei Lehre von Gott, Erster Halbband. Zollikon, Zürich: Evangelischer Verlag A.G., 1948.

————. *Dogmatique.* Vol. 1-2. Translated into French by M. Fernand Ryser. Geneva: Editions Labor et Fides, 1954-1956.

Bloesch, Donald G. *A Theology of Word and Spirit.* Downers Grove, IL: InterVarsity Press, 1992.

Boice, James Montgomery. *Foundations of the Christian Faith.* Downers Grove, IL: InterVarsity Press, 1986.

Berkhof, Hendrikus. *Christian Faith.* Grand Rapids, MI: Eerdmans, 1979.

Berkhof, Louis. *Systematic Theology.* 1st British ed., 1958. 3d reprint, London: Banner of Truth Trust, 1966.

Chafer, Lewis Sperry. *Systematic Theology.* 8 vols. Dallas, TX: Dallas Theological Seminary, 1948. 11th reprint, 1973.

Clouse, Robert G., ed. *The Meaning of the Millennium.* Downers Grove: InterVarsity Press, 1977.

Calvin, John. *Institutes of the Christian Religion.* Translation by Henry Beveridge. 2 vols. London: James Clarke, 1953.

Carter, Charles W., R. Duane Thompson and Charles R. Wilson, eds. *A Contemporary Wesleyan Theology.* 2 vols. Grand Rapids, MI: Zondervan, 1983.

Erickson, Millard J. *Christian Theology.* Grand Rapids, MI: Baker Book House, 1985. 3rd reprint, 1987.

Finger, Thomas. *Christian Theology: An eschatological approach.* 2 vols. Nashville, TN: Thomas Nelson Publications, 1985.

Gentile, Panfilo. *Il Cristianesimo Dalle Origini a Costantino.* Collana di studi storici e filosofici. Carlo Antoni, ed. Firenze: Le Monnier, 1946.

Grenz, Stanley J. *Theology for the Community of God.* Nashville, TN: Broadman, 1994.

Grossi, Vittorino and Angelo Di Berardino. *La chiesa antica: ecclesiologia e istituzioni.* Roma: Borla, 1984.

Grudem, Wayne. *Systematic Theology: An Introduction to Biblical Doctrine.* Leicester: Inter-Varsity Press, 1994.

Hanson, R.P.C. *Allegory and Event, A study of the sources and significance of Origen's Interpretation of Scripture.* Richmond, VA: John Knox Press, 1959.

Harnack, Adolf. *Manuale di Storia del Dogma.* 1st Italian ed. from the 4th German ed. 7 vols. Mendrisio: Casa Editrice Cultura Moderna, 1912-1914.

Hodge, Charles. *Systematic Theology.* 3 vols, 1872-1873. Reprint, Grand Rapids, MI: Eerdmans, 1975.

Jay, Eric G. *The Church: its changing image through twenty centuries.* Atlanta, GA: John Knox Pess, 1978.

Kelly, J.N.D. *Early Christian Doctrines.* 3d ed., London: Adam & Charles Black, 1965.

Lewis, Gordon R. and Bruce A. Demarest. *Integrative Theology.* 3 vols. Grand Rapids, MI: Zondervan, 1994.

Lindsay, Thomas M. *The Church and the Ministry in the Early Centuries.* The 18th series of the Cunningham Lectures, 1902. 3d ed., London: Hodder & Stoughton, 1907.

McClendon, James Wm, Jr. *Systematic Theology.* 2 vols. Nashwille, TN: Abingdon Press, 1994.

McGrath, Alister. *Christian Theology: An Introduction.* London: Blackwell, 1994.

Moody, Dale. *The Word of Truth: A summary of Christian doctrine based on biblial revelation.* Grand Rapids, MI: Eerdmans, 1981.

Murray, Iain. *The Puritan Hope.* London: The Banner of Truth Trust, 1971.

Noll, Mark A., ed. *Confessions and Catechisms of the Reformation.* Grand Rapids, MI: Baker Book House, 1991.

Oden, Thomas, C. *Systematic Theology.* 3 vols. New York: HarperCollins, 1992.

Oliver, W. H. *Prophets and Millennialists: The uses of Biblical Prophecy in England from the 1790s to the 1840s.* Auckland: Auckland University Press, 1978.

Pelikan, Jaroslav. *The Christian Tradition.* 5 vols, Chicago: University of Chicago Press, 1971-1989.

Rahner, Karl. *Foundations of Christian Faith.* Translated by William V. Dych, New York: Crossroad, 1982.

Robertson, Archibald, *Regnum Dei.* Eight lectures on the Kingdom of God in the History of Christian Thought. The Bampton Lectures 1901. London: Methuen & Co., 1901.

Spykman, Gordon J. *Reformational Theology: A New Paradigm for doing Dogmatics.* Grand Rapid, MI: Eerdmans, 1992.

Strong, A. H. *Systematic Theology.* 3 vols in 1. Westwood, NP: Fleming & Revell, 1907.

Thiessen, Henry Clarence. *Lectures in Systematic Theology.* Revision by Vernon D. Doerksen, Grand Rapids, MI: Eerdmans, 1979.

VanGemeren, Willem. *The Progress of Redemption: the story of salvation from creation to the new Jerusalem.* Grand Rapids, MI: Zondervan, 1988.

Whiston, William, translator and ed. *Works of Josephus.* 4 vols. Grand Rapids, MI: Baker Book House, 1974.

Williams, Rodman. *Renewal Theology.* 3 vols. Academie Books. Grand Rapids, MI: Zondervan, 1988-92.

5. General works, Monographs, Historical Romance

Barker, William S. & W. Robert Godfrey. eds. *Theonomy: A Reformed Critique.* Grand Rapids, MI: Zondervan, 1990.

Barth, Markus. *The People of God. Journal for the Study of the New Testament.* Supplement series, no. 5. Sheffield: The University of Sheffield, 1983.

_____. *Rediscovering the Lord's Supper.* Louisville, KY: John Knox Press, 1988.

Baum, Gregory O.S.A. *Is the New Testament Anti-Semitic?* Glen Rock, NJ: Paulist Press, 1960.

Bentwich, Norman. *The Jews in our Time.* Penguin Books, 1960. Italian translation by Lia Moggi. *Gli Ebrei nel nostro tempo,* Florence: Sansoni, 1963.

Beyerhaus, Peter P. J. *God's Kingdom and the Utopian Error.* Wheaton, IL: Good News Publishers, 1992.

Blum, Erhard, Christian Macholz and Ekkehard W. Stegemann (eds.). *Dei Hebräische Bibel und ihre zweifache Nachgeschichte.* Festschrift für Rolf Rendtorff. Heukirchen, Vluyn: Neukirchen Verlag, 1990.

Bright, John. *A History of Israel.* London: SCM Press, 1960.

Bruce, F.F. *Israel and the Nations.* Exeter: The Paternoster Press, 1963.

_____. *The Spreading Flame.* The Paternoster Church History. Vol. 1. Exeter: The Paternoster Press, 1958.

Bunk, B. "L'élection d'Israel/Analyse critique de la position de K.B. sur le rôle d'Israel dans l'histoire du salut." Unpublished thesis. Lausanne: Fac. Théol. Eglise Libre Canton de Vaud, 1966.

Charlesworth, James H., Frank X. Blisard & Jeffrey S. Siker, eds. *Jews and Christians.* New York: Crossroad, 1990.

Clowney, Edmund P. *The Church.* Contours of Christian Theology. Gerald Bray, ed. Downers Grove, IL: InterVarsity Press, 1995.

Collins, R.F. *Studies on the First Letter to the Thessalonians.* Louvain, University Press 1984.

Davenport, Rowland A. *Albury Apostles.* United Writers, 1970. Revised ed. London: Neilgo Publications, 1974.

Davies, Alan T. ed. *AntiSemitism and the foundations of Christianity.* New York: Paulist Press, 1979.

de Waard, J.A. *Comparative Study of the Old Testament Text in the Dead Sea Scrolls and the New Testament.* Leiden: Brill, 1965.

Dunn, James D. G. *The Partings of the Ways.* London: SCM Press, 1991.

Ellison, H.L. *The Mystery of Israel.* Exeter: Paternoster, 1966.

Evans, Craig A. & Donald A. Hagner, eds. *Anti-Semitism and Early Christianity.* Minneapolis, MN: Fortress Press, 1993.

Fackre, Gabriel. *Ecumenical Faith in Evangelical Perspective.* Grand Rapids, MI: Eerdmans, 1993.

Feinberg, John, ed. *Continuity and Discontinuity.* Westfield, IL: Crossway Books, Good News Publishers, 1988.

Flusser, David. *Jesus.* Jerusalem: The Magnes Press, The Hebrew University, 1997.

Frend, W.H.C. *The Rise of Christianity.* Philadelphia, PA: Fortress Press, 1984.

Giles, Kevin. *What on earth is the Church?* Downer's Grove, IL: InterVarsity Press, 1995.

Gonzàlez, Justo L. *The Story of Christianity.* 2 vols. San Francisco, CA: Harper, 1984-1985.

Harvey, Graham. *The True Israel.* Leiden: E.J. Brill, 1996.

Hengel, Martin. *Judentum und Hellenismus.* Tübingen: J. C. B. Mohr (Paul Siebeck), 1973. English ed. by John Bowden. *Judaism and Hellenism.* 2 vols. London: SCM Press, 1974.

Johnson, S. Lewis Jr. *The Old Testament in the New.* Grand Rapids, MI: Zondervan, 1980.

Jules, Isaac. *Genèse de L'Antisémitisme.* Paris: Calmann Lévy, 1956.

Käsemann, Ernst. *New Testament Questions of Today.* Philadelphia, PA: Fortress Press, 1969, pp. 183-187.

Lacunza y Diaz, Manuel de. *Venida del Mesìas en gloria y majestad.* 1811. English translation, with Introduction, of the 11th ed. by Edward Irving. *The Coming of the Messiah in Glory and Majesty.* 2 vols. London: L.B. Seeley & Sons, 1827.

Langmuir, Gavin I. *History, Religion, and Antisemitis.* Los Angeles: Center of Medieval and Rennaisance Studies, 1990.

Lapide, Pinchas & Jürgen Moltmann. *Monoteismo Ebraico – Dottrina Trinitaria, Un dialogo.* Brescia: Queriniana, 1980.

LaRondelle, Hans K. *The Israel of God in Prophecy.* Berrien Springs, MI: The Seventh-Day Adventist Andrews University Press, 1983.

Leighton, Robert. *The Whole Works of Robert Leighton D.D.* Included is "A Life of the Author" by John Norman Pearson. New York: J.C. Riker, 1855.

Luz, Ulrich. *Das Geschichtsverständnis des Paulus.* Beiträge zur evangelischen Theologie. Theologische Abhandlungen. von E. Wolf., ed. Vol. 49. Müchen: Chr. Kaiser Verlag, 1968.

McComisky, Thomas Edward. *The Covenants of Promise: A Theology of the Old Testament Covenants.* Grand Rapids, MI: Baker Book House, 1985.

Moore, George F. *Judaism in the First Three Centuries of the Christian Era. The Age of the Tannaim.* 2 vols, 1927. 3d ed. New York: Schocken Books, 1971.

Motyer, Steve. *Israel in the plan of God.* Leicester: Inter-Varsity Press, 1989.

Munck, Johannes. *Paulus Und Die Heilsgeschichte.* 1954. Eng. Trad. *Paul and the salvation of mankind.* By Frank Clarke, 1959. Paperback ed. Atlanta: John Knox Press, 1977.

Newell, J. Philip. "A. J. Scott and his circle." Unpublished Ph.D. thesis. University of Edinburgh, 1981.

Parkes, James. *The Conflict of the Church and the Synagogue.* New York: Hermon Press, 1934.

_____. *A History of the Jewish People.* Penguin Books. Middlesex: Harmondsworth, 1964.

Perkins, William. *The Workes of That Famous and Worthy Minister of Christ in the Universitie of Cambridge, M.W. Perkins.* 3 vols. Cambridge, 1626-1631.

Plag, Christoph. *Israels Wege zum Heil,* Eine Untersuchung zu Römer 9 bis 11. Stuttgart: Calwer Verlag,1969.

Ramm, Bernard. *Protestant Biblical Interpretation.* Grand Rapids: Baker, 1970.

Refoulé, François. *"...Et ainsi tout Israël sera sauvé".* Paris: Les Éditions du Cerf, 1984.

Roth, Cecil. *A Short History of the Jewish People.* 1936. 6th revised ed. Hartmore: Hartmore House, 1969.

Ruether, Rosemany R. *Faith and Fratricide.* New York: The Seabury Press, 1974.

Sachar, Howard M. *A History of Israel: from the rise of Zionism to our Time.* New York: Alfred A. Knopf, 1993.

Saucy, Robert. *The Case for Progressive Dispensationalism.* Grand Rapids, MI: Zondervan, 1993.

Schaff, Philip. *History of the Christian Church.* 8 vols. Charles Schribner's Sons, 1910. Reprint ed. Grand Rapids, MI: Eerdmans, 1967.

Scott, Sir Walter. *Ivanhoe.* Nelson Classics. T. Nelson & Sons, 1830.

Sibbes, Richard. *The Complete Works of Richard Sibbes.* A.B. Grosart, ed. 4 vols. Edinburgh: James Nichol, 1862.

Siker, Jeffrey S. *Disinheriting the Jews Adraham in early Christian Controversy.* Louisville, KY: Westminster/John Knox Press, 1991.

Schmid, Herbert. *Dei christlich-jüdische Auseinandersetzung um das Alte Testament in hermeneutischer Sicht.* Zürich:Theologischer Verlag. 1971.

Soulen, R. Kendall. *The God of Israel and Christian Theology.* Minneapolis, MN: Fortress Press, 1996.

Toon, Peter, ed. *Puritan Eschatology 1600-1660.* Cambridge: James Clarke, 1970.

Ucko, Hans. *Common Roots New Horizons.* Geneva: WCC Publications, 1994.

Williamson, Clark M. *A Guest in the House of Israel.* Louisville, KY: Westminster/John Knox Press, 1993.

Wistrich, Robert S., ed. *Anti-Zionism and Antisemitism in the Contemporary World.* London: The Macmillan Press, 1990.

6. Articles

Atwell, R.R. "From Augustine to Gregory the Great: an Evaluation of the Emergence of the Doctrine of Purgatory." *JEH* 38/2 (1987): 173-186.

Beale, G.K. "An Exegetical and Theological Consideration of the hardening of Pharaoh's heart in Exodus 4-14 and Romans 9." *Trinity Journal* 5 NS (1984): 129-154.

Bianchi, Enzo. "Israele e la chiesa." *Storia cristiana* 10 (1989): 77-106.

Carbone, Sandro. "Israele nella Lettera ai Romani." *Rivista Biblica* XLI (1993): 139-170.

Castellina, Paolo. "La salvezza di Israele: un inno alla sovranità di Dio." *Studi di teologia.* NS. III (1991): 190-198.

Cousins, Ewert. "Judaism–Christianity–Islam: Facing Modernity Together." *JES* 30 (1993): 417-425.

Davies, W.D. "Paul and the People of Israel." *New Testament Studies* 24 (1977-1978): 4-39.

Demson, David E. "Israel as the Paradigm of Divine Judgement: An examination of a theme in the Theology of Karl Barth." *JES* 26 (1989), pp. 611-627.

Drane, John W. "Why did Paul write Romans?" In *Pauline Studies.* Donald A. Wagner, and Murray J. Harris, eds. Exeter: The Paternoster Press, 1980, pp. 208-227.

Droge, Arthur J. "Justin Martyr and the Restoration of Philosophy." *CH* 56 (1987): 303-319.

Dunn, James D.G. "Echoes of Intra-Jewish Polemic in Paul's Letter to the Galatians." *Journal of Biblical Literature* 112/3 (1993): 459-477.

Evans, Gillian R. "The Beginnings of Christian Philosophy." In *The History of Christian Theology,* Paul Avis, Series ed. Vol. 1. *The Science of Theology.* Gillian R. Evans, Alister E. McGrath and Allan D. Galloway, eds. Basingstoke: Marshall Pickering, 1986.

Fuller, Daniel P. "Interpretation, History of." In *The International Standard Bible Encyclopedia.* Fully revised. Geoffrey W. Bromiley, ed. 4 vols. 1982.

Garrone, Daniele. "Il regno di Dio nell'antico e nel nuovo testamento." *Certezze,* n. 150 (1996): 7.

_____. "Protestanti ed ebrei: alcuni nodi del confronto attuale." *Protestantesimo* XVIIV (1989/2): 82-89.

_____. "Considerazioni sul sussidio ecclesiastico per il rinnovamento del rapporto di Cristiani ed Ebrei," *Protestantesimo* XLIIV (1989/2): 98-100. Translation of "Christen und Juden. Schwerpunkt-Tagung der Landessynode der Evangelischen Landeskerche in Baden" with notes (Bad-Herrenalb, 1980, pp. 182-183).

_____. "Chiesa – Israele: nuove prospettive teologiche, *Protestantesimo* 52 (1977/4): 303-305.

Georgi, Dieter. "The Early Church: Internal Jewish Migration or New Religion?" *Harvard Theological Review* 88/1 (1995): 35-68.

Harrington, Daniele J. "Israel's Salvation according to Paul." *Bible Today* 26 (1988): 306-307.

Hempton, D.N. "Evangelicalism and Eschatology." *JEH* 31/2 (1980): 179-194.

Johnson, S. Lewis, Jr. "Evidence from Romans 9-11." In *A Case for Premillennialism: A New consensus.* Donald K. Campbell and Jeffrey L. Townsend, eds. Chicago: Moody, 1992, pp. 199-223.

Jospe, Raphael. "The Concept of the Chosen People: An Interpretation." *Judaism* 43 (1994): 130-135.

Katz, David S. "The Abendana Brothers and the Christian Hebraists of Seventeenth-Century England." *JEH* 40/1 (1989): 28-52.

Klein, Charlotte. "From conversion to dialogue – The Sisters of Sion and the Jews: A paradigm of Catholic-Jewish Relations?" *JES* 18 (1981): 388-400.

Lapide, Pinchas. "Christians and Jews – A New Protestant Beginning." *JES* 12 (1975): 485-492.

Levy, David. "A History of Anti-Semitism." *Israel My Glory* 51 (1993/2): 16-18.

Longenecker, Bruce W. "Different Answers to Different issues: Israel, the Gentiles and Salvation History in Romans 9-11." *Journal for the Study of the New Testament* 36 (1989): 95-123.

Molari, Carlo. "L'elezione d'Israele nell'autocomprensione cristiana." Unpublished paper presented on 4 November, 1995 at the SIDIC Center, Rome.

Osborne, William L. "The Old Testament Background of Paul's «All Israel» in Romans 11:26A." *Asia Journal of Theology* 2 (1988): 282-293.

Parmentier, Martin. "Greek Church Fathers on Romans 9. Parts I & II," *Bijdragen* 50 (1989): 139-154; 51 (1990): 2-20.

Pawlikowski, John T. "Contemporary Jewish-Christian Theological Dialogue Agenda." *JES* 11 (1974): 599-616.

_____. "Toward a Theology for Religious Diversity: Perspectives from the Christian-Jewish Dialogue." *JES* 26 (1989): 138-153.

Reeve, Simon. "Heartless Haven". *Time,* Jan. 26, 1998, pp. 24-27.

Reichrath, Hans L. "Dei Geschichtlichkeit der Kirche war und ist eine Israelgeschichtlichkeit", *Judaica* 52/1 (1996): 40-58.

Riggans, Walter. "Messianic Judaism: A case of Identity Denied." *IBMR* 16 (1992): 130-132.

Schariah, Zechariah. "Development of epiclesis in the liturgy." Unpublished paper presented at the Doctoral Colloquium, September 1992. Evangelische Theologische Faculteit, Louvain, Belgium.

Schmid, Herbert. "Die Wurzeln des Zionismus im Alten Testament", in *Befreiungsbewegung des jüdischen Volkes.* Veröffentlichungen aus dem Institut Kirche und Judentum 5. Zionismus: Berlin, 1977, pp. 23-29.

Taylor, Howard. "The Continuity of the People of God in Old and New Testaments." *The Scottish Bulletin of Evangelical Theology* 3/2 (1985): 13-26.

Timmer, D.E. "Biblical Exegesis and the Jewish-Christian Controversy in the Early Twelfth Century." *CH* 58 (1989): 309-321.

Trevett, Christine. "Prophecy and Anti-Episcopal Activity: a Third Error Combatted by Ignatius?" *JEH* 34/1 (1983): 1-18.

Van Buren, Paul M. "Covenantal Pluralism?" *Common Ground* (1990/3): 21-27.

Vanlaningham, Michael G. "Romans 11:25-27 and the Future of Israel in Paul's Thought." *The Master's Seminary Journal* 3 (1992): 141-147.

Vleugels, Gie, "Οὔτως," unpublished notes, Evangelische Theologische Faculteit, Louvain, n. d.

Walker, David. "Thomas Goodwin and the Debate on Church Government." *JEH* 34/1 (1983): 85-99.

Weiss, Andrea L. "Creative Readings of the Covenant: A Jewish-Christian Approach." *JES* 30 (1993): 389-402.

7. Pamphlets

Bicheno, James. *The Restoration of the Jews,* 1800.

Faber, George Stanley. *A General and Connected view,* 1808.

Gli Israeliti: il nuovo amore per essi, e il loro avvenire. Florence: Le Monnier, 1847.

Priestly, Joseph. *Letters to the Jews,* 1794.

8. Joint Statements

Declaration of the Regional Synod of the Evangelical Church of Renania, 11 January, 1980. "Zur Ermenerung des Verhaltnisses von Christen und Juden," *Handreichung Nr. 39 für Mltglieder der Landesssynode, der Kreissynoden und der Evangelischen Kirche in Rheinland,* Düsseldorf, 1985²: 9-11. Italian translation and notes by Daniele Garrone. "Risoluzione sinodale sul rinnovamento del rapporto fra Cristiani e Ebrei." *Protestantesimo* XLIIV (1989): 96-97.

"L'accordo fondamentale tra la Santa Sede e Israele." Jerusalem, 30 December, 1993. *Il Regno-attualità* (1994/2): 1-3.

"The Churches and the Jewish People: Towards a New Understanding." Resolution adopted by the WCC Consultation on the Church and the Jewish People on 4 November, 1988. *IBMR* 13 (1989): 152-155.

The Theology of the Churches and the Jewish People: Statements by the World Councl of Churches and its member churches. Comments by Brockway, Allan, Paul van Buren, Rolf Rendtorff & Simon Schoon, eds. Geneva: WWC Publications, 1988.

Tutti i documenti del Concilio, Rome: U.C.I.I.M., 1972.

9. Reference Works

A Greek-English Lexicon of the New Testament and Other early Christian Literature. Walter Baur, William F. Arndt and F. Wilbur Gingrich, eds. Translated, revised and augmented by F. Wilbur Gingrich and Frederick W. Danker from Walter Bauer's 5th ed. Chicago: The University of Chicago Press, 1979.

A Hebrew and English Lexicon of the Old Testament. Francis Brown, S. R. Driver, Charles A. Briggs, eds. Oxford: Clarendon Press, 1975.

An Analysis of the Greek New Testament. Maximillian Zerwick S.J., and Mary Grosvenor. Revised ed. Rome: Biblical Institute Press, 1981.

An Idiom Book of New Testament Greek. C.F.D. Moule. 2d ed. 7th reprint, Cambridge: Cambridge University Press, 1959.

Enclyclopedia Britannica. 29 vols. London: Enclyclopedia Britannica (1994).

Encyclopaedia Judaica. 16 vols. Jerusalem: Encyclopaedia Judaica (1971).

Encyclopedia of Judaism. Geoffrey Wigoder, ed. Jerusalem: Jerusalem Publishing House, 1989.

Evangelical Dictionary of Theology. Walter A. Elwell, ed. Grand Rapids, MI: Baker Book House, 1984.

Gesenius' Hebrew and Chaldee Lexicon to the Old Testament Scriptures. William Gesenius. Translater by S. P. Tregelles. Samuel Bagster & Sons, 1847. Reprint, Grand Rapids, MI: Baker Book House, 1979.

Handbook of Evangelical Theologians. Walter W. Elwell, ed. Grand Rapids, MI: Baker Book House, 1993.

Liddell, Henry George & Robert Scott. *A Greek-English Lexicon.* 1897. 8th revised ed. Oxford: Clarendon Press: 1901.

New Catholic Encyclopedia. 15 vols. New York: McGraw Hill Book Company, 1967.

New International Dictionary of the Christian Church. J.D. Douglas, ed. Exeter: The Paternoster Press, 1978.

New International Dictionary of New Testament Theology. Translated and revised, with additions. Colin Brown, ed. 3 vols. Exeter: Paternoster Press, 1975-1978.

Theological Dictionary of the New Testament. Gerhard Kittel and Gerhard Friedrich, eds. Translated by Geoffrey W. Bromiley. 9 vols. Grand Rapids, MI: Eerdmans, 1964-1972.

Zerwick Max and Mary Grosvenor. *An Analysis of the Greek New Testament.* Rome: Biblical Institute Press, 1981.

SUBJECT INDEX[1]

Aaron, *122*
Abendana, Isaac, *24*
Abraham, *7-9,20,27,36-37,50,77,79,81*
Abraham's children, offspring, seed, *17,36-38,44,59*
Adam and Eve, *89,105*
Adversus Judaeos, 75,96,118,138
Alsted, Johann Heinrich, *166*
Altar, *112, 128,134,139*
Allegorism, *86-87,163-164*
Ambrose, *120*
Antichrist, *157,161*
Anti-Jewish legislation, *98-101*
Anti-Judaism, anti-Judaic, *50,70,75,96-97,103*
Antisemitism, *24,129-131*
Apostles Creed, *169*
Arethas of Cesarea, *57,58*
Augustine, *38,67 (n.114),76,92-96,120,139,164-174*
Augustinian Tradition, *5,169*
Augsburg, *160(n.76)*

Balaam, *10-11*
Barabbas, *90*
Barbarians, *79*
Bar Kochba, *73*
Baptism,*118,125,126-127,132-132*
Bishop, bishops, *98,107,109,114-115,127*
Boniface VIII, *171*

Calvin, John, *19(n.17), 67(n.114)*
Canon, canonical status of, *78,82*
Catholicity, *128*
Children of God, *37-38,59*
Children of the Devil, 36-38
Christ, Christology, *33,130 et passim*

[1]For the names of recent and contemporary authors consulted during the course of this study, see *Bibliography*.